Radical Enactivism

Consciousness & Emotion Book Series

Consciousness & Emotion Book Series publishes original works on this topic, in philosophy, psychology and the neurosciences. The series emphasizes thoughtful analysis of the implications of both empirical and experiential (e.g., clinical psychological) approaches to emotion. It will include topical works by scientists who are interested in the implications of their empirical findings for an understanding of emotion and consciousness and their interrelations.

Volume 2

Radical Enactivism: Intentionality, Phenomenology and Narrative
Edited by Richard Menary

Radical Enactivism

Intentionality, Phenomenology and Narrative

Focus on the philosophy of Daniel D. Hutto

Edited by

Richard Menary
University of Hertfordshire

John Benjamins Publishing Company
Amsterdam / Philadelphia

∞™ The paper used in this publication meets the minimum requirements of American National Standard for Information Sciences – Permanence of Paper for Printed Library Materials, ANSI Z39.48-1984.

Library of Congress Control Number: 2006043044

ISBN 90 272 4151 1 (Hb; alk. paper)

John Benjamins Publishing Co. · P.O. Box 36224 · 1020 ME Amsterdam · The Netherlands
John Benjamins North America · P.O. Box 27519 · Philadelphia PA 19118-0519 · USA

Table of Contents

Author's addresses

Professor Tim Crane
Professor of Philosophy/Director of the Institute of Philosophy, School of Advanced Study
Department of Philosophy
University of London
Gower Street
London WC1E 6BT, England
Email: tim.crane@ucl.ac.uk

Dr. Erik Myin
Department of Philosophy
Center for Philosophical Psychology
University of Antwerp,
City Campus, Hof Van Liere,
Prinsstraat 13
2000 Antwerp, Belgium
Email: Erik.Myin@ua.ac.be

Mr. Lars De Nul
Research Assistant
The Research Foundation Flanders
Department of Philosophy
University of Antwerp,
City Campus, Hof Van Liere,
Prinsstraat 13
2000 Antwerp, Belgium
lars.denul@ua.ac.be

Professor Shaun Gallagher
Professor and Chair of Philosophy,
University of Central Florida
Philosophy and Cognitive Science
University of Central Florida
4000 Central Florida Blvd.
Orlando, Florida, 32816
USA
Email: gallaghr@mail.ucf.edu

Professor Peter Goldie
Samuel Hall Professor of Philosophy,
Department of Philosophy
The University of Manchester
Manchester, M13 9PL, England
Email: peter.goldie@manchester.ac.uk

Professor Peter Hobson
Professor of Developmental Psychopathology
Brain and Behavioural Sciences Unit,
Institute of Child Health,
University College, and Tavistock Clinic, London
Email: r.hobson@ich.ucl.ac.uk

Professor Daniel D. Hutto
Professor of Philosophical Psychology
School of Humanities
University of Hertfordshire
De Havilland Campus, Hatfield,
AL10 9AB, England
Email: d.d.hutto@herts.ac.uk

Dr. Richard Menary
Senior Lecturer in Philosophy
School of Humanities
University of Hertfordshire
De Havilland Campus, Hatfield,
AL10 9AB, England
Email: r.menary@herts.ac.uk

Dr. Anthony Rudd
St. Olaf College,
1520 St. Olaf Avenue,
Northfield,
Minnesota 55057
USA
Email: rudd@stolaf.edu

For Emerson

Introduction

What is radical enactivism?

Richard Menary

1. Varieties of enactivism

Enactivism offers an important challenge to traditional ways of thinking about cognition and the mind. But enactivist approaches come in more than one form. In this special issue, Daniel Hutto defends a radical version of the approach in an attempt to explicate emotional experience, expression and response. The main features of his account are developed in his target paper and in greater detail in his responses to commentators. Before attending to these, it is important to be clear about the general character of enactivist approaches and what they have to offer.

In fulfilling this task, this introduction divides into five sections. The first of these outlines what is distinctive about the enactivist approach and how it is supposed to differ from traditional cognitivist approaches to the mind and cognition. Since the main bone of contention for enactivists is the role of internal representations in cognitivist explanations, the second section looks at ways of classifying different types of representation. Section three clarifies the nature of representation further by using some of the criteria for representation first introduced by Charles Sanders Peirce; a biological version of this can be found in the work of Ruth Millikan. Section four focuses particularly on the symbolic 'encoding' type of representation which is ubiquitous in cognitivist theorising. It is this type of representation which is the particular bugbear of enactivists. However, the encodings are still found to be lurking even in some enactivist theories of perception and a warning to enactivists to avoid encodings is enjoined here. The final section begins the job of outlining the main commitments of radical enactivism as they are played out by Hutto in his target paper and responses to critics. I briefly summarise the main tenets of his radical version of enactivism and point the reader to where they may find some of these tenets being elaborated upon in the responses.

2. What is enactivism?

Enactivism, as a term of art, was first introduced in Varela, Thompson and Rosch's book *The Embodied Mind* (1991). A good way to understand the enactive approach is to contrast it with more traditional approaches to the mind. For example, we find that it "questions the centrality of the notion that cognition is fundamentally representation" (Varela, Thompson & Rosch 1991: 9). A more programmatic statement of this difference in approach can be found in the following:

> We propose as a name enactive to emphasize the growing conviction that cognition is not the representation of a pregiven world by a pregiven mind but is rather the enactment of a world and a mind on the basis of a history of the variety of actions that a being in the world performs (Varela, Thompson & Rosch 1991: 9).

Enactivism is based on the notion of cognition as emerging out of embodied action. Cognition emerges from processes of perception and action that give rise to recurrent sensorimotor patterns. Thus:

> the enactive approach consists of two points:
>
> (1) perception consists in perceptually guided action and (2) cognitive structures emerge from the recurrent sensorimotor patterns that enable action to be perceptually guided. The overall concern... is not to determine how some perceiver independent world is to be recovered; it is, rather, to determine the common principles or lawful linkages between sensory and motor systems that explain how action can be perceptually guided in a perceiver-dependent world. (Varela, Thompson & Rosch 1991: 173)

As such, enactivists hold that for an agent to be cognitive, it must have a body; and that the embodied agent is embedded in an environment such that it must be able to interact with that environment.

Enactivism, as introduced by Varela, Thompson and Rosch, took an autopoietic route to the sensorimotor interactions of the organism with its environment. On this view a physical structure with an autopoietic organization is one that is self-producing and self-maintaining – it is both living and cognitive. The components of autopoetic systems "must be dynamically related in a network of ongoing interactions" (Maturana & Varela 1992: 43–44). The components interact and are mutually dependent, they also maintain the boundary of the autopoietic system. A cell is a case in point, because it produces its own boundary – the membrane.

> An autopoietic machine is a machine organised (defined as a unity) as a network of processes of production (transformation and destruction) of components that produces the components which: (i) through their interactions and transformations continuously regenerate and realise the network of processes (relations) that

> produced them; and (ii) constitute it (the machine) as a concrete unity in the space in which they (the components) exist by specifying the topological domain of its realisation as such a network (Maturana & Varela 1980: 78–79).

However, more recent 'enactivist' projects such as Alva Noë's (Noë 2004) enactive account of perception do not depend upon an autopoietic conception of the organism. Noë's account of perception only invokes sensorimotor contingencies to explain perceptual experience. Thus, there remains a link between Noë's enactivist account of perception and the programmatic conception of enactivism that issues from Varela, Thompson and Rosch, but these emphasise different things. For example, in a forthcoming book Thompson makes it clear that autopoiesis is a fundamental basis for enactive studies of the mind and cognition. He argues that there is a deep continuity of life and mind. This is because the self-producing autopoietic organization of living systems already implies cognition. Clearly, there is some disagreement about how central autopoiesis is to the enactivist programme. As we shall see, Hutto's variant of radical enactivism, like that of Noë, does not depend upon the autopoietic conception of the organism, but it is in tune with the enactivist hostility to the 'cognitivist' conception of mind as involving internal representations of the environment, as well as taking seriously sensorimotor interactions with the environment. I shall focus on this in the remaining sections.

3. Representation

Noe (2004, 2) claims that enactivists are hostile to the view of perception inspired by the work of Marr (1982), whereby perceptual processes in the brain create detailed inner representations of the external environment.

This rejection of detailed inner representations is in line with other enactivist accounts of perception, such as those developed by Ellis (1995, 2005) and Newton (1996, 2004), where action imagery is used to ground perceptual image schemas; they then argue that these image schemas ("representations") in turn play a role in perception by allowing us to "look for" motivationally salient items in the environment. The general hostility of enactivists to the cognitivist conception of internal representations is maintained since image schemas are not to be thought of as internal representations with content and truth conditions.

Yet to properly understand what is being rejected requires getting clear about what internal representations are supposed to be. Wilson provides a three part classification of representational types (2004: 187):

- Reactive – Reflexes.
- Enactive – Bodily skills/abilities.

– Symbolic – Linguistic tokens/concepts.

A paramecium oriented towards magnetic north/south would be an example of the first. The paramecium registers a state of its environment and reacts to this. The paramecium has no real control over its behaviour – it is reactive – and its registration of the environmental state is extremely simple and limited (Wilson 2004: 185). It is closer to the truth to say that the paramecium is directed at a state of its environment, rather than represents it – there is no obvious sense in which the internal state of the paramecium carries any 'content'.

Enactive representations involve bodily skills, such as those required to ride a bicycle. Enactive representation is closely tied to bodily activities (Wilson 2004: 186). It goes beyond simple reflexive reactions to environmental stimuli, but it is not yet conscious or reflective thought. In fact, as Wilson points out, such reflective thought often intrudes into enactive performance: when performing a bodily skill, it is better to let the body get on with it than to consciously direct the activity.

By contrast, symbolic representations can be divorced from their bodily and contextual origins (Wilson 2004: 186). For example, my belief that Chicago is windy[1] can be thought about whilst sitting in my study in Berkhamsted, whilst I am doing nothing more than relaxing in an armchair with a glass of whisky in hand. It is in this sense that symbolic representations are autonomous of the here and now; whereas reactive representations are entirely dependent upon the here and now and enactive representations almost entirely. Although with enactive representations, there is the possibility for mimetic rehearsal and off-line imagining of the kind often used by sports men and women for calibrating their performances.

I would suggest that enactivists are unlikely to be hostile to the first two categories of representational type[2], indeed Noë's enactivist conception of perception reconstrues perceptual experience entirely in terms of enactive representations – bodily skills – rather than internal symbolic representations. So their hostility must be directed at the third class of representation – symbolic representations.

Although this tri-partite classification tells us something about the types of representation that there are, it still doesn't give us any insight into the general conditions for what it is to be a representation. Before considering further the nature of symbolic representations, in the next section I propose such a set of conditions.

4. The Peircean principle

The Peircean principle maintains that any representation must involve the following three components[3]: The first condition is that the vehicle has certain intrinsic or relational properties that make it salient to a consumer. The second condition is that the vehicle is exploited by a consumer in virtue of its salient properties, thereby establishing the vehicle's representational function (the function of representing an object/environmental property). The third condition is that a representational triad (a genuine representation) is established only when the representational function is recruited for some further end (such as the detecting of food). The recruitment of the representation in virtue of its function is established as a norm; Millikan (1984, 1993) shows how such norms are established as proper biological functions, but the norm might very well be conventional. The conditions can be unpacked in the following way.

1. A token vehicle Φ is a representational vehicle when it has properties that can *potentially* be exploited by a representational consumer. For example: Φ is salient because it is reliably correlated with an object/environmental property X, or with objects/environmental properties X, Y, Z….
2. Φ has a representational function when its salient features are exploited by some consumer Ψ. For example: Φ has the function of representing X for consumer Ψ, because Φ is reliably correlated with an object/environmental property X.
3. Φ represents X for consumer Ψ in the performance of some biological function.

The conditions for representation are simple: a vehicle has properties that are potentially exploitable by a consumer, call these its representationally salient properties. It is consumed in virtue of its salient properties. However, for the repeatability of this representational triad we need the co-ordination of producer and consumer mechanisms, a vehicle is produced which is consumed for some further end. This process is established as a teleonomic norm if it is adaptively successful as in Millikan's bee dance example, which is discussed by Hutto in the target paper.

The very same conditions for representation are the basis for teleological representational triads and repeatability requires the co-ordination of producer and consumer. However, the process is established as a teleological norm by being part of a conventional system such as language or mathematics. How we get from teleonomic norms to teleological norms need not detain us here (Hutto sketches a possible answer in his reply to Hobson).

The Peircean principle is valuable because it allows us to explain how representation works in both natural and social environments. It demonstrates the commonalities and differences between teleonomic and teleological representation and provides the very fundamental conditions under which representation is possible. It makes no commitment to whether representational triads are internal, external or distributed across body and world.

Having clarified this we can better understand the nature of symbolic representation, especially as it is understood by cognitivists.

5. Cognitivism and representation as encoding

For cognitivists, mental representations rely on encoded 'information' – these supply their content. They have formal or syntactic properties and are constructed from constituents. Symbols refer or denote a property, state or possibly an event in the world. In principle this can also allow them to have a truth condition.[4] Encodings are usually a part of a wider system of representation, such as natural language or a computer language[5]. Reflexes and bodily skills are not really representational in the cognitivist's sense. They don't have content, they don't *encode* information. Symbols in contrast are uncontroversially contentful and representational.

It appears that the encoding view of representation is the one to be avoided by enactivists. This is particularly so when considering perception, which is not to be construed as the encoding of information from the environment in some symbolic representation in the head. Despite this, there is evidence of a tendency of some enactivists to rely on this very notion of representation in the literature (as pointed out by Hutto 2005 and Rowlands 2006). This can be found in the way the enactivist account of perception of Noë (2004) and O'Regan and Noë (2001) gets expressed in terms of 'mediating knowledge'.

Enactivist accounts of perception generally conceive of these as abilities that are "largely a matter of readiness to hand or 'knowledge how' based on the accumulation of experience in a vast number of cases" (Varela, Thompson & Rosch 1991: 148). O'Regan and Noë also make this claim:

> Visual experience is a mode of activity involving practical knowledge about currently possible behaviours and associated sensory consequences. Visual experience rests on know how, the possession of skills (O'Regan & Noë 2001: 946).

In this they seek to robustly reject the cognitivist construal of perception as the construction of detailed inner symbolic representations. However, critics (Hutto 2005, Rowlands 2006) point out that the examples they give and the claims they make about the laws of sensorimotor contingencies and the practical or implicit knowledge of them allows symbolic representation, or knowing that, to enter in through the back door, as it were. This is evident in the following quotation for example.

> In what does your focussing on the red hue of the wall consist? It consists in the (implicit) knowledge associated with seeing redness: the knowledge *that* if you were to move your eyes, there would be changes in the incoming information that are typical of sampling with the eye; typical of the nonhomogenous way the

> retina samples color; knowledge *that* if you were to move your eyes around, there might be changes in the incoming information typical of what happens when the illumination is uneven, and so on (O'Regan & Noë 2001: 961 emphasis added).

Enactivists should take heed of the warning signs. Knowledge of the laws of sensorimotor contingencies had better not be construed as knowledge of symbolic representations of the encodings of those laws. Otherwise enactivism will just be another species of cognitivism and the genuinely radical nature of enactivism will be lost: Hence, Hutto's distinction between conservative and radical versions (Hutto 2005).

The rest of this volume is concerned with trying to work out what a thoroughgoing radical enactivism would look like, especially when it comes to understanding emotional experience and its expression.

5. What is radical enactivism?

Hutto's radical enactivism offers a non-cognitivist way of understanding experience and intentionality that focuses on the embodied as opposed to the thinking organism. It sharply distinguishes between basic visceral responding and linguistically mediated thought. The former involves organisms being intentionally directed at aspects of their environment in ways that are *not* contentful – i.e. their intentionality is not to be understood as a property of their mental states or mental representations. Nor does it involve the acquisition or manipulation of encoded information content. As such, basic forms of perceptual and emotional responding do not involve or instantiate truth conditions; we only find such properties at the level of linguistically mediated thought.

The nature of this intentional directedness is cashed out in terms of a biosemiotic account. Biosemiotics can be most easily understood as biosemantics without the semantics; there being no truth or reference at this level. However, there is determinate intentional directedness, as illustrated by Millikan's bee dance example which Hutto discussed in the target paper. Hence, the kind of determinate intentional directedness that characterises perceptual and emotional responding also falls under the Peircean principle. Even so, Hutto does not think that we are warranted in calling Millikan's intentional icons or his own local indexical and iconic guides (LIGs) representations, because they lack content and properties of truth or reference (*pace* Millikan). If such a view can be made to work it has important implications for cognitive science. For example, it does away with the idea of perceptual modules that take in low-level informational contents, converting these into representations. Hutto argues for this in response to Goldie, where he also shows how the biosemiotic approach can be used to explain how, in basic emotional engagements, we are directly responsive to the minds of others as opposed to reading them.

The idea of a contentless intentional directedness makes its initial appearance in Hutto's first book, *The Presence of Mind*. It is discussed in the target paper but is developed more fully in the final section of Hutto's response to Crane where it is christened 'Biosemiotics'. Both Rudd and Crane take issue, in different ways, with Hutto over the claim that intentional directedness does not involve content, truth conditions and reference. For Rudd conceptual content is key to all forms of human responding that can enter into the 'space of reasons', including basic perceptual and emotional responding. Taking an essentially McDowellian line, he presents transcendental and phenomenological arguments against Hutto. Crane, in contrast, defends an account of phenomenal experience and intentionality that necessarily involves a form of non-conceptual content. Hutto clarifies and develops arguments against this idea in his reply to Crane's, where he also argues that these nonconceptual contents should not be thought of as objects to which we are psychologically related.

This complaint ties in with Hutto's views about how best to understand the character of phenomenal experience. He is particularly concerned to reject what he calls the Object Based Schema (OBS), which is essentially committed to the view that contents and experiences are kinds of objects of some kind; typically, these are imagined to be mental objects with which we are directly phenomenally acquainted (such as qualia) or intentional contents to which we are psychologically related. Arguments against the OBS made their debut in Hutto's early writings – being discussed most fully in Chapter 4 of his *Beyond Physicalism*. They are further developed in the target paper, where it is argued that on a radical enactivist construal, basic acts of experience of either the perceptual or emotional variety are best identified with embodied responding. Relatedly, our understanding of the character of experience must be nonconceptual and nontheoretical; to know-what-it-is-like to have experience requires directly enacting or imaginatively re-enacting it. The role and importance of the OBS in Hutto's thinking about the metaphysics of consciousness and how we acquire our concepts of experience is clarified in important ways in his replies to the commentaries by Myin and De Nul, Crane, Goldie and Rudd.

In the exchanges with Hobson and Gallagher we begin to see how basic forms of interpersonal responding provide a platform for and connect with the ways in which we understand others using propositional attitudes and ultimately folk psychology. Hutto argues that these capacities are quite distinct and that they develop over time, building upon our more basic, embodied modes of expression and response. Thus, in his reply to Hobson, he makes it clear that children have a practical mastery of the concepts of desire and belief and that they use these to understand others before they can make sense of intentional actions in *bona fide* folk psychological terms. In his response to Gallagher he describes his Narrative Practice Hypothesis (NPH) which challenges the orthodox view that our mind-reading skills are a biological inheritance from our hominid forerunners. Building on his other writings on this topic, Hutto argues that understanding others folk psychologically is always an essentially narrative business, theory and simulation are just supplementary heuristics used to aid in the construction of the relevant narratives when we are forced to adopt a third-personal, speculative stance (Hutto 2004). He develops and expands on this idea in his reply to Gallagher.

With these clarifications in hand, it is perhaps worth providing a slightly more detailed prelude as to how the commitments of radical enactivism get developed by Hutto in his target paper and his responses to critics. The target paper advances the claim that the intentionality and characteristic phenomenology of basic non-verbal emotional experience, expression and response is not content-involving; it is best understood in purely actional ways. In elucidating his radical enactivist approach, Hutto provides a first sketch of how it enables us to understand the phenomena which Goldie calls 'feeling towards'. Its distinctive offering is revealed by locating it in the conceptual landscape in relation to positions such as Crane's strong intentionalism and O'Regan, Noë and Myin's sensorimotor contingency approach. More substantially, he argues that the intentional directedness and structural causes of basic responding as well as its role in intersubjective engagements are ultimately best understood in terms of biologically proper functions.

In 'Feelings and Objects' Myin and De Nul raise two questions about Hutto's radical enactivist understanding of the character of experience; one relates to his diagnosis and treatment of 'hard' problems and the other concerns his critique of the existing versions of the Sensorimotor Contingency approach (SMC). In reply Hutto clarifies in what ways he sees commitment to the Object Based Schema (OBS) as fostering the metaphysical variant hard problem of consciousness (and how best to avoid it). He also describes, in greater detail than in the target paper, in what precise ways he would want to see the SMC modified in line with a more radical enactivism.

In 'Unnatural Feelings', along broadly McDowellian lines, Rudd identifies two worries about Hutto's general approach. These concern: (1) its commitment to a dualism of the conceptual and non-conceptual (and how these relate), and (2) the putative role Hutto sees for evolutionary considerations in understanding human experience. In responding to these concerns Hutto attempts to demonstrate that his enactivist position is consistent with the Bradleyean metaphysics he has espoused elsewhere. For Rudd's overarching concern is that there may be a fundamental tension in what Hutto hopes to achieve on this front, and the means by which he seeks to achieve it. Hutto's reply concludes with a discussion of how the development of a socio-cultural second nature importantly transforms the character of emotional responding and what we value.

In 'Intentionality and Emotion' Crane takes issue with Hutto's appraisal of the current situation in the philosophy of mind; in particular he objects to the claim that much existing philosophical confusion can be traced to a commitment to the Object Based Schema (OBS). In the first section of Hutto's reply he argues that Crane's assessment is based on a mischaracterisation of the OBS and the role Hutto sees it playing. In subsequent sections of the reply Hutto corrects aspects of his presentation of Crane's account (as it appears in the target paper) in order to get at the real issue between the two – the existence of content in basic perceptual and emotional responding. Importantly, he concludes by showing that in essence his critique of Crane on this issue also applies to other prevalent cognitivist views about content and its acquisition.

In 'Emotional Experience and Understanding' Goldie asks exactly what kind of account Hutto intends to offer based on the programmatic sketch provided in the target paper. In clarifying his views on this Hutto resists endorsing a single approach, promoting a kind of pluralist pragmatism instead. He then addresses Goldie's suggestion that enactivism might be best understood in terms of direct, non-inferential perception of other minds. Against this, Hutto develops and clarifies his understanding of the embodied character of non-verbal emotional responding and its transformational character. Finally, although he denies that basic responding is based upon or yields propositional knowledge, he says something about its role in guiding one's responses and those of others; and also how more detached forms of responding become possible through symbolic mediation.

Hobson and Hutto agree in large part about the nature of basic emotional responding and the forms of interpersonal interactions it fuels, as is made clear by the former's 'From Feelings to Thinking (through others)'. After clarifying in what way Hutto thinks his approach does away with the conceptual problem of other minds, he takes up the challenge of addressing four major challenges that Hobson sets for him. For Hobson asks how embodied modes of interpersonal responding, those that allegedly characterise our primary unprincipled engagements, lead to the development of concepts (in general); concepts of mind that are applicable both to self and other; and concepts of the propositional attitudes. Additionally, he wonders what Hutto would say about the effects of their impairment in certain conditions, such as autism. In his long reply, Hutto attempts to address most of these questions in some detail.

In his 'The Narrative Alternative to Theory of Mind' Gallagher makes it clear that he and Hutto agree that primary interpersonal engagements culminate in discursive modes of understanding others that are narratively-based. Gallagher picks up a thread in the target paper that relates to these issues, and in reply Hutto elaborates on the precise version of an idea he has been developing in various other writings in the form of his Narrative Practice Hypothesis (NPH). In response to prompts from Gallagher, he explains how this more discursively based capacity builds upon more mimetically grounded skills for dramatic re-enactment and how it is bound up with phenomena such as childhood amnesia, which relates to a lack of autobiographical memory and narrative self-consciousness.

In all, it should be evident from the above that radical enactivism not only retains the enactivist's hostility to cognitivism, it defines itself in such terms. It is quite in line with other forms of enactivism such as sensorimotor theories of perception, so long as the relevant responses are not thought to involve anything more than abilities of the organism; i.e. they do not involve propositional *knowledge* of sensorimotor laws – (see the response to Myin and De Nul). Radical enactivism attempts to account for the nature of experience by showing that at root it is a kind of nonconceptual embodied engagement, rather than a McDowellian presentation of the world that is conceptually saturated. It therefore occupies a unique and interesting place in today's conceptual geography and, as the rich debates of this volume demonstrate, it is a position well worth exploring in more detail.

Notes

1. Which is a false belief when taken literally, if the origin of the nickname is accurate. The nickname is thought to be based not on wind velocity, but on loud and windy boosterism. A Chicago Daily News article from Sept. 22, 1969 gives this origin: Blame it on John Stephan Wright and William (Deacon) Bross, two local boosters (windbags, some might say), who went up and down the East Coast yelling about the wonders of Chicago, according to Daily News library clippings.... Because of their loud boasts of the virtues of the city, Chicago was dubbed the "Windy City" after its "windy" citizenry in the 1850s, according to stories.

2. If indeed it is questionable whether they can be construed as representations at all, given that they appear to lack identifiable contents.

3. A fuller version of this account of representational criteria can be found in Menary 2007 and 'in development'.

4. Agreement on precisely what properties symbols have is not always to be found amongst cognitivists.

5. Although an atomist such as Fodor would not be content with the holistic overtones here.

References

Hutto D.D. 1999. *The Presence of Mind.* Amsterdam: John Benjamins.

Hutto D.D. 2000. *Beyond Physicalism.* Amsterdam: John Benjamins.

Hutto D.D. 2004. "The Limits of Spectatorial Folk Psychology". *Mind and Language* 19: 548–73.

Hutto D.D. 2005. "Knowing What?: Radical versus Conservative Enactivism". *Phenomenology and the Cognitive Sciences* 4: 389–405.

Maturana H. and Varela, F. 1980. *Autopoiesis and cognition: The Realization of The Living.* Boston: D. Reidel.

Maturana, H. and Varela, F. 1992. *The Tree of Knowledge: The Biological Roots of Human Understanding.* Revised edition Boston and London: Shamabala.

Maturana, H. 1987. "Everything Said is Said By An Observer". In *Gaia: A way of knowing,* W. Thompson (ed.), 65–82. Hudson, NY: Lindisfarne Press.

Menary, R. 2007. *Cognitive Integration: Mind and Cognition Unbounded.* Basingstoke: Palgrave Macmillan.

Menary, R. (in development) The Peircean Principle.

Millikan, R.G. 1984. *Language, Thought, and Other Biological Categories.* Cambridge, MA: MIT Press.

Millikan, R.G. 1993. *White Queen Psychology and Other Essays for Alice.* Cambridge, MA: MIT Press.

Noë, A. 2004. *Action in Perception.* Cambridge, MA: MIT Press.

O'Regan, J. K. and Noë, A. 2001. "A Sensorimotor Account of Vision and Visual Consciousness". *Behavioural and Brain Sciences* 24: 939–1031.

Rowlands, M. 2006. "Understanding the 'Active' in 'Enactive'". *Phenomenology and the Cognitive Sciences.*

Thompson, E. (in press) *Mind in Life: Biology, Phenomenology, and the Sciences of Mind.* Harvard University Press.

Varela, F. (1987). "Laying Down a Path in Walking". In *Gaia: A way of Knowing,* W. Thompson (ed.), 48–64. Hudson, NY: Lindisfarne Press.

Varela, F., Thompson, E., and Rosch, E. (1991). *The Embodied Mind: Cognitive Science and Human Experience.* Cambridge, MA: MIT Press.

Wilson, R.A. 2004. *Boundaries of The Mind: The Individual in the Fragile Sciences.* Cambridge: Cambridge University Press.

Unprincipled engagements

Emotional experience, expression and response[1]

Daniel D. Hutto

1. Introduction: The trouble with emotions

Philosophically speaking, emotions are a nuisance, even the good ones. There are several reasons for this. First, it is thought that they are a hangover of our animal natures that interfere with our rationality: they gum up our reasoning. This verdict has been familiar since the time of Greek philosophy, which is no doubt why being a cognitive scientist appears a respectable occupation, but being an 'emotive scientist' sounds like a blemish on one's capacity for professional judgement.

Second, emotions are paradigmatic experiential phenomena, i.e. they involve the having of *feelings* of guilt, anguish, fear, sorrow and the like. Our emotional life, *par excellence*, is tinged and coloured with phenomenality. Failure to account for this, as is the legacy of reductive behavioural or functional approaches, hardly yields a satisfactory philosophy of psychology. This is, of course, also true of certain other psychological phenomena, such as seeing, hearing and so on, which are sometimes billed as 'purely cognitive'. These too clearly involve sensations, yet it is somehow easier to imagine that these might be carved off or at least go unmentioned when it comes to studying such phenomena scientifically. It is harder to ignore or deny 'feelings' in the study of the emotions.

But the very idea that such a selective carving off of specific 'aspects' or 'objects' of study is possible is what fuels fears of a potential explanatory gap and the so-named hard problem of consciousness. For once we begin to think this way, we are driven to wonder why there would be any need for the experiential aspects if the underlying mechanisms alone are capable of doing all the important causal work. Worse still, if we imagine experiences to exist as objects and as playing a causal role, we wonder how they can be identified with (or generated by) the purely physiological, neural or more neutrally, 'physical' activity.

If this were not enough, emotions force us to confront two age old problems concerning other minds, those of the epistemological and conceptual varieties. The first is very familiar. It is a concern about justification, which starts from the seemingly reasonable assumption that we lack direct access to the 'inner mental life' of others. For example, claims to know that another is feeling *thus* and *so* are open to serious challenge since our evidence about another's state of mind is allegedly always mediated by uncertain signs and outward expressions: it is thus inconclusive. Worse still, we might wonder how we ever get into a position even to frame such claims since the extensions of the concepts of emotion must either be 'inner' states or the 'outward' behaviour of others: indexing one or the other of these seems to have been the basis for first learning the concepts of emotion. This suggests that our ordinary concepts of emotion, which appear to cover *both* first and third person cases, are necessarily equivocal. They have different meanings when applied to oneself as opposed to others, even though we tend to think that such concepts apply to and mean just the same for all. But how, given options presented by the received view about how they are learned, is that possible? This is the conceptual problem of other minds.

Although initially compelling, all of these philosophical puzzles have important and questionable frames. I have argued at length elsewhere that the hard problem of consciousness, conceived of as a problem about intelligibility, and the problem of the explanatory gap stem directly from our tendency to employ an object-based schema when characterising experience (Hutto 2000). We tend to think of experiences as inner objects (states, processes or events – or more commonly, determinable properties of these). As with all other objects or objective features, we are licensed to ask seemingly legitimate questions about their location, duration and independent causal effects. Thus, we begin to wonder: Where do experiences reside? Who views them? How can they be the very same as what goes on in our brains?

This whole way of thinking about experience is encouraged by and mutually reinforces the common idea that our experiential concepts grasp (or pick out) determinate objects or determinable objective features. This idea comes easily to those who already think that this is how we learn our concepts in general, experiential concepts being no exception. In the course of drawing a distinction between knowing what-it-is-like to be conscious (in general) and what-it-is-like to be conscious *of* something (i.e. transitively), Velmans sums up the 'standard view':

> As with *any term that refers to something* that one can observe or experience, it is useful, if possible, to begin with an ostensive definition – that is to point to or pick out the phenomena to which the term refers and, by implication, what is excluded (Velmans 2000: 6, emphasis added).

A yet more recent example of how this idea plays out with respect to 'qualia', conceived of as a kind of isolatable referent, comes from Chalmers:

> A direct phenomenal concept is formed by attending to a quality and taking up that quality into a concept whose content mirrors the quality, picking out instances of the quality in all epistemic possibilities (Chalmers 2003: 236).

These authors are not alone in unflinchingly regarding our terms and concepts of experience to be grounded in ostensive definitions that refer to objects of some kind (or qualities, properties, etc.). But the point is that once experiences are so reified, debates ensue about where they are located, as do the familiar and seemingly well-defined dichotomies of 'inner and outer' and 'mind and world'. Ironically, this understanding of concepts leads us to model experiences on the oxymoronic category of the objective-subjective.

As noted above, this way of thinking is also responsible for setting up questions about how our experiential concepts can apply to both ourselves and others (indeed how they can be shared concepts). Once experiences are seriously, not metaphorically, modelled on objects – only now 'interior' or 'private' ones – we are faced with the question of what *common* 'possession' or 'grasp' of such concepts comes to. The tension is that whereas, for example, Frege would have insisted that concepts, which comprise complete thoughts, can be commonly grasped because they are public objects, if experiences are cast as graspable 'private' objects as opposed to public ones, it becomes problematic to see how they can be shared. If experiences are indexed by their inward phenomenal properties then sharing concepts of experience cannot be like sharing an ice cream. Either that or we are saddled with the opposite problem: the concepts of experience index something public and hence are shareable and universally applicable. But this comes at the cost that they wind up being *about* something that is publicly identifiable – e.g. outward behaviour, stripped of phenomenology. If our concepts of experience are based on a grasp of either one or the other or both sorts of extension they would either be special purpose or incompatible: we would necessarily be operating with a different sets of concepts when, say, ascribing pain to ourselves as opposed to ascribing it to another. Something has gone deeply wrong.

Confusion on this score also infects standard views about how we *deploy* our concepts. It is typically supposed that we do so in purely spectatorial contexts – ones in which we are at a necessary remove from others: the only access we have to their 'inner lives' is through their outward behaviour. It is assumed therefore that we ascribe mental states to them by means of the cold inferential, processing of 'exterior' signs. Such attributions are imperfectly justified by analogy with our own case. Thus, Jackson, like Russell before him, has recently claimed that when we 'see' another's anger or annoyance, we are in fact making a series of assumptions that licence our inference from others' behaviour to beliefs about their psychological states. He cites the following four putative facts in making his case:

(i) Perceptual inferences depend on our folk knowledge that our judgements are 'typically causally sourced' in behaviour;
(ii) The judgements that people's behaviour tend to induce in us are, by and large, reliable;
(iii) For these inferences to be rational we must have other, independent means of certifying their truth;
(iv) Facts (i-iii) form part of our implicit folk theory, which links behaviour and psychological states (Jackson 1999: 84).

Importantly, for Jackson, as a theory-theorist, 'seeing' another's emotion must always be inferentially mediated. Interestingly, even supporters of projectivist versions of simulation are apt to accept at least the first three of these claims. For instance, Goldman holds that when simulating we first identify, by means of introspection, what our own mental states would be in the circumstances of those of the target individual. In the next step we feed these pretend inputs into the relevant psychological mechanisms and run them off-line. The resulting outputs will then take the form of inferences, predictions or explanations, as opposed to actions or responses. It is thought that by putting these psychological mechanisms to this sort of alternative use enables rudimentary forms of social co-ordination. The outputs provide a reliable guide to how things are with the other, based on the relatively safe assumption that the others in question are enough like us to justify such projections. Given that many simulationists often describe this process as one of 'putting oneself in the shoes of the other', they must, at least, implicitly endorse Jackson's claim that 'assumption' and 'inference' are involved even in our most basic interactions (cf. Hutto 1997: 63–4).

My contention is that standard views about the nature of concepts and concept learning (which promote the object-based schema) are complicit in generating the so-called 'hard' problem of consciousness, the explanatory gap, and both problems of other minds. These views are deeply rooted and I do not imagine that any brisk treatment will be convincing. Nevertheless, in what follows, by concentrating on explicating the nature of *basic* forms of emotional experience and response (and the role they play in our lives) I hope to encourage a rethink. For if we can abandon certain misguided assumptions about the 'extensions' of experiential concepts and how they are acquired, we can put certain of the concerns that give emotions a bad name to rest.

2. Intentional directedness and characteristic phenomenology

It will prove useful to say a word or two about the nature of emotions and to make a few distinctions that will help to keep the important issues in focus. In his recent study, Goldie rightly resists over-intellectualised accounts of the emotions, such as Solomon's cognitivism, that would render emotions as nothing but kinds of judgement. Equally, he rejects belief/desire approaches that attempt to analyse emotions entirely in terms of propositional attitudes (see Goldie 2000: 22–4).

Instead of treating these proposals about the emotions as mere rivals to his own, he recognises that they also touch on phenomena that are bound up with the emotions. He accepts that sometimes beliefs, desires and judgments comprise proper parts of an emotion. For example, your ire at a specific person *may* involve a whole series of beliefs and desires about them (e.g. beliefs about what they have done, desires about what you would like to see happen to them, etc.). It *may* also include judgements, say, about their character, motives or their capacity to respond to you (should you act against them) and so on. These may be part and parcel of one's anger in a particular case or it may be that you are unreflectively angry at someone – for no reason that can be articulated; perhaps your emotion involves no explicit judgements or beliefs about the other but it is expressed in your actions towards them all the same. There are a number of possibilities here. Goldie's account accommodates this because, for him, emotions are "typically *complex, episodic, dynamic* and *structured*" (Goldie 2000: 16). Eschewing the object-based schema, on this account, emotions, like acts of perception, are not synchronic occurrences but are extended over time. For this reason, an emotion can constitute:

> part of a narrative – roughly, an unfolding sequence of actions and events, thoughts and feelings, in which the emotion is embedded. The different elements of the emotion are conceived by us as all being part of the *same* emotion, in spite of its complex, episodic and dynamic features. The actions which we do out of an emotion, and the various ways of expressing an emotion, are part of the same narrative, but are not themselves part of the emotion itself (Goldie 2000: 13, 102).

Or, as I would prefer to say, emotions and their consequences have a kind of structure that is ripe for narration.

What allows for these varying degrees of sophistication? Goldie's answer is that culture makes an important difference in shaping our emotional responses in ways that are locally deemed to be appropriate and proportional (Goldie 2000: 23, 28). Yet he objects to what he calls the avocado pear conception, according to which evolutionary pressures provide a distinguishable 'hard' core of primitive or basic emotions which is then encompassed by a soft core of culturally determined sophisticated emotions. Instead he maintains that, although evolution will have provided the basis for our emotions and emotional responses, these are 'developmentally open and plastic', such that once they become influenced deeply by local culture, normally *via* education, it is not possible to disentangle or separate the elements (see Goldie 2000: 98–100). Either way, given that the philosophical 'hard problems' of interest concern the phenomenal character of emotional experience and issues about the ontogenesis of our concepts, for our purposes it is useful to look at proposals about our most basic or primitive forms of response.

Goldie approves of Griffiths' appeal to 'affect-programme responses' when it comes to understanding those hard-wired episodes of emotional experience and response which are at once "complex, coordinated and automated" (Griffiths 1997: 105). This, he thinks, helps to stave off confusion with culturally-influenced emotions 'proper'. Yet even basic hard-wired responses have a kind of 'script' structure. Goldie reformulates this idea as follows (he acknowledges that Griffiths does not concentrate much on steps 1 and 5):

> Step 1: paradigmatic recognitional element involved in X
> Step 2: paradigmatic outward expression of X
> Step 3: paradigmatic bodily changes and feeling of those changes;
> Step 4: paradigmatic motivational response involved in X;
> Step 5: paradigmatic action out of X (Goldie 2000: 94).

This looks pretty much like good old fashioned functionalism, even if of a non-reductive sort, since it combines both bio-physiological and phenomenal elements. Goldie goes further and effectively allies his approach to a kind of teleo-functionalism by holding that Griffiths' affect-programmes provide "a good characterization of some short-term episodes of emotional experience involved in the recognition-response tie, which could be a suitable object of study for evolutionary science" (Goldie 2000: 105). But it is important to realise that it is the *whole* embodied attitude of a creature that exhibits intentionality and not some functionally specified 'mental state'.

Importantly, in distinguishing 'emotions proper' from 'episodes of emotional experience', Goldie insists nevertheless that the latter necessarily involve what he calls 'feeling towards'.

> What I want to do is to emphasize an intentional element which is neither belief nor desire, and which is, in many respects more fundamental to emotional experience than either of these ... To reflect the fact that this intentional element is *both* intentional *and* involves feelings, I will call it *feeling towards* (Goldie 2000: 19, cf. Ellis and Newton 2000: 6).

This capacity for 'feeling towards' is thus basic to the emotions. Any full account of emotions proper must account for their intentional and experiential aspects, since even sophisticated or educated emotions must involve episodes of directed emotional experience. All emotions are directed at things and involve feelings, *inter alia*, just as acts of perceiving are directed at things and involve sensations. Citing Crane, Goldie endorses the idea that, in instances of 'feeling towards', we need not be directed at propositions, even in sophisticated cases (I discuss this again later).[2]

> When you are asked, for example, 'What are you afraid of?', you are being asked to state the object of your fear; the reply will specify something – the object – or, more specifically, some feature of the object of which you are afraid. An object of an emotion, in this sense, could be a particular thing or person (that pudding, this man), an event or an action (the earthquake, your hitting me) or a state of affairs (my being in an aeroplane) (Goldie 2000: 17).

Goldie's purpose is, in large part, to provide a means of understanding the intentionality of emotions in a way that does not route them through 'feelingless' belief and desire psychology. Thus, "Feeling towards is *thinking of* with feeling, so that your emotional feelings are directed towards the object of your thought" (Goldie 2000: 19). This single notion is meant to encompass both the directedness and characteristic phenomenology of primitive forms of experience. There are various ways of making sense of this important idea. Conservatively, one might endorse weak intentionalism, which is the view that although experiences (such as feelings and bodily sensations) are intentional, this "does not rule out their having (narrowly) qualitative properties (qualia) in addition to their intentional character" (Crane 2003: 37). Of course, invoking 'qualia' as non-optional extras only fuels our need to address the 'hard' problem and to bridge the explanatory gap. Thus, if for no other reason, we might be inclined towards strong intentionalism according to which "mental states only have intentional mental properties" (Crane 2003: 37). I reject this view too (and especially this way of formulating it). Saying why will aid in sketching my alternative.

Firstly, when setting out his account, Crane follows the tradition and defines intentionality as the mind being directed at or upon objects, augmenting this with the idea that such objects have aspectual shapes or modes of presentation – the idea that objects are "presented under a certain aspect, or in a certain way" (Crane 2003: 38). But concerns about non-existent objects quickly drive him away from the simple account. For example, he recognises that it is possible to feel pain in body parts that do not exist, as in phantom limb cases. Thus he feels compelled to say that "An intentionalist cannot say that pain is a relation to a body part. Rather, pain is a relation to an intentional content, where the content is the way things seem to the subject" (Crane 2003: 54). To accommodate this he offers a tripartite analysis of the requirements of intentionality, treating it as a relation holding between:

> Subject – Intentional mode – Intentional content (Crane 2003: 39).

On this rendering, the object at which the 'subject' is directed fails to appear as a *relata*. But right here something has gone badly wrong. Firstly, whereas talk of being directed at an object is relatively straightforward, we might wonder what being related to 'contents' consists in. Interestingly, Crane accepts that "the content of a sensation-state is a matter of its object *being presented in a certain way*. This content need not be propositional" (Crane 2003: 44). Construed thus, it may be difficult to see what distinguishes mere modes and non-propositional contents, since modes are defined as "a way of being aware" (Crane 2003: 52).[3] And despite allowing for the possibility of such content being non-propositional, Crane borrows from Valberg, explicating the nature of such content in the following counterfactual fashion: "The content is what one *would* put into words, if one were to have the words into which to put it" (Crane 2003: 39, emphasis mine). Unsurprisingly, this foreshadowing of the conceptual is brought out in the following characterisation of the content and object of pain: "the content of the sensation is *that* one's ankle hurts, the object of the sensation is the ankle (apprehended *as* one's ankle) and the mode is the hurting" (Crane 2003: 53).

Introducing content into the equation is an unnecessary and potentially confusing extra step when it comes to understanding *feeling towards*, at least in the most basic cases involving nonconceptual responses. For in such cases the object (or putative content) of experiences is not in fact put into words (nor for non-verbal animals is it clear what this would come to, even potentially). Talk of 'content' is appropriate *only* in characterising the conceptual aspects of experiential modes, as is necessary for distinguishing between 'seeing' and 'seeing as'. But if we accept that the basic capacities for experience are nonconceptual – and do not involve forming any kind of judgement –then, by my lights, these experiences will lack 'content' altogether.

Secondly, *contra* Crane, I want to retain the simpler idea that we are only ever directed at those items that we are meant to be directed at. When we are misdirected (so to speak), perhaps by responding to something else, nothing in our experience alone allows us to recognise this. I deny therefore that the possibility of misdirection, however frequent, gives us reason to think that we are directed at 'contents' (propositional, conceptual or otherwise) rather than at the objects or states of affairs that we are meant to be directed at when things are as they should be. In setting out his self-styled 'perceptual' variant of strong intentionalism, Crane observes that we cannot perceive without perceiving *something*. That is an analytic truth. But we can fail to perceive something while *believing* that we are (or otherwise responding as if we are). This is typically where appeal to experiences comes into its own. For what usually explains mistaken beliefs (or responses) is that things are not as they seem to us (see Hutto 2006a). We normally account for straightforward perceptual error by invoking experiences that make sense of why such beliefs seemed justified, given how things *looked* to us at the time.

By tying intentionality and phenomenology too tightly together, Crane's analysis threatens the possibility of explanations of this variety. To accommodate them properly requires endorsing a position that Crane summarily dismisses when considering the options. He writes, "The second view, that the phenomenal character of the state of mind is fixed purely by the mode, has little to be said for it; obviously, any plausible intentionalist view must allow that the intentional object and content contribute to phenomenal character" (Crane 2003: 50, emphasis mine).

In my view, object and content do not contribute to the phenomenal character by being part of what is experienced. I may have the feeling of being hit on the leg, even if I lack the concept of 'leg' or the means to articulate such a feeling in words (even potentially) and even if this gets the 'intentional object' or focus completely wrong (i.e. perhaps this feeling is caused by a nervous spasm). Ridding myself of all talk of 'states', 'qualia' etc., I say that our experiencing is directed towards objects or features of objects and that they have the characteristic feel that they do precisely *because* of the history that established this directedness. Intentional objects therefore fix the character of experience at a temporal distance. We can say that the distant objects at which our ancestors were directed contributed to the shaping of the experiential character of our experience without assuming that these are, in any way, *part* of our experience.

Thirdly, we are not *related* to the modes by which such objects are perceived, as Crane's analysis implies. These are the media through which we are related to the objects in question.

> Experiences are not seen; they are the *media through which we see*. In taking this line, we can see why the representationalists get the story generally right about the distal objects – internal or external – at which we are directed. But … even if we recognise this, it is still a mistake to confuse experience with intentional directedness, intentional objects or bodily or neural mechanisms. If we wish to avoid a host of intractable difficulties, it is better to regard consciousness, not as what is experienced, but as *how* things are experienced (Hutto 2000: 135, emphasis added).[4]

In proposing that basic experiences should be regarded as modes of presentation, I want to emphasise that they are not referents; appearances don't appear; things appear (cf. also Rowlands 2002: 174). That is, in understanding primitive experiential episodes as belonging to the category 'nonconceptual mode of presentation' in this way, we must beware of reifying them. If we take the metaphor too seriously, we will be tempted to imagine 'the way the world is presented' as an object appearing before the mind's eye of a passive observer – as a kind of 'calling card'. Talk of 'contents' and 'presentation' can encourage just this by conjuring up the wrong images. I want to emphasise the phenomenal character of experiential modes by insisting that we think of them in the context of actions done by or done to experiencers (i.e. be they agents or patients). Importantly, we can still refer to 'experiences' but rather than treating these as free-standing objects or qualitative items of select attention (such as 'redness' or 'pain') we would do better to give descriptions of the character of specific actions such as, 'Her seeing the red card' or 'My feeling of pain in my shoulder'.[5]

In line with this, I have elsewhere argued in favour of what is, effectively, a non-reductive variant of the ability hypothesis. It bids us to *understand* the character of experiences in terms of our active engagement with things and their features, without claiming that experiences are nothing but abilities. In short, viewed as a reductive account of what experiences are, the 'ability hypothesis' is circular, since the notion of a particular sort of experience (e.g. recognising red, re-identifying red) must be invoked in order to characterise the abilities in question. I endorse a version of this idea, which does not fall foul of such circularity because it surrenders all explanatory ambition, suggesting instead that in order to understand experience we must give attention to what is involved in the exercise of certain abilities descriptively. Hence, my insistence that we recognise both that experiences exist and that they matter (Hutto 2000: 53–55, 2006a). What we must not do is to think of them as 'existents', modelling these as inner objects, properties, and so on.

3. Getting in on the act

To clarify my position further, it will prove useful to contrast it with the sensorimotor contingency (SMC) approach to perceptual experience. This has been recently put forward by O'Regan and Noë and has been grabbing headlines. At first glance, it may look as if my position and theirs are much the same since they stress that experiences are not objects of perception but rather '*the way in which we perceive*'. Refreshingly, the SMC approach openly opposes the object-based schema and its use in understanding experiential activity.[6] Indeed, their rejection of this familiar way of understanding experience forms the basis for their critique of endeavours to identify neural correlates of consciousness. Their basic challenge to the tradition and the central idea of their alternative approach is encapsulated in the following passage:

> From the point of view of the brain, there is nothing that differentiates nervous influx coming from retinal, haptic, proprioceptive, olfactory, and other senses, and there is nothing to discriminate motor neurons that are connected to extraocular muscles, skeletal muscles, or any other structures. Even if the size, the shape, the firing patterns, or the places where the neurons are localized in the cortex differ,

> this does not in itself confer them with any particular visual, olfactory, motor or other perceptual quality.
>
> On the other hand, what *does* differentiate vision from, say, audition or touch, is the *structure of the rules* governing the sensory changes produced by various motor actions, that is, what we call the *sensorimotor contingencies* … Because the sensorimotor contingencies within different sensory domains (vision, audition, smell, etc.) are subject to different (in)variance properties, the structure of the rules that govern perception in these different modalities will be different in each modality (O'Regan & Noë 2001: 941).

While I endorse this basic message of the SMC approach – i.e., that the character of experiences is determined by sensorimotor contingencies specific to the various modalities – I reject many of the particulars of the account. Its proponents maintain that perceptual experience implicates (or equates to) a kind of skilled practical knowledge. I am unclear about the precise content of the claim as they set it out. To the extent that I do understand it, I am deeply sceptical of its truth. In setting it out, O'Regan and Noë tell us:

> The central idea of our new approach is that vision is a mode of exploration of the world that is *mediated by knowledge* of what we call sensorimotor contingencies (O'Regan & Noë 2001: 940).

What does '*mediated* by knowledge' mean in this instance? We are told that we 'draw on our mastery of relevant laws' when perceiving. As presented, 'knowledge' at this level appears to boil down to the brain's mastery of contingencies concerning the structure of the various modalities as they relate to the attributes of specific types of objects.

Also, ironically – given that the authors accuse their opponents of committing a naïve 'homunculus error' – all their examples of how the brain performs its operations involve unabashed talk of its assuming, judging and concluding all manner of things about observers and objects. This suggests that it employs 'propositional knowledge' or uses semantically evaluable subpersonal representations (O'Regan and Noë 2001: p. 950, 951).[7] If so, the knowledge upon which its mastery depends is therefore hardly 'practical'. We are told:

> The question nevertheless arises of how the *brain is able to accurately judge* whether an object is stationary (O'Regan & Noë 2001: 949, emphasis mine).

> If the retinal receptors did not signal a global smear during saccades, then the *brain would have to assume that* the observer was not seeing and that he or she was perhaps hallucinating or dreaming (O'Regan & Noë 2001: 950, emphasis mine).

> ...if retinal sensation were not to change dramatically when an object falls into the blind spot, then the *brain would have to conclude that* the object was not being seen, but was being hallucinated (O'Regan & Noë 2001: 951, emphasis mine).

Perhaps all this is shorthand and not meant to be taken too seriously. But if so, it is not clear what it is shorthand *for* or what the SMC view implies about *how* the brain achieves its various feats. Moreover, certain passages give the impression that the laws concerning the attributes of objects and their effects on our various perceptual systems exist independently, for its proponents say that "the animal, or its brain, must be 'tuned to' these" (O'Regan & Noë 2001: 943). If this talk of being attuned to (or more strongly having skilful mastery of) SMC laws is not meant to be *merely* metaphoric, the account is implausible. For we must ask, what could possibly motivate us to postulate the independent existence of laws to which organisms or brains are attuned? Certainly we need not do so in order to accept the weaker claim that the character of our experiences is determined by the structure of our perceptual modalities.

Objects, as we sometimes say, obey basic physical laws. What does that amount to? Take the relatively simple case of the effect of gravity. We can, of course, describe the rate of acceleration at which bodies move towards one another, expressed in the form of an equation. The so-called Law of Gravity applies to all falling bodies equally causing them to accelerate at a rate of 32 feet per second squared on Earth. Of course, in making their descent, falling objects are neither attuned to, nor do they represent, either this local variant or a more universal law. This law does not describe an external force, as Newton originally thought when he included it in his calculations alongside acceleration and mass. The 'force of gravity' was postulated as something external that explained why all bodies, despite their differences in mass, fall at the same rate. Tellingly, the only *evidence* for the existence of such a force was this uniform rate of acceleration itself, which troubled astute physicists. It wasn't until Einstein reformed our understanding of physics by introducing us to the idea of general relativity (and the concomitant notion of curved space time) that it became clear why there was no need to postulate any such force of gravity. This much is common knowledge. What then does the 'Law of Gravity' so accurately describe? It is neither an internal rule, the common following of which causes bodies to fall uniformly, nor it is some exogenous force that externally governs the motions of all such bodies. It simply describes (in an idealised fashion) the behaviour of bodies when accelerating, nothing more.

No one in this day and age would be tempted to explain the behaviour of a falling rock by suggesting that it, or any of its integral parts, is attuned to such laws or that it exhibits a mastery of them. Why then should operations of our sensory systems be regarded as essentially different, despite the fact that these too can be described mathematically, as exemplified by the specification that can be given of the operations of the simple arm-mounted photocell? (O'Regan & Noë 2001: 957) The mere fact that they are more complex or inside the 'skin' or 'skull', provides no justification for treating their operations differently than the behaviour of other physical bodies. Perhaps, the fact that they generate reliable effects suggests that the 'internal' changes must be using *special means* to keep pace with environmental changes, implying a special type of attunement. But it is easy enough to understand this type of more complicated attunement without introducing the idea that directed behaviour is law *governed* (internally or externally).

In avoiding this view I want to call on Millikan's account of simple 'intentional icons', which she holds are paradigms of our 'cover-all notion of a sign'.[8] According to her, such icons have the proper function of mapping on to specific features or objects and they are consumed by co-operating devices. These respond appropriately to such icons (in Normal circumstances), which is *their* proper function. As such, intentional icons have the following essential features:

1. They are relationally adapted to some feature, object or state of affairs.
2. The relation described in (a) can be characterised by means of a mapping rule.
3. They have the direct proper function of guiding co-operating (consumer) device(s) in the performance of its (or their) direct proper function(s).

Thus even the simplest type of intentional icon has both indicative and imperative aspects, which is why Millikan calls them pushme-pullyu devices. The figure eight dance of bees is a very clear example. These dances are meant to generate an appropriate response in a co-operating consumer mechanism (s); the watching bee or bees. The watcher(s) generate a patterned flight response that leads to the location of nectar (see Figure 1.1). If the conditions are historically Normal for this characteristic type of dance it will succeed in directing the icon-consuming bee(s) to the nectar's location. Natural history explains how the bees came to be attuned to each other and their normal environment in this way.

Crucially, however, there are no laws 'governing' the bee's behaviour or to which they are attuned; rather any laws we might construct when describing such antics will be a kind of fallout – fallout explained by their activity. Millikan's remarks concerning 'proximal' and 'distal' rules prove apposite. Using the male hoverflies as an example, she explains that their distal rule for action can be effectively rendered as 'if you see a female catch it' (Millikan 1993: 222). In the course of 'following this rule' a number of lower-level devices will need to effectively 'follow' more complex rules. Here is her example of a 'proximal rule':

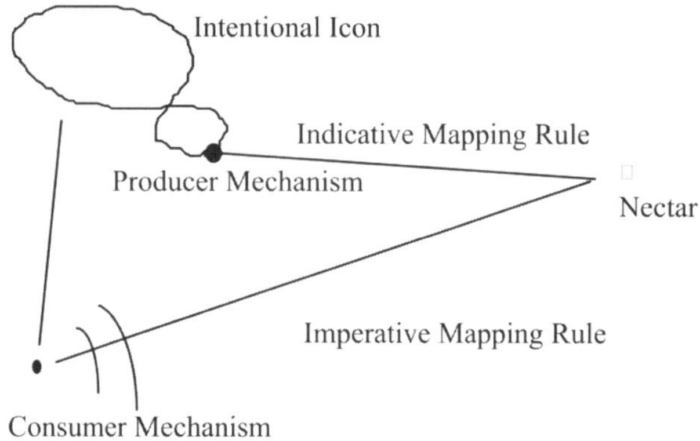

Figure 1.1 The intentional directedness of the bee dance

> Rather than turning toward the target in order to track it, the hoverfly turns away from the target and accelerates in a straight line so as to intercept it. Given that (1) female hoverflies are of uniform size, hence are first detected at a roughly uniform distance (about. 7 m), (2) females cruise at a standard velocity (about 8m/sec), and (3) males accelerate at a constant rate (about 30–35 m/sec2), the geometry of motion dictates that to intercept the female, the male must make a turn that is 180 degrees away from the target minus 1/10 of the vector angular velocity (measured in degrees per second) of the target's image across his retina... Taking note that this rule is not about how the hoverfly should behave in relation to distal objects but rather how he should react to a proximal stimulus, to a moving spot on his retina, let us call this rule 'the proximal hoverfly rule' (Millikan 1993: 28).

Again, the point is that neither the bees nor their lower level devices 'follow' these rules in performing their duties – they are not internally or externally represented, consulted, mastered or obeyed. Rather they are products of activity and, although they instantiate real patterns, these are only described for *our* benefit.

Although the example of co-operating 'mechanisms' in the bee dance is that of distinct organisms, we can see from Millikan's discussion of proximal rules that the account works just as well for distinct devices operating *within* a single organism. She is explicit about this intended use when she writes:

> Put (an analogue of) the bee dance inside the body so that it mediates between two parts of the same organism and you have... an inner representation (Millikan 1993: 164).[9]

For reasons I will make clear shortly, I am uncomfortable about talk of 'inner representations'. Nevertheless the basic point is all we need. For if different perceptual modalities developed to permit organisms to respond to salient features of their environments, then sensorimotor contingencies too will have been shaped in this way over the ages, as constrained by the nature of other 'internal' devices. Why do we experience certain features as 'green' rather than as 'red'? Or, why do we experience these as 'green' rather than as not experiencing them at all? Ultimately, we should answer with reference to facts concerning our natural history.

For these reasons we must treat with caution the claim of the SMC proponents that "visual exploration *obeys* certain laws of sensorimotor contingency" (O'Regan & Noë 2001: 941). Yet there is some evidence that the authors do not wish to commit themselves to anything extravagant in saying this. For in the very next sentence we are told that "The laws *are determined by* the fact that exploration is being done by the visual apparatus" (O'Regan & Noë 2001: 941). This last remark could be interpreted as the utterly innocuous claim that the laws in question are nothing other than what can be 'read off' the activity of perceptual systems as they respond to different types of objects.

This reading is in keeping with the idea that "even the out-of-order missile guidance system has a kind of ineffectual mastery of its sensorimotor contingencies" (O'Regan & Noë 2001: 943). Yet if there are no independently established laws, what does its 'ineffectual mastery' amount to (other than merely failing to meet *our* stipulated designs)? Since the missile is still operating, to some extent, why not say it has a competent or effective grasp or a sound mastery of a *different* set of sensorimotor contingencies? These might be determined by what the malfunctioning system actually does. This underlines, once again, that talk of such 'laws' lacks any normative or prescriptive force. Nothing in any purely descriptive comparison of the 'structure of the rules' of a properly functioning as opposed to the malfunctioning missile guidance system would enable us to tell which one was breaking *the* law. To do that we would need independent grounds for determining how the systems are *meant* to respond. In the case of artefacts deciding this is easy because we know in advance what ends they are supposed to serve. It is different with the products of Mother Nature. Still, as we have seen, it is possible to understand natural systems, such as our perceptual systems, as end-directed in a way that does allow for talk of them functioning properly or otherwise.

This brings us to another virtue of the proper functions approach. It permits talk of devices being ineffectual in achieving their ends without introducing the notion of '*skilful* mastery'. For example, my ability to breathe is not an exhibition of practical knowledge; it is not an achievement of mine, skilful or otherwise. It is not something that I have learned how to do, nor is it the result of training (contrast this with learning how to control one's breathing for deep sea diving or in response to an asthma attack). But is it then an achievement of my body or my lungs? Is it evidence of a kind of know-how of theirs? At best, this would be to speak metaphorically – at worst, it is simply confused. My lungs can fail to perform as they ought. They have biological proper functions and in this sense they may not operate as they should; they can fail to carry out these functions by not producing the kinds of results that items of this type have historically produced. The point is that such failure is not to be explained in terms of lack of knowledge or an ineffectual application of knowledge on the part of lungs. If they fail it will be due to mechanical malfunction or breakdown or because they find themselves in an 'abnormal' environment (e.g. if they have been artificially removed from their usual partner devices). Whether or not they are fulfilling their proper biological functions, we can still describe their operations. If we like, we can use our understanding of their proper functions to determine what their motor contingencies *should* be.

By taking this approach we can do away with the idea that our perceptual systems have a skilful practical mastery of subpersonal knowledge of SMC laws. But this enables us to accept the weaker claim that the basic *character* of our perceptual experiences is determined by the features of the various sensory modalities and the specific objects to which they respond. Rejecting the 'skilful mastery' account makes room for the possibility that even if a creature fails to perceive what it ought, it still might (depending on the nature and the extent of the failure) have perceptual experiences.

Finally, returning to the concern I raised about Crane's account, modestly understood, this approach gives us everything we need in order to understand the directness and phenomenal character of basic experiential responses, without introducing 'contents' into the equation. For what contents would such devices be 'directed at' or 'related to'? In *Language, Thought and Other Biological Categories* Millikan misleadingly spoke of 'producer and interpreter devices'. But given that she explicitly did not require the interpreter devices to 'understand what the sign signs', she later adopted the more appropriate term 'consumer' (Millikan 1984: 96). With direct reference to bees she writes:

> Bee dances, though (as I will argue) these are intentional items, do not contain denotative elements, because interpreter bees (presumably) do not identify the referents of these devices but merely react to them appropriately (Millikan 1984: 71).

In the case of the bees, figure eight icons are meant to direct the watching bees to nectar. But they cannot do this by 'indicating nectar' alone; to act appropriately they must be informationally sensitive and responsive to the relations holding between the sun, hive and nectar. This can make it seem as if successful action depends on the icons 'encoding' information about such complex relations. But bees have no 'understanding' of these or their 'significant parts', which are neither separately distinguishable nor substitutable. It is not possible to replace 'sun' with 'moon' in a bee dance. Instead transformations to the size and shape of *the whole* icon merely make a difference to the behaviour of these well-designed 'consumers'.

Nor does the bee dance as a whole 'stand for' anything – rather it is a device that should have the effect, if all is Normal, of guiding certain types of well-calibrated creatures to a particular goal. To the extent that it is correct to say that these dances 'carry' information, they might do so for someone who sees and understands the *whole* of this activity and its point; someone with this background knowledge can use the dances as reliable indicators, as they might use tree rings as an indicator of age. In both these cases, such information is a by-product. The bees themselves do not *use* one another's dances as reliable indicators *in this way*. Indeed their antics, honed over eons, *establish* or *generate* this indicative relationship; it is not something found and pressed into service for their purposes. This goes directly against Dretske's claim that such responses are grounded in the recruitment of intrinsic indicators, according to which "A sign is given a job of doing what it (suitably deployed) can *already* do" (Dretske 1988: 59).

In light of all this, it is at best misleading to talk of "the kinds of mapping functions that correlate intentional icons with the things they are icons of" (Millikan 1984: 104). For this encourages us to think of signs and things signified. And this in turn bids us to try to explicate the former using the 'words' that 'one' *would* use to describe such contents "if one were to have the words into which to put it" (Crane 2003: 39). Consider Elder's awkward attempt to provide such a designation in the case of the marina bacteria. He writes:

> The bacteria have not a single thought about oxygen, and could not recognize it if it were right in front of them. So it is misleading to suggest that the content of a given tug is 'oxygen-free water thither'; it would be better to say, 'safe travel that-away' (Elder 1998: 360).

It would be better still to say nothing at all. Once again, I see no reason to attempt to introduce talk of content in such cases, other than to satisfy our own interpretative needs (Hutto 1999, Godfrey-Smith 2002).

4. The ties that bind

It should now be clear how the above framework can help us to understand the connection between intentionality and the phenomenal character of basic forms of experience so as to make sense of emotional capacities for *feeling towards*, while doing away with many of the assumptions that give life to some of the 'hard' problems of consciousness. Rethinking the nature and function of experiencing along the lines suggested above shows many familiar philosophical worries to be misguided. For example, rejecting the object-based schema reveals as nonsensical questions about the location of conscious experiences; how they are bound together in the mind/brain; and how and why they relate to the nervous, physiological and neural mechanisms that underpin them.

Still, it might be wondered how advancing what is effectively a 'perceptual model' could help with the problems of other minds discussed at the outset. It may be hard to see how this might be done given the tendency to think of recognition-and-response patterns in individualistic and unidirectional terms. But we should resist both of these temptations; and resisting the first is particularly important if we are to understand aright the kinds of ends that emotional experiences and their expressions are likely meant to serve.

It is revealing that nearly all of Goldie's examples of sophisticated emotions, involving cases of love, anger and jealousy, speak to their social import. However, this aspect is much less prominent when he speculates about their likely evolutionary basis. Thus, he reminds us that "Darwin argued, some sorts of facial expression – for example barring of the teeth in anger – which were serviceable for some purpose in our remote ancestors, may in humans have taken on the secondary function of signalling an emotion to other members of the same species" (Goldie 2000: 97).

In some cases, this may be the right sort of account. Yet there is no reason to think that the functions of signals or other emotional expressions to produce effects on other organisms are necessarily *secondary* adaptations. It is possible that emotional recognition and response is something for which social animals have selectively been calibrated for directly. Once we surrender individualism, there is no reason to deny that the function of at least some of our capacities for emotional recognition and response are primarily social, not simply expressions designed to indicate 'internal' states (see Costall 1995). For example, whereas certain animals, such as frogs, may lack any need to express anger, pack animals such as wolves, need to employ a whole series of signals of graduated intensity, from mere annoyance to rage, in order to navigate their much more socially complex worlds. Thus, perhaps the *having* and *expressing* of certain *feelings towards* will *only* have become adaptations for creatures in which coordinated social activity is a must. Perhaps this will have *directly* "improved the average chances of survival and reproduction" (Goldie 2000: 95). It is easy enough to imagine that the having or lacking of such capacities could have had such an immediate impact on reproductive success and competition (sexual or otherwise) for social creatures.

The basic emotional expression of intentional attitudes may have the direct proper function of having particular effects on consumer organisms. The mere fact that such effects would have to be inter-organismic is no bar to this possibility. Consideration of the bee dance, in which the producer and consumer devices involve the interaction between whole organisms, is enough to remind us that there is no need to think that natural signs need be reproduced 'inside the skin'. Given this, it is plausible that seeing or recognising emotion in another's expressions has the function of producing characteristic emotional reactions and responses in certain perceivers, provoking both characteristic feelings and actions.

The thought I want to promote is that facts about our natural history can ultimately account for our primitive psychological reactions to others, both in the sorts of cases in which emotions are shared and those in which they contrast. The scripts of affect routines are flexible enough to explain both the cases of embodied responding in which we mirror others and those in which we do not. For, as Smith rightly observes, "We sympathize with people's plight and in doing so we are not required to share their feelings. When I observe someone's humiliation, it is pity I feel, not humiliation" (Smith 2002: 120). In a similar vein, your anger might fuel my anger or it might induce fear in me, depending on our characters. Even in the wild, this sort of variation is typical of the responses of individuals.

Importantly, although Mother Nature will have initially 'tied' these tendencies for recognition and response together, these can be put asunder; this happens, for example, in abnormal circumstances or when the lower-level devices that underwrite such activity go awry. More interestingly, these patterns can be re-tied such that our recognitional capacities come to yield new or additional responses (and *vice versa*), through education or habitual training (cf. Goldie 2000: 12). It is because of this that the emotions can be enculturated, in response to the canonical demands of local norms. The very fact that recognition-and-response ties *can* be undone shows that Wittgenstein was right in resisting behaviourism; he was right to insist that the characteristic expressions of emotion must be treated as *symptoms* of their associated emotions and not as *criteria* for them. With respect to sophisticated emotions, this is what makes it possible for stage actors to ply their trade. But even in nature – when it comes to simpler forms of response – there are other 'actors' who take on the symptomatic outward expressions of other species in order to gain advantages.

None of what I have said above should lead us to deny that it is the individual creatures that *feel* emotions by way of response to the expressions of others or features of worldly objects. Nevertheless, acceptance that emotionally charged social effects are proper functions – whether primary or secondary – is enough to upset the traditional understanding of the boundaries between self and other. For it follows that strong individualism does not make sense at this fundamental level. Crucially, the 'perception of emotion' can be accounted for without introducing anything like the idea that the creature doing the signalling is doing so knowingly or that in responding appropriately the consuming creature is making any inferences.

It is unfortunate that such capacities are often gathered together under the heading of 'mind reading' by today's behavioural ecologists and developmental psychologists, for it suggests a misleadingly individualistic picture of the way in which we engage with one another.[10] It would be wrong to think that infants and animals are using some kind of theory, inferential reasoning or projective type of simulation procedure in order to make *ascriptions* on the basis of observed behaviour – and only thereby bridging an existing gap between self and other (see Hutto 2002, 2003, 2006b). In line with the account sketched above, in the basic cases there is no need for such ascriptions since there is no such gap to bridge. It is much more plausible to think that cases of emotion sharing, imitation, motor mimicry and even more sophisticated contrastive emotional responses are better explained as instances of naturally calibrated reactions to the circumstances and actions of others; in normal environments we engage practically and emotionally with each other, without the need for theoretical mediation.

We should follow Gordon who, in promoting his peculiar variant of the simulation theory, has argued that the process should be understood as a *hot* methodology precisely because the imaginative transformations it involves require that one "exploit one's own motivational and emotional resources" (Gordon 1996: 11). He rejects the introspectionism found in many other simulationist accounts, persistently stressing that simulation should not be understood as a process of transportation but rather one of transformation. Crucially, he maintains that such transformations do not involve, as he puts it, any inference from me to you (Gordon 1995; Gordon 1996: 12).[11] To think otherwise gets the direction of affection back-to-front, since what is needed is a reliable method of indicating the *other's* perspective on events, not a projection of our own on or into theirs. This is especially important in the kinds of cases that we are considering. For on Gordon's account it is not necessary for a simulator to make an assumption of analogy between themselves and the other (not even an implicit one) in order for this type of procedure to work. In sum, we have strong grounds for doubting that appeals to tacit knowledge are necessary in order to explain how, in our normal environments, we reliably respond to the actions and expressions of others to whom we are calibrated and *vice versa*.[12]

This does away with the strong first/third person divide at least with respect to our basic emotional responses and expressions. Thus the conceptual problem of other minds evaporates: there is no reason to think that, as children, we ever faced a hard choice in the learning of our basic perceptual or emotional concepts – that of ostensively focusing on their introspected, internal, qualitative characters or the outward behaviours of others when establishing their conceptual extensions. Similarly, if these basic systems of emotional expression and response subtend our normal adult interactions, the epistemological problem of other minds also loses its teeth. On this account we do not neutrally observe the outward behaviour of another and only then infer coldly that they are in such and such an inner state, on less than certain grounds, as, say, justified by analogy with our own case. Rather we react and feel as we do because it is natural for us to see and be moved by specific expressions of emotion in others.

5. Full circle

In closing, I also want to correct any residual impression that the capacities for recognition and response should be thought of in unidirectional or in crude input-output terms. Sticking with the perceptual model set out in section 3, we must not underestimate the importance that attention plays in directing acts of perception. Indeed, the authors of the SMC approach have argued explicitly cognitive engagements involving explicit attending are what make experience possible. By their lights, perceptual awareness is a bifurcated one: not entirely unlike the position promoted by higher-order thought (or perception) theories of consciousness. Accordingly, although the sensorimotor contingencies account for the characteristic *feel* of specific types of awareness we are only ever conscious of these when we attend to certain features or things.

Acts of attention are typically characterised as involving full-fledged propositional thoughts, as, say, when I am specifically hunting for my missing spectacles. But my actions need not be framed in this way. We often unintentionally or unknowingly attend to features and things; sometimes, we are drawn to them despite ourselves. One notices or catches oneself looking at something or someone, often despite oneself. Examples of this, some quite embarrassing, are all too easy to come by.

What explains this? Megill has recently argued that emotions, as opposed to merely cognitive factors, ought to be recognised for their role in driving selective attention. On his account there must be "something about a first-order thought… that draws the attention of the internal attention mechanism" (Megill 2003: p. 85). He proposes that emotional import may be responsible for this, if we conceive of emotions as forming part of the very meaning of the concepts that go to make up our thoughts. Thus, the 'something about P' that grabs our attention could then be its emotional 'element'. In this way, as per the tradition, he is inclined to reify emotions by thinking of them in terms of properties, parts and constituents (in effect, they are conceived as proper parts of objective Fregean *senses*).

Although I think he is right to link attention and emotion, this tendency to objectify, along with several other features of his approach, should be rejected. For, along with this reification of the 'emotional elements' comes the idea that they are 'internal', as indicated in the quotation above. Thus he elsewhere claims that emotions shape the meaning of the "narrow content of P" (Megill 2003: 91). Here, once again, 'contents' are made substantial: they are located, have proper parts and we can be directed at or related to them. This leads to confusions, also witnessed earlier, of the following sort:

> ...emotions are highly contextual phenomena. For example, I am not afraid of the polar bear at the zoo. I.e. I don't associate fear with the 'polar bear' concept in this context. However, if a polar bear somehow made its way into my apartment, I probably would associate fear with the 'polar bear' concept. This is to say: I associate fear with the proposition 'A polar bear is in my apartment', but not with 'A polar bear is in the zoo'... (Megill 2003: 92).

Sticks and stones! Polar bears themselves are quite worthy of fear, but propositions in and of themselves will never hurt us – nor should or do we fear them. I may *fear* that a polar bear is in my apartment, but that is to be afraid of a certain state of affairs obtaining, not an 'internal proposition' or 'narrow content' which represents or presents it (cf. Stout 2004: 230).[13] Failure to rid ourselves of such notions of cognitive content and this internal/external imagery leads to other problems as well. For example, there is also an obvious regress on the horizon if we try to explicate what is involved in 'grabbing the attention of the attention mechanism' in terms of *its* capacity to attend.

Megill does well to remind us that when something is of emotional import, it tends to be or becomes the focus of attention. But he does not go far enough. He implies that his sort of approach has the potential to solve part of the frame problem since one aspect of it concerns the "question of how we know what to pay attention to in our environment, i.e. we seem to naturally pay attention to the more salient aspects of our environment" (Megill 2003: 98). However, merely noting that certain salient features of things or states of affairs elicit emotional responses does not make it less mysterious *why* this is so. Presumably, we want to know *why* these features, objects, actions or situations are perceived of as important or in an emotionally charged way. Or, using Megill's language, we would like to know *why* our 'attention mechanism' finds certain Ps, but not others, important. The problem is that Megill is attracted to a sort of functional flowchart boxology, of the sort inspired by a traditional input-output functionalism. And the trouble with such boxology is that it encourages lots of pre-packing activity, such as labelling and putting things into boxes, but rarely results in any serious explanatory unpacking.

In contrast, by adopting a proper function view, the question of ends is always in the forefront; the means follow in train. Approaching matters in this way not only forces one to go beyond static labelling, but it also reveals that it may not be possible to distinguish cleanly between inputs and outputs. For example, as I argued above in responding to simple signs (or signals), organisms and their devices are not engaged in acts of interpretation. If these signs have no 'content' it becomes an important question as to what such signals are input *for* and output *from*. As a consequence, as Hurley has suggested, we may be required to question the idea that perception and action are strongly 'independent'. Having said this, it is but a small step to add affect to this equation.[14] Although I will not pursue it further here, one might think that if such things cannot (and should not) be neatly distinguished, it may be a mistake to think that acts of perception are ever truly emotionless or value-free.

Notes

1 I am grateful to the Mind Association for providing me with a Research Fellowship in 2004 that gave me the time to finalise this paper. Many of the views expressed in it have been influenced by comments and discussions that took place at the following conferences where earlier versions or aspects of ideas within were presented: Enactive Perception Symposium, organised by Centre for Research in Cognitive Science, Sussex and the Consciousness and Experimental section of the British Psychological Society, March 2004; Eastern Division Meeting of the American Philosophical Association, Washington, DC., December 2003 and the Embodiment and Intersubjectivity, Leuven, Belgium, September 2003.

2. He writes, "once it is accepted, as it should be, that the object of an emotion need not be a proposition, and can be, for example, a person, then it becomes clear that I can perfectly coherently say that you are angry with James (adding, perhaps, that this is because you think he stole your shoelaces) whilst at the same time insisting that your emotion is ungrounded" (Goldie 2000: 22).

3. He provides the following example of the mode of pain: "The hurting … is the way the body part or location is (so to speak) forcing itself into one's consciousness" (Crane 2003: 54).

4. Unlike Crane I want to keep the elements of the intentionalist account separate. Thus, in *Beyond Physicalism*, I wrote: "If we wish to talk of experiences as modes of presentation, we must distinguish: the object itself and its properties, the intentionality that directs us at this rather than that object, and the way in which the object is presented to a subject" (Hutto 2000: 134, emphasis added).

5. Crane goes against one version of the object-based schema when he observes that the 'property'-based understanding of experiences is misguided, arguing that they are in fact 'covertly relational'. He writes, "it does not take much reflection to realize that the way a perception 'feels' is different from the way a bodily sensation feels; we can talk about how it feels to see red, so long as we do not think of this in terms of a certain 'feel' of redness (say) around one's eyes" (Crane 2003: 35). However, ultimately he fails to free himself from using that schema altogether. For by endorsing intentionalism, the idea that experiences are in fact intentional states, he continues to accept that, "Pain is a state of consciousness, or an event in consciousness" (Crane 2003: 31). For example, while he denies that pains are a kind of qualia – which would make them higher-order properties of intentional states – he nevertheless falls in line with the standard idea that "states are normally understood as instances of properties" (Crane 2003: 45).

6. The authors are equally concerned to reject the conception of visual experience as the harbouring of inert or passive 'inner' representations of external scenes. They amass a great deal of empirical evidence, including experiments concerning change and inattentional blindness, which they marshal, successfully, to discredit this idea.

7. Thus despite promoting the idea that experience requires practical knowledge, O'Regan's and Noë's talk of mastering laws appears to be exactly the kind of conflation of practical and propositional knowledge that Ryle anticipated and to which he objected. His reason for introducing the know-how and know-that distinction was precisely to attack what he called the 'intellectualist legend'. He predicted however that "Champions of this legend are apt to try to reassimilate knowing how and knowing that by arguing that intelligent performance involves the observance of rules, or the application of criteria" (Ryle 1949: 29). He cautioned us that if we are to avoid regress, knowing how could not be defined in terms of knowledge that – since even if we could make sense of the idea of 'regulative propositions' knowing how and when to apply them could not be a matter of knowing yet another set of 'regulative propositions' (Ryle 1949: 31–2). Indeed, he took this to be the 'crucial objection' to the intellectualist legend.

8. She borrows the term 'icon' from Peirce because it does not carry with it the same legacy of confusion and disagreement as the term 'representation'.

9. Millikan writes, "Roughly indeed, the idea is this. Cognitive systems are designed by evolution to make abstract pictures of the organism's environment and to be guided by these pictures in the production of appropriate actions" (Millikan 1993: 11, cf. Rowlands 1997: 283).

10. The very fact that Nichols and Stich regard the term mindreading to be 'theoretically' neutral, is evidence of the pervasive influence of this unquestioned assumption (Nichols and Stich 2003: 2). That is to say, they assume that all engagements are of a mentalistic variety, involving attributions, predictions and explanations. Their theoretical neutrality therefore, only extends to allowing the possibility that these ends might be achieved either by means of 'a theory-like body of information' or simulative 'role-taking'.

11. He also denies that simulation is not an intellectually governed enterprise, holding that it "operates primarily at the sub-verbal level" (Gordon 1986: 170).

12. Others have advocated a similar approach under the heading of 'primary intersubjectivity'. Accordingly, they use the lingo of 'body reading' to remind us that our basic interactions with others are such that, "one perceives the emotion in the movement and expression of the other's body" (cf. Gallagher 2001: 90).

13. As Stout rightly observes, "To treat practical rationality as simply concerned with the rational responses to different psychological states would be a crude form of psychologism every bit as bad as the psychologism that Frege objected to concerning the principles of logic" (Stout 2004: 230).

14. Providing us with a lovely bit of word play, Hurley reminds us that in resisting the idea of pure input (the myth of the given) we must equally take care to resist the idea of pure output (the myth of the giving) (Hurley 1998: 240–1).

References

Chalmers, D. 2003. "The Content and Epistemology of Phenomenal Belief." In *Consciousness: New Philosophical Perspectives*, Q. Smith and A. Jokic (eds), 220–72. Oxford: Oxford University Press.

Costall, A. 1995. "Socializing Affordances." *Theory and Psychology* 5 (4): 467–81.

Crane, T. 2003. "The Intentional Structure of Consciousness." In *Consciousness: New Philosophical Perspectives*, Q. Smith and A. Jokic (eds), 33–56. Oxford: Oxford University Press.

Dretske, F. 1988. *Explaining Behaviour: Reasons in a World of Causes*. Cambridge, MA: MIT Press.

Elder, C. 1998. "What Versus How in Naturally Selected Representations." *Mind* 107 (426): 349–63.

Ellis, R. and Newton, N. 2000. "The Interdependence of Consciousness and Emotion." *Consciousness and Emotion* 1 (1): 1–10.

Gallagher, S. 2001. "The Practice of Mind: Theory, Simulation or Primary Interaction?" *Journal of Consciousness Studies* 8(5–7): 83–108.

Godfrey-Smith, P. 2002. "On the Evolution of Representational and Interpretative Capacities." *The Monist* 85 (1): 50–69.

Goldie, P. 2000. *The Emotions: A Philosophical Exploration*. Oxford: Oxford University Press.

Goldie P. 2003. "One's Remembered Past: Narrative, Thinking, Emotion and the External Perspective". *Philosophical Papers* 32: 301–20.

Goldman, A. 1989. "Interpretation Psychologized." *Mind and Language* 4: 161–85.

Gordon R M. 1995. "Simulation without Introspection or Inference from Me to You". In *Mental Simulation*, M. Davies and T. Stone (eds), 53–67. Oxford: Blackwell.

Gordon R. M. 1996. "Radical Simulationism". In *Theories of Theories of Mind*, P. Carruthers and P. Smith, (eds), 11–21. Cambridge: Cambridge University Press.

Griffiths, P. 1997. *What Emotions Really Are*. Chicago/London: University of Chicago Press.

Hurley, S. 1998. *Consciousness in Action*. Cambridge, MA: Harvard University Press.

Hutto, D.D. 1997. "The Story of the Self: The Narrative Basis of Self-Development." *In Critical Studies: Ethics and the Subject*, K. Simms (ed.), 61–75. Amsterdam: Rodopi.

Hutto, D.D. 1999. *The Presence of Mind*. Amsterdam: John Benjamins.

Hutto, D.D. 2000. *Beyond Physicalism*. Amsterdam: John Benjamins.

Hutto, D.D. 2002. "The World Is Not Enough: Shared Emotions and Other Minds." In *Understanding Emotions*, P. Goldie (ed.), 37–53. Aldershot: Ashgate.

Hutto, D.D. 2004. "The Limits of Spectatorial Folk Psychology." *Mind and Language* 19: 548–73.

Hutto, D.D. 2006a. "Turning Hard Problems on Their Heads." *Phenomenology and the Cognitive Sciences* (forthcoming).

Hutto, D.D. 2006b. "Knowing What?: Radical versus Conservative Enactivism." *Phenomenology and the Cognitive Sciences* (forthcoming).

Jackson, F. 1999. "All That Can Be at Issue in the Theory-Theory Simulation Debate." *Philosophical Papers* 28(2): 77–96.

Megill, J. 2003. "What Role Do the Emotions Play in Cognition? Towards a New Alternative to Cognitive Theories of Emotion." *Consciousness and Emotion* 4 (1): 81–100.

Millikan, R. G. 1984. *Language, Thought and Other Biological Categories*. Cambridge, MA: MIT Press.

Millikan, R. G. 1993. *White Queen Psychology and Other Essays for Alice*. Cambridge, MA: MIT Press.

Nichols, S. and Stich, S. 2003. *Mindreading: An Integrated Account of Pretence, Self-Awareness and Understanding of Other Minds*. Oxford: Oxford University Press.

O'Regan, J. K. and Noë, A. 2001. "A Sensorimotor Account of Vision and Visual Consciousness." *Behavioural and Brain Sciences* 24: 939–1031.

Rowlands, M. 1997. "Teleological Semantics." *Mind* 106(422): 279–303.

Rowlands, M. 2002. "Two Dogmas of Consciousness." *Journal of Consciousness Studies* 9 (5–6): 158–80.

Ryle, G. 1949. *The Concept of Mind*. London: Hutchinson.

Smith, B. 2002. "Keeping Emotions in Mind." In *Understanding Emotions*, P. Goldie (ed.), 111–121. Aldershot: Ashgate.

Stout, R. 2004. "Internalising Practical Reasons." *Proceedings of the Aristotelian Society* CIV (3): 229–43.

Velmans, M. 2000. *Understanding Consciousness*. London: Routledge.

Feelings and objects

Erik Myin and Lars De Nul

1. Introduction

One of the things Dan Hutto warns us against in 'Unprincipled Engagements' is of committing a category error in the realm of emotions. Once one misconstrues emotions as objects, so Hutto argues, the door is open for a series of traditional philosophical 'hard problems' about whether and how other minds 'feel'. In particular, once emotions are construed on the object-model, it becomes almost compelling to adopt an inferential theory of how one comes to know someone else's emotions.

Hutto proposes to consider emotions in a framework in which experiences are not thought of as objects that appear, but rather as the ways in which the world, as a complex of actual spatial objects, appears. This is not to characterise emotions as experiences, for emotions, while containing experiential episodes, have a complex, episodic structure, dynamically extended over time. In this respect, emotions are like acts of perception, with which they also share the characteristic of intentionality.

In construing emotions on the basis of perception, and perception as action, Hutto's approach thus seems to have affinities with the recently proposed sensorimotor contingency theory of perception. Though Hutto acknowledges parallelisms, he also discerns remnants of the object-model in the sensorimotor theory, and criticises it for that. His own way of developing the 'perceptual model' of emotion is to apply Ruth Millikan's idea of 'proper functions'. Once one describes emotions as having the proper function of negotiating social life through directly arousing other, and often different, emotions in fellow humans, the motivation to think about emotions in terms of inner objects no longer gets a foothold.

2. Hard problems and object-based schemas

A first issue we would like to raise concerns the precise link between what Hutto calls the object-based schema and the family of 'hard problems' about consciousness (including the 'problem of phenomenal experience' as well as the 'other minds problem'). It seems to us that the source of the hard problems might be a more general 'objectivism', of which the use of 'object-based schemas' is but a particular manifestation. The broader 'objectivism' we have in mind is the thesis that there exist objective (as opposed to subjective) descriptions of anything that is real. A common motivation behind what we mean by objectivism goes as follows: everything real is physical. Everything that is physical has an objective description. So everything real must have an objective description. Applied to experience and emotions, objectivism will lead us to expect that, as emotions are (ultimately) identical to physical processes, there could be some objective description of these physical processes. It seems to us that objectivism, thus characterised, is considerably broader than the use of object-based schemas. That is, one could agree that experience and *a fortiori* emotions, should not be construed as (inner) objects, but as dynamic and temporally extended processes, ripe with narrative structure, and yet endorse the objectivist thesis that an objective description of these processes is in principle possible. More specifically, one could embrace an idea of perception-as-action, and transfer it to emotion-as-action, and simultaneously believe that objective descriptions of perceptual or emotive acts are principally possible.

For example (to stick with perception), one might insist that feeling the softness of a sponge lies in the process of actively exploring it (O'Regan, Myin and Noë, in press), while also believing that some objective description of that exploratory process, involving perhaps both bodily, environmental and neural elements, could be provided. The family of hard problems arises, or so it seems to us, from intuitions that such objective descriptions do 'leave something out', or offer an 'incomplete description' of reality. Various attitudes can be adopted here. Some philosophers vehemently defend that there is indeed something missing, which can lead either to despair about the limits of objectivism, or to attempts to devise ways in which the missing aspect could be grasped. Quite a different option, while admitting that (perhaps) some objective description of experience-as-action is not precluded, is to question whether there is any serious problem of 'something that is left out' at all. Here, one could point out that the intuition of something missing in objective descriptions springs from a mistaken attempt to recover, in reflecting on experience (that is, in one's objective description), what is obviously only present in 'living' the experience. Or: in actually exploring a sponge, one does (under additional conditions, such as not being too distracted by something else) relate to the experience of the softness in a unique way, which differs significantly from the way one relates to that experience later. To use some of Hutto's phrases: in the first case (of being the experiencer), the experience is the medium through which one relates to the sponge, in the second case (in reflecting upon the experience), the experience rather becomes the (intentional) object of one's reflection.[1]

Notice that even if one takes the latter option, one can still proclaim the existence of an 'even harder' hard problem, namely the problem of how it is possible that such two different ways of relating to an experience (can) exist (Rowlands 2002).

Whatever stance one takes, it seems to us that the 'hard problems' of consciousness arise and should be treated at the more general level of 'objectivism', rather than at the level of 'object-based schemas'. That is, questions about how we can know about the (quality of) the experiences of other minds, seem to spring from the issue whether objectivist descriptions 'leave something out'.
Insofar as Dan Hutto, in 'Unprincipled Engagements', attempts to address the hard problems by treating of object-based schema's, we suspect his goals will only be partially reachable.

3. Skill in perception and emotion

This brings us to a second, related, issue. It seems to us there is no a priori problem with 'object-based schemas' in science, including 'cognitive science' and neuroscience. By this we simply mean that one should allow the various sciences, including 'sciences of the mind', to invoke all kinds of objects (from neurons to – perhaps – inner representations[2]). The recourse to such inner objects only becomes problematic, so it seems to us, once they are 'overinterpreted': i.e. once the objects that figure in them are identified with experience.

Identification is problematic for two distinct reasons. Firstly, because it is quite plausible that an active, perceptual model of experience is correct, and that experience thus is a dynamical and extended process. This would mean that when identifying experiences with objects, we are simply using the wrong conceptual tools to get an explanatory grip on what experience is. And secondly, it is problematic for all the reasons why objectivism is problematic. That is so, irrespective of which of the two previously described attitudes towards 'hard problems' one adopts. Identifying experiences with something like objects unavoidably results in an attempt to provide an objective description of these experiences. We are then either 'leaving something out', i.e. every link to the qualitative aspect of experience, or we are mistakenly assuming that the unique relation to experience present in the lived perspective can be totally grasped from within a reflective framework.

We suggest that Hutto may be overinterpreting the sensorimotor contingency theory in this way. He warns for problematic identifications where they are absent or, at least, not intended to be read that way. As Hutto concedes, the idea that 'experience is in the act' is central to the sensorimotor contingency approach. It is by our active exploration of the environment, our acting in the world, that experience comes into being. But in order to gain additional insight in why our phenomenal experience is the way we know it to be, it seems perfectly legitimate to appeal to an analysis of the kinds of capacities we bring into play in this interactive encounter with the environment. And that is precisely where talk of sensorimotor contingencies fits in. We think these should not be interpreted in any object-based 'internalistic' way, but rather as patterns that structure perceiver-environment interaction. Mastery of sensorimorimotor contingencies, in our preferred reading, just indicates the ability of a perceiver to engage in specific interactions. And where in various presentations of the theory, it is emphasised that experience lies in exercising one's mastery, we read this as pointing to the unique relation to experience one has in living it: it serves to remind us that the 'feel' of softness is present only in the active exploration of a concrete sponge, and warns against the idea that that feel should be fully recoverable from any other perspective.

Not overinterpreted, the sensorimotor approach seems perfectly compatible with the 'proper function' account that Hutto proposes. Moreover, the idea of 'skill' might prove to be a necessary ingredient even for the rather basic functions that Hutto considers, namely negotiating social relations through directly arousing a (possibly different) emotion. In order to have the required sensitivity for the arousing emotion, it might be a precondition that one has abilities, comparable to skills, to engage in quite complicated natural and social interactions. To refer to an example of Merleau-Ponty: an erotic scene might have no emotional meaning for a young child, just because it does not participate in the 'way of life' which is constitutive for sexuality, and the emotional sphere surrounding it (Merleau-Ponty 1945).[3]

Notes

1. In reflection the thought can be considered to be the medium through which one relates to the (now past) experience.

2. There might be plenty of other problems with representations, but they seem independent of the existence of 'hard problems'.

3. Erik Myin would like to thank the University of Antwerp for Financial support (BOF kleine projecten 2005). Many thanks also, for stimulating discussions and providing intellectual context, to the participants at the two conferences on Enactive Perception organised by Steve Torrance in 2003 and 2004 in Oxford and Sussex and to his colleagues at the Centre for Logic and Philosophy of Science of the Department of Philosophy at the University of Brussels, with which Erik Myin has an additional affiliation. Lars De Nul is Research Assistant of the Research Foundation – Flanders (FWO – Vlaanderen).

References

O'Regan, J.K., Myin, E. and Noë, A. (2005). "Skill, corporality and alerting capacity in an account of sensory consciousness." *Progress in Brain Research (-)*, 150, 55–68.

Merleau-Ponty, M. 1945. *Phénoménologie de la Perception*. Paris: Gallimard.

Rowlands, M. 2002. "Two Dogma's of Consciousness." *Journal of Consciousness Studies* 9, (5–6): 158–180.

Impossible problems and careful expositions

Reply to Myin and De Nul

Daniel D. Hutto

1. Intelligibility and impossible problems

Myin and De Nul suggest that there may be no "precise link between what Hutto calls the object-based schema and the family of 'hard problems' about consciousness (including the 'problem of phenomenal experience' as well as the 'other minds problem')." They hold that the true source of these problems might be a more general 'objectivism'. I do not think that the hard problems can be solved but I do hold that adherence to the object-based schema (OBS) is the source of such problems when it comes to thinking about experience because it is the source of *the temptation to think* that they admit of straight solutions, at least possibly. That is and has long been my claim about the precise link between the OBS and much current thinking about consciousness.

I take it that Myin and De Nul are falling in with a fairly common misunderstanding of my ambitions when they claim that in attempting to "address the hard problems by treating of object-based schemas" my "goals will only be partially reachable" (Myin and De Nul: this volume).[1] I have consistently said that hard problems cannot be solved. And because they cannot be solved, we are best advised to avoid trying to deal with them. This is not a 'cop out'. It is the exercise of practical wisdom: Do not try to solve problems that cannot be solved. The *really* hard problem is getting a certain class of thinkers to see that the hard problems in question are not ones that *can* be solved. Thus a major aim of *Beyond Physicalism* was to articulate the conditions under which a satisfying account of the relation between the 'mental' and the 'physical' might be obtained. In particular, my aim was to reveal that in order to make consciousness intelligible in physical terms requires showing how it could be captured within the object-based schema. By demonstrating that this *cannot* be achieved – not even in principle – my ultimate goal was to enable my readers to purge themselves of the misbegotten ambition to 'explain consciousness' once and for all.[2]

In illustrating this in more detail, in this reply I focus exclusively on what I call the metaphysical problem – which concerns providing an intelligible representation of the relation between the mental and the physical – in this section, and the phenomenology problem – which concerns the correct way in which to understand the character of conscious experiences – in the next. In addressing the latter I say more about how and why I think the SMC approach should be modified in order to do proper service. I lack space to discuss the conceptual problem of 'other minds' and what Myin and De Nul identify as the 'even harder' problem: "How it is possible that two different ways of relating to an experience – [the unreflective and the reflective] (can) exist" (Myin and De Nul: this volume). But I try to do so in my reply to Hobson, where I make clear the need both to deal with philosophical puzzles as well as to answer the challenges of how we should understand the development of concepts. I see these as complementary tasks – indeed the latter presupposes getting a clear head about the former.

Turning to the metaphysical problem first, let us consider the reasoning that Myin and De Nul see as promoting 'objectivism'. For them it goes like this:

1. Everything real is physical.
2. Everything that is physical has an objective description.
3. So everything real must have an objective description.

This sort of argument might get someone who is already a physicalist to endorse objectivism. But since physicalism is a form of objectivism this would be a question-begging argument *from* physicalism. Because of this I doubt this could be the kind of thinking that is responsible for promoting objectivism at large. Here is an argument *for* physicalism that would seemingly lend better support to 'a general objectivism':

1. Everything that happens occurs in space-time (or, all events occur in space-time);
2. Anything that happens in space-time can be given a physical description;
3. Anything that can be described in a physical vocabulary is physical;
4. Everything that happens is physical (or, all events are physical events).

There is a way of agreeing with all of this while rejecting physicalism (for full details see Hutto 2000: ch. 5). For one may agree with the conclusion that all events are physical without accepting that they are exclusively so. Events can be properly characterized in many other ways than by using the vocabulary of physics and how we talk about them matters to the inferences we can draw and this matters, for example, to what explanations and predictions we can make about events, so described. When events are described in different ways, different features are on exhibit: attending to these requires the use of different methodologies and vocabularies. Non-reductive physicalists hold this – but I think that position, when understood as sponsoring explanatory ambitions is hopeless and when it is not it collapses into a more neutral and absolute form of monism. Thus:

> however perfect we might think physical explanations might become for certain purposes, it must be recognised that such explanations are just as limited and interest-sensitive as all others. If this is right, then even if every spatio-temporal event had a potential physical description, it would not follow that all of their salient features could be understood within an ideal physics. If certain phenomena resist incorporation into the object-based schema, we would have reason for thinking that physical descriptions, however useful, would be incomplete, for they do not provide a transparent window through which to view every aspect of an event's nature.
> The point is that the extensional manoeuvre does nothing to clear the air of the mystery that hangs over psychophysical causation. This is hardly surprising since *a suitably cautious minimal physicalism makes no attempt to resolve the intelligibility problem*. To solve this problem would require providing an explanatory theory of consciousness. The point is that postulating identities makes no advance in this regard. For merely stipulating that Y and F are identical provides no clearer understanding of the psychophysical relation since such understanding rests on having an explanation at the level of *sense* (cf. Lowe 1996: 75). What then, if anything, is the advantage of endorsing minimal physicalism, as opposed to substance dualism?
>
> Minimal physicalism is attractive, not because of explanatory virtues, but for its metaphysical economy. The fact that it is monistic enables us to postulate, for example, the existence of causal closure, even if we cannot fully comprehend the nature of causal interaction in extension. But this raises the question: If monism is all we are after or all we can legitimately have, what entitles us to endorse the physicalist claim that physics provides a privileged, true picture of the universe in all its nakedness (cf. Putnam 1988: ch. 1)? It is the inability to give a convincing answer to this question that makes the physicalist construal of the token identity thesis questionable. The minimal physicalist is faced with the following dilemma. On the one hand, if they hold that the world in extension is in most full and complete sense nothing but the world described by an ideal physics, how then can consciousness be a genuine phenomenon? On the other hand, if we reject the claim that the world in extension can be correctly characterised *exclusively* by any one discourse, then what is 'physicalist' about the token identity thesis? Indeed, to drop the claim that ideal physical descriptions are privileged when it comes to describing reality is, in effect, to endorse some variety of idealism (Hutto 2000: 152, with changes).

I endorse an identity thesis – though, to be sure, it is one of my own peculiar Bradleyian as opposed to a *prêt-a-porter* physicalist variety. Thus I endorse what Myin and De Nul are here calling 'objectivism'. That is, I accept that experiences are happenings. They are events – and as such they have physical descriptions (at least potentially). Nevertheless, I reject all versions of explanatory physicalism, both reductive and non-reductive. Something is left out – unmentioned – in purely physical descriptions and explanations of what goes on when one experiences. What is 'left out' by adopting an exclusively physical view of things is the possibility of describing the character of experience (the phenomenology problem) and the possibility of having an *intelligible* understanding of how experiences can be 'understood' in such terms (the metaphysical problem). Knowing that experiences are events that have potential physical description provides no illumination about how or why this should be so. For this reason *the* hard problem of consciousness should be cast as a problem about *intelligibility*. At bottom it asks, can consciousness be made intelligible in terms of something else (traditionally, purely functional or physical categories)?

I argue that it cannot – not even in principle. My diagnosis, given in my previous writings, was designed to show that those physicalists who think otherwise must be, at least implicitly, committed to the OBS. For adherence to that schema is what encourages one to treat the following questions as well-formed: Where are experiences located? How are they unified in consciousness? How do phenomenal properties make a causal difference? And so on. Yet if the OBS cannot be rightly applied to experiences these questions don't make sense. Attachment to the object-based schema makes it seem *as if* certain questions, such as those exemplified above, can be answered if we develop a successful explanatory theory of consciousness: one that demonstrates how our understanding of experience can be incorporated, without residue, into a yet more fundamental theory or theories. As is well known, theories of consciousness have been advanced from a variety of angles, including: the neurobiological (Crick 1994, Churchland 1989), the quantum mechanical (Penrose 1994), the functional (Dennett 1991, Lycan 1996) and the representational (Dretske 1995, Tye 1996). In the preface to his book, *Psychoneural Reduction*, Bickle identifies the crucial background assumption made by those engaged in such explanatory projects. It is that: "The question of how psychological theories relate to neuroscience is no different from, e.g. the question of how theories in chemistry relate to their counterparts in physics. The object-level theories are different, and maybe the relationship between the levels is different, but the question at issue is the same" (Bickle 1998: x).

This assumption only holds good in some cases, not all. As a matter of fact, there is:

> no intellectual puzzle in understanding the relation between the entities described by physics and chemistry. It is possible to see, in a fully transparent fashion, how chemical molecules are composed of particular types of atoms with specific atomic weights. The connections between these can be described by certain valence rules (cf. P.S. Churchland 1986: 279, Kitcher 1993: 106–109). Thus at the atomic

> level, we can specify all the necessary conditions required in order to form particular chemical molecules. A chemical compound is nothing but certain kinds of atoms, in the right numbers, linked together in the right kind of way. It is an easy matter to make this kind of compositional claim intelligible because both chemistry and classical physics are part of a *common conceptual framework*, despite their divergent explanatory interests and methods (Hutto 2000: 113, emphasis added).

It is a condition on obtaining satisfying reductions of any kind that the theories in question share a common conceptual schema. One way of thinking that this condition can be met when it comes to thinking about consciousness – the one most commonly supported – is to imagine experiences or their qualitative features as 'inner' objects of some kind. For if experiences were objects there would be no barrier, in principle, to *understanding* them – at least, ultimately – in physical terms. Thus for those who think it is possible to 'explain' consciousness in the sense of making it intelligible in other terms, the true underlying requirement – which must be presupposed (at least tacitly) as being met – is that the OBS applies to our understanding of experience.

But just what is the OBS? What are its contours? I tried to be as liberal as possible in characterising it. When first coining the label, I proposed that talk of adherence to the 'object-based schema' would be a charitable and reasonable way to put some much-needed meat on the bones of the physicalism – protecting it from the charge of vacuity. Hence:

> The point is that if we take physicalism to be committed to the object-based schema, which minimally requires a selective interest in the objects of space-time, we have the means for non-vacuously formulating it. We can mark its concern to a particular domain without foreclosing entirely on the possibility of conceptual development. For example, no matter how indifferent the mathematical formalisms of classical physics may appear to be with respect to certain qualities of objects, as opposed to their quantifiable features, the object-based schema used in classical physics *derives from* and remains *distinctively applicable to* objects in the spatio-temporal domain…
>
> If physicalism is to be a substantive doctrine, then, even allowing latitude for conceptual change, there must be a limit to what can constitute a physical concept. This is so even if the boundary cannot be fully stated in terms of necessary and sufficient conditions (cf. Mills 1997: 181). The fact that physics has *developed from*, and *applies to*, the world of spatio-temporal objects provides a tethered, but reasonably flexible way of characterising that limit. Yet it still provides grounds for meaningful contrast such that certain phenomena might be regarded as non-physical. Specifically, any phenomenon that systematically resists capture or incorporation into the object-based schema will be regarded thus. If we accept this, then physicalism can be formulated in a way that is not so freewheeling that it becomes

> meaningless, while at the same time allowing the notion to develop in theoretically projectible ways along a continuum (Hutto 2000: 115–116, with changes).

Consciousness is not the only phenomenon to resist capture in the OBS.

The very same problems (and standard patterns of reply) emerge when philosophers attempt to understand the metaphysics of the denizens of the quantum realm – for in that domain too the 'subject matter' cannot be modelled on anything found in our familiar 'object-based' schema (see Hutto 2000: ch. 4, but especially: 179–181). The 'hard problem' is not a 'metaphysical' problem that is special to consciousness. Thus, the explanation of why it is possible to obtain a satisfying explanation of relations between the constructs of chemistry and classical physics (on the one hand) is directly linked to explanation of why it is impossible to provide intelligible accounts of the relations between the constructs of quantum physics or consciousness and those of classical physics (on the other). In the first case, the domains in question do share a common framework in the second case, they do not.

With this observation in mind, I hold that theories of consciousness are not just ill-motivated – they are doomed to fail: they are literally nonsensical attempts to produce fantastical products. We cannot solve the 'hard problem' of consciousness, not even in principle. There can be no genuine solution. It is not just 'hard', it is *impossible*. No one will solve the 'hard' problem any more than they will square a circle. Unexamined attachment to the idea that conscious experience can be modelled on objects (or, more likely, a tendency to model it so without realising that one is so doing) is what misleads many into thinking otherwise. If the OBS 'is but a particular manifestation of objectivism' then it is *the* troublesome one.

Some may feel I have been too quick in ruling out the possibility of such an explanation *a priori*. Perhaps, I should say 'as things stand'. For, if I am right that the problem is a conceptual one then it is at least possible to 'solve' – or better, to dissolve – it by changing the current rules of the game. If the issue is finding a common conceptual framework perhaps we can fiddle with the relevant concepts in question until this is achieved. This is Humphrey's strategy. He realises that we will only see the back of the metaphysical problem by recasting "the terms on each side of the mind-brain identity equation, phantasm, p = brain state, b, so as to make them look more like each other" (Humphrey 2000: 15). In praising Humphrey's approach, Van Gulick observes that this tactic is already familiar and that it "even has a name: Pat Churchland (1986) dubbed it 'co-evolution', reflecting the way in which our conceptions and theories on both sides of the divide change over time as we bring them into correspondence" (Van Gulick 2000: 94, Hutto 2000: 205–216).

On a co-evolutionary proposal there are three possible ways that experience might be made intelligible: (1) concepts of consciousness could alter in ways that would make them amenable to the object-based schema; (2) the physical concepts might abandon that schema, bringing them in line with our existing understanding of conscious experience (this is what inspires and gives hope to those who pursue quantum theories of consciousness. But, note, saying that two theories do *not* share a particular conceptual framework is not the same as saying they share one); or (3) concepts of consciousness and physical concepts could both alter significantly, coming into alignment in the right way.

Consequently, even if one accepted my diagnosis of the reason why solving the hard problem is impossible and the role I see the OBS as playing in this, surely an explanatory theory of consciousness is still a legitimate possibility after all. If one, the other, or both set of concepts were shifted in the right way then making consciousness intelligible in naturalistic terms may be on the cards. What right have I to rule it out? Why is even this hope forlorn? The fact is that everyday concepts of experience are not theoretically based: they are not part of a commonsense theory – certainly not one that *speculates* about the nature or character of experiences. If so there will be no theoretically-driven adjustments to our understanding and concepts of experience. Concepts of experience cannot be revised based on changes to our existing theory if there is no such 'theory' to change. Rather, such concepts are linguistically based, serving to describe or express the character of our nonconceptual modes of responding. This is true even of our most sophisticated and refined concepts of experience, those deployed in the fine arts; these are nothing like the speculative postulates of the sciences even though they are associated with more trained and educated forms of response.

For example, our colour concepts and their subtleties are *primarily* bound up with the capacities that we have for discriminating and recognising things. Our concepts of experience are thus fundamentally anchored to our nonconceptual ways of getting around in and feeling our way through the world. To understand experiences conceptually at all requires taking up a *reflective* stance on such events. And, as Myin and De Nul note, having experiences does not involve adopting such a stance. The rub is that to the extent that experiential concepts are open to revision, growth and development then the way in which they are is nothing like that in which theoretical concepts are. The concepts of experience are in this respect quite different from those of the 'physical' or 'chemical' variety. Thus we cannot expect them to 'co-evolve' alongside with or even after the fashion of the *bona fide* theoretical constructs of the sciences.[3] Putting all of this together, we can know *in advance* that the intelligibility problem will not dissipate with the coming of any hoped for 'theoretical' adjustments or developments.

It follows that if we are to approach the study of consciousness properly, the first step is to free ourselves of the tendency to imagine experiences as 'inner objects' or 'properties' in their own right – as substantive entities that can be explained in terms of yet other properties or states. We must also rid ourselves of the unrealisable and distracting goal of making experience intelligible in terms of something else. A strong dose of philosophical therapy is therefore a necessary prelude to conducting clarifying investigations on this important topic (Hutto 2003/2006: ch. 6). But the therapy is *just* a prelude. Dealing with what I call the 'phenomenology' problem requires something more; it requires developing a better methodology for addressing the question of "how to characterise the nature of consciousness itself" (Hutto 2000: 2).

I hold that it is not possible to explicate the qualitative or phenomenal aspects of experiences – the characteristic feels – the somethings-that-it-is-like to engage with worldly offerings in purely *intellectual* terms (see my reply to Crane).[4] As I see it some form of ability hypothesis is the correct alternative approach. I have recently tried to explicate this calling on enactivist insights (see Hutto 2000: ch. 2, 2005, 2006).[5] Briefly and in sketch, the first step to understanding the enactivist proposals is to steer clear of the practice of imagining experiences in the abstract – experiences are not posits or theoretical constructs to be understood *in vacuo*. The only way to understand 'what-it-is-like' to have an experience is to actually undergo it or re-imagine undergoing it. Gaining insight into the phenomenal character of particular kinds of experience requires *practical* engagements, not theoretical insights. The kind of understanding we seek when we want to know 'what-it-is-like' to have such and such an experience requires responding in a way that is enactive, on-line and embodied or, alternatively, in a way that is re-enactive, off-line and imaginative – and still embodied. It involves undergoing and/or imagining experiences both of acting and of being acted upon. It is for this reason that attempts to 'understand' the character of certain types of conscious experience have *natural* limits – as Nagel's musing about bats reveals.[6]

Since the greatest barrier to accepting this is our tendency to 'reify experiences', it is crucially important to give a correct diagnosis of the *source* of that temptation: I identify this as a misplaced attachment to the 'object-based' schema. And that attachment is itself typically fostered by a commitment to a certain, misguided explanatory project. In surrendering to this temptation one is driven to talk of distinct phenomenal qualities, such as 'redness' or 'softness', that come before the 'mind' – those which are presented to subjects. In my view, this should always be traded in for more homely talk of 'seeing something red' or 'being tickled by something soft' in *such*-and-*such* circumstances. In imagining what-it-is-like to have such experiences one must imagine them *in situ*, against a complex backdrop – even if what concerns us is only a particular quality of the experience that is attended to (for even the character of such 'qualities' are affected by background conditions). Experiencing is here understood as an extended, temporal activity not as momentary inner occurrences. Likewise, experiencers must be understood as embodied and situated beings – whole organisms – not imaginary inner subjects or brains. So in all, I fully agree with the following passage from Myin and De Nul:

> It is by our active exploration of the environment, our acting in the world, that experience comes into being. But in order to gain additional insight into why our phenomenal experience is the way we know it to be, it seems perfectly legitimate to appeal to an analysis of the kinds of capacities we bring into play in this interactive encounter with the environment. And that is precisely where talk of sensorimotor contingencies fits in (Myin and De Nul, this volume).

Nevertheless, I have concerns about the way the core claim of the sensorimotor contingency theory is characterised. I make clear why and in what sense in the next section.

2. Interpreting the Sensorimotor Contingency 'theory'

My commentators observe that "Hutto's approach thus seems to have affinities with the recently proposed sensorimotor contingency theory of perception. Though Hutto acknowledges parallelisms, he also discerns remnants of the object-model in the sensorimotor theory, and criticises it for that" (Myin and De Nul, this volume). This is not so. As I said in my target paper, I endorse the general spirit and direction of the SMC approach – i.e. the idea that the *character* of experiences is determined by sensorimotor contingencies specific to the various sense modalities. Indeed, the reason why I like it so much is that it openly and thoroughly rejects the object-based schema. Read in the right way, I think it also provides a healthier way forward for investigating the mechanisms of consciousness.

Let me be clear. Nothing I have said here or in previous writing about the impossibility of a 'theory of consciousness' of either the metaphysical or phenomenological sort should lead us to deny that we can investigate some aspects of consciousness third-personally. Indeed, this is the only way to learn more about the mechanics of experience and their evolutionary history. We should not doubt the prospects of future scientific work yielding more and more detail about the specific mechanisms that underpin certain types of experiences – as, for example, in the study of different sense modalities and their links to other brain and nervous systems. Knowledge of this kind will surely permit greater control, prediction and manipulation of experiences (understood as embodied actions). Such developments will rightly be regarded as constituting an increase in 'our understanding of experiences' – but such claims must be handled with great caution if they are not to inspire philosophical confusion. Such investigations will only tell us more about the *causes* of experience, be these of the triggering or structuring sort (see my reply to Rudd for more detail). It bears repeating that attention to these could never give us any insight into the character of 'what-it-is-like' to be an experiencer *per se* (though it might enable us to extend our existing enactive and imaginative capacities, offering up new possibilities for experience and our capacity to understand those of others).

My worry about the existing SMC approaches is not therefore that they make improper use of the object-based schema, but rather that they appear to be committed to a kind of intellectualism, despite themselves. This is brought out when its proponents explicate their claims about *mediating knowledge* that is the keystone of their account. In elaborating the core claim of the SMC approach two of its original founders write:

> Visual experience is a mode of activity involving *practical knowledge* about currently possible behaviours and associated sensory consequences. Visual experience *rests on know-how, the possession of skills* (O'Regan & Noë 2001: 946, emphases mine).

The trouble is that when they attempt to explain the character of this knowledge the authors typically revert to giving examples of propositional knowledge or some confused mix of practical and propositional knowledge (see also Hutto 2005, Rowlands 2005).[7] This suggests that, despite advertisements and avowals of anti-intellectualism, the account as presented seems to rest on a tacit appeal to 'inner representations and rules' after all.[8] This is deeply ironic given that, in line with enactivism generally, its supporters claim that their position is:

> distinctive in at least two respects compared to more traditional and still 'mainstream' cognitive science. First, by emphasising that perception concerns the activity of an organism in an environment, the traditional focus on the 'inner' as the locus of importance is abandoned. This implies – and this is the second respect – that perception is not, as in many traditional approaches seen as the establishment of inner representations of the outside world, but rather engagement with this outer world (Myin & O'Regan 2002: 32–3).

Importantly, as above, where the emphasis is on 'interaction with the world' mention of 'knowledge' *per se* need not figure at all. Trouble starts when attempts are made to coherently and non-vacuously explicate the *mediating* role that knowledge is meant to play. In the target paper I briefly examined the implications of the claim about mediating knowledge at the sub-personal level and found it wanting (a much fuller examination of this, citing more instances of the tendency to fall back on a kind of intellectualism, can be found in Hutto 2005, see also O'Regan, Myin & Noë 2005 for a re-statement). I argued there that the commitment to 'mediating knowledge' is treacherously misleading in more than one way and, ultimately, unnecessary. I stand by that assessment.

I also proposed that we can get by without positing any such 'knowledge' by appeal to what I now call a 'bio-semiotic' approach (see my reply to Crane). With this in hand we can get by without claiming that our perceptual and emotional abilities rest on a *skilful practical mastery* of SMC laws on the part of brains or their owners. Nevertheless, we can still accept the weaker claim that the basic *character* of perceptual experiences is determined by the features of the different sensory modalities and how they are affected by and respond to specific objects, as fixed by our biological history. To understand this we do not need to invoke talk of a 'skilful mastery' of SMC laws. According to this more modest approach even if a creature fails to perceive what it ought – fails to successfully exercise its abilities properly – it can nevertheless have perceptual experiences. Depending on the reason for and extent of its failure, these may be of a different character than in the normal case.

For reasons of space, in making this suggestion I focused almost entirely on the subpersonal and did not provide a detailed analysis or critique of the claim made by SMC proponents that experience rests on *personal level implicit knowledge*. It is worth saying more about this however since according to the SMC theorists 'the brain's mastery of laws' at the subpersonal level is only necessary and not sufficient for perceptual experience (I discuss this in greater depth in Hutto 2005). We are told:

> ...there are facts about what experiences are like. But these, however, are facts not about a person's qualia or raw feels. They pertain, rather, to the person's (or animal's) active engagement with the world he or it inhabits. They are facts at the personal (as opposed to subpersonal) level (O'Regan & Noë 2001: 965).

It is therefore a red herring to think that the true focus of the SMC account is on explicating the know-how of the brain's mastery of a set of laws (though this is part of the story told by its proponents). For, despite advancing the claim that the brain is skilfully attuned to sensorimotor contingencies, this 'being attuned' – on its own – does not fix the character of the perceptual experiences. As the above quotation makes clear, it is practical knowledge at the personal level that makes acts of perceiving into full blown experiential ones. It is claimed that this too is a kind of *know-how*. Yet, once again, the examples employed point in a different direction. Thus:

> Having the feeling of seeing a stationary object consists in the *knowledge that* if you were to move your eyes slightly leftwards, the object would shift one way on your retina, but if you were to move your eye rightwards, the object would shift the other way. The knowledge of all such potential movements and their results constitute the perception of stationarity (O'Regan & Noë 2001: 949, emphases mine).

> ...the experience of red, for example, arises when we know, though this is not propositional, but rather *practical knowledge that*, for example, if we move our eyes over a red region, there will occur changes typical of what happens when

> our non-homogenously sampling retinas move over things whose color is red (O'Regan & Noë 2001: 963). [9]

Protestations to the contrary aside, the cases cited apparently involve propositional knowledge of the very sort that is derived by consideration of what typically 'goes on' mechanically when we look at things. After all, we are told that "to reflect on the character of experience is to reflect on the character of one's law-governed exploration of the environment, on what one does in seeing" (O'Regan and Noë 2001: 961).

One natural way to take these remarks – understood now as concerning personal level knowledge – is to treat them as referring to run-of-the-mill *propositional knowledge about* our practices – of the sort obtained by reflecting on what we do – after the fashion of Aristotle's attempt to articulate the principles of logic or Walton's prescriptions about angling. This would be a straightforward case in which "Efficient practice precedes theory of it" (Ryle 1949: 30). But this cannot be what enables us to experience, *simpliciter*. The authors claim that it is the organisms' *attending* (their cognitive engagement) that ultimately makes for experiential perception – and for them that this is equivalent to perceptual awareness. Yet any kind of theoretical reflection that would make us *skilful* attenders would have to be based on *attending* to more *basic* acts of attention. So surely this proposal is heading for trouble.

In one way, this observation won't trouble defenders of SMC theory. They clearly would not want to endorse this rendering of their claim in any case – for that would be to treat know-how as explicit propositional knowledge gained through reflection. They adamantly insist that the implicit knowledge to which they refer should be "understood as *literally constituting* a perceptual skill, analogous to a skill such as tying one's shoelaces" (Myin & O'Regan 2002: 34, emphasis mine). So is this just an over-interpretation on my part? I do not think so. For even with this relevant adjustment, there are still problems for the account. This is because the equation of know-how and experience does not hold up well. In line with the spirit of what SMC theorists want to claim, let us re-evaluate the above quotation after having replaced all instances of talk of knowledge *that* with those of knowledge *how*, as in this rewritten quotation.

> Having the feeling of seeing a stationary object consists in [knowing how] to move your eyes slightly leftwards, so that the object would shift one way on your retina, and [knowing how] to move your eye rightwards, so that the object would shift the other way (O'Regan & Noë 2001: 949).

The problem is that on this new formulation it is easy to see that it is not remotely plausible to say my capacity for visual experience depends on or equates to *my knowing how* to move eyes in any way that relates to the behaviour of my retina at all. Of course, in an important sense, I can and do move my eyes, especially during acts of attention, but there seems to be no good reason to think of this as a kind of skill-based, personal level knowledge.[10]

What 'skill' is exercised in seeing that is fundamentally different to those involved in breathing or walking? Or are these cases meant to be equivalent? If so, in what possible sense should we regard 'seeing' as a kind of know-how expressed in action? Do I learn *how* to see skilfully? Certainly, this ability develops over time – but it is hardly dependent upon 'training' in the normal sense of the word. In contrast, the ability to tie my shoelaces rests on my previous training. Perceiving is – unless we are prepared to stretch the analogy too far – an unlearnt ability. Certainly seeing, although it involves complicated activity and co-ordination, is more like breathing than, say, dancing in this regard.

While I endorse the idea that experiences are enactive and depend on our specific kinds of abilities, I clearly agree that for experience it is "a precondition that one has abilities" (Myin & De Nul: this volume). Still, I deny that in the basic perceptual and emotional cases these "are comparable to skills" (Myin & De Nul: this volume). This way of putting things invites confusion. Some basic and unlearnt abilities exhibited by certain creatures, for example the social coordination abilities of certain primates, are very complex and in this sense perhaps they are 'comparable to skills' in their degree of sophistication. But they do not rest on skilful mastery or know-how: they are basic, untrained abilities for all that. This is not to say that some abilities cannot be trained. Nor is it to deny that training can extend and indeed radically alter the quality and nature of our experiences (see my replies to Rudd and Goldie).

If we consider cases of trained skills that involve implicit knowledge, it is clear that such knowledge can be demonstrated if not stated. Although I may not be able to say quite how I tie my laces I can *show* you how I do it and I can train others to tie theirs too. But with respect to abilities such as the basic capacity to see things, it is perfectly intelligible to say that although I can Φ, I don't know how I Φ nor can I show you how to Φ. It is just something I am able to do. My worry can be expressed in another way: What kind of failure is it to *see* badly or imperfectly? What is it that organisms do not *know* or do not *know how to do* in such cases? And even if there were some answer to these questions, given that such knowledge is meant to be *constitutive* of perception, the follow-up is quite serious: Why doesn't a lack of knowledge result in a lack of experience altogether?[11] I think the answer is because seeing is not a skill-based achievement in the same way as dancing or tying one's shoelaces are.

It should now be evident why the SMC claim, as stated, is too strong. Being able to see does not depend on our having skilful knowledge *"about how* sensations will change when you move your eyes, or move the object" (O'Regan & Noë 2001: 946, emphasis mine). If it did, visual experience would be very limited indeed, since very few of us have either explicit propositional or even implicit but demonstrable skill-based knowledge of this kind. For example, I know that if I take an object from a well-lit room to a poorly lit one it will look different. In which ways, I cannot say exactly – even when the object is familiar to me. This does not mean that the way I experience it is independent of the relevant sensorimotor contingencies, only that it is not knowledge of them, at any level, that matters to my perceiving it in the way I do.

In my view, with some important pruning we can modify the original SMC claim so as to address this shortcoming by removing references to the adjective 'skillful' as follows:

> "seeing is [a form of] activity whereby one explores the world..." (O'Regan & Noë 2001: 966).

Recast thusly, we can now press for the simpler claim that the sensorimotor contingencies of the various modalities account for the qualitative differences in the character of particular perceptual experiences (in conjunction with the features of the particular things encountered, see sec. 3 of my reply to Crane). And this is in line with the following claim:

> Under the present view of what seeing is, the visual experiences of a red colour patch depends on the structure of the changes in sensory input that occur when you move your eyes around relative to the patch... (O'Regan & Noë 2001: 951).

The point is that this much weaker rendering of the SMC 'core claim' does not make any reference to 'practical knowledge' or 'skillful mastery' of laws, at any level. Know-how does not come into it at all. In some places, the authors present their main thesis in a weak form that is entirely consistent with this. For instance, we can uncover this idea at the heart of a truncated version of the claim we examined earlier:

> ...there are facts about what experiences are like... They pertain, rather, to the person's (or animal's) active engagement with the world he or it inhabits (O'Regan & Noë 2001: 965).

Presented in this way, it is not knowledge – nor embodied *know-how per se* – that gives perceptual experiences their character but facts about the nature of our embodiment in relation to particular active engagements. Let us now rewrite the earlier claim once more, removing all reference to knowledge, so it reads as follows:

> Having the feeling of seeing a stationary object consists in [the fact that] if you were to move your eyes slightly leftwards, the object would shift one way on your retina, but if you were to move your eye rightwards, the object would shift the other way (O'Regan & Noë 2001: 949).

I take this to be uncontroversial. All it commits one to is the idea that perceptual experience is a mode of activity, requiring a certain set of abilities. The point is that even with these somewhat dramatic modifications the revised approach still stands opposed to the *ultra-passive* view according to which seeing involves nothing more than the having of static inner representations. It seems that Myin and De Nul and I agree about this.

> It seems perfectly legitimate to appeal to an analysis of the kinds of capacities we bring into play in this interactive encounter with the environment. And that is precisely where talk of sensorimotor contingencies fits in. We think these should not be interpreted in any object-based 'internalistic' way, but rather as patterns that structure perceiver-environment interaction. Mastery of sensorimotor contingencies, in our preferred reading, just indicates the ability of a perceiver to engage in specific interactions (Myin & De Nul: this volume).

However, they also say that "one should allow the various sciences, including 'sciences of the mind', to invoke all kinds of objects (from neurons to – perhaps –inner representations). The recourse to such inner objects only becomes problematic, so it seems to us, once they are 'overinterpreted': once the objects that figure in them, are used to identify experience with" (Myin & De Nul: this volume). On this I do not agree. I am driven by the reformist zeal to clarify our terms – to 'clean up' our language – since how we are inclined to talk affects our understanding and our method. Indeed I take such clarificatory activity to be the prime business of philosophy. And in this case, I hold that the sensorimotor proposal has a great deal more to offer when carefully presented.

4. New theory or reformed thinking?

So far I have been trying to clarify, explicate and evaluate the SMC proposal about perceptual experience as if it were a sort of theoretical hypothesis with a clear content. But perhaps it is better to understand it not as an unambiguous new theory but as a rejection of the misleading 'copy view' of visual experience: i.e. the idea that experience is somehow constituted by the formation of passive, internal representation of outer scenes. This proposed interpretation is surely not *wholly* off the mark. Its authors harbour transformative ambitions for their approach of the magnitude that Newton's introduction of the notion of a field of force had in physics. Of Newton's idea they claim, it was "not a theory at all, just a new way of defining what is meant by force. It is a way of abandoning the problem being posed, rather than solving it" (O'Regan & Noë 2001: 949). Seen in this light, the work of O'Regan, Myin and Noë is also meant to provide "a general framework for the study of vision... [in which] old problems appear as non-problems" (O'Regan & Noë 2001: 948).

We can best see this aspect of their work in their attack on 'qualia', as motivated by the realisation that *understanding* experience is equivalent to *understanding* the temporally extended perceptual activity of organisms. Once we better understand our quarry we will come to recognise that the experiences in question are already rich and diachronically stretched or extended in time. Experiences can only be understood by giving attention to such activity: they cannot be reduced to a collection of discrete sensations in the brain which are somehow bound together. This point has been familiar to phenomenologists, pragmatists and even a few reflective artists, for some time.

It is wrong to imagine experiences as reduced to sets of 'sense data' alone or modelled as inner objects or representations. Yet even if we accept this, it does not automatically lend support to the claim that "experience *derives* not from the sensation itself, but from the rules that govern action-related changes in sensory input" (O'Regan & Noë 2001: 956, emphasis added). Nor does it directly support the idea that "the experience of perception *derives from* the *potential* to obtain changes in sensation, not from the sensations themselves" (O'Regan & Noë 2001: 956, emphasis added). Although, we may agree that the very possibility of experiencing in a temporally extended way depends upon the potential for such changes, it is quite another thing to say that such experiencing consists in the manipulation of rules or the potential for making changes in any explanatorily interesting way.

A note of caution is in order about sensations. For, in rejecting this false picture, we must take care to check the bathwater for babies. Focusing on the character of sensations is not to tell the whole story concerning experience. But in acknowledging this we should not be led to think that sensations are not an essential part of it. To see why, we have but to consider O'Regan and Noë's discussion of the use of echolocation device to somewhat compensate for the lack of sight in blind patients. According to them, what makes this an alternative form of 'seeing' is the fact that "the brain extracts the same invariants from the structure of the sensorimotor contingencies" (O'Regan & Noë 2001: 956). And they acknowledge that this echolocation device "*obviously* cannot provide visual experiences" (O'Regan & Noë 2001: 956, emphasis mine). I suggest the reason why this is *obvious* is precisely because such devices do not generate the characteristic types of visual sensation that are part and parcel of normal sight. Nor would this be surprising, for isn't it the difference in these sensations partly what distinguishes echolocation from normal modes of seeing?

We should accept that differences in the various modalities (coupled with particular objects perceived through them) determine which sensations we enjoy. Aristotle proposed something like this in *De Anima*, long ago. There is nothing wrong in accepting such a view, provided we neither imagine sensations to be strange types of objects or properties nor suppose that visual experience should be understood in terms of sensations *alone* (see O'Regan & Noë 2001: 940). Sensations are part and parcel of the character of our experience – part of what it is to act and be acted upon. Formulated properly, we can keep this idea and use the SMC idea to counter the claim that experience is 'something extra' that is added to otherwise undifferentiated neural activity.

All of this is consistent with the much edited version of the core claim of the SMC approach presented in the previous section. Once again, with appropriate adjustments, the main thesis looks less exciting. It is recast as:

> 'vision is a mode of exploration of the world...." (O'Regan & Noë 2001: 940).
>
> Or:
>
> "seeing is an ...activity whereby one explores the world..." (O'Regan & Noë 2001: 966).

It would be hard to disagree with these remarks. Indeed, they could almost serve as definitions of 'seeing'. They are hardly philosophical theses that one would be tempted to dispute, unless one was under the spell of a certain picture and driven to try to explain what seeing 'really' is – despite appearances. If properly interpreted the SMC revolutionaries are reduced to making claims such as this, they have hardly offered a 'new definition of visual experience' – rather they will have reminded of something we ought to already know. I take it that the real payoff is that it reminds us that perception is an activity – not that it provides the basis for yet another new theory of experience. Rather, if treated with care, it acts as a prophylactic against certain standard philosophical confusions about the nature of experience. It also provides insight into the only genuine way we have of understanding the character of experiences (for it brings to light the natural limitations in this domain): Don't think, but act, interact or re-enact.

Notes

1. Thus in a recent review of *Beyond Physicalism* Robinson makes the following assessment: "On the central claim of the book, however, a sense of disappointment seems likely. The motivation for a way out was that dualism makes interaction mysterious and physicalism either tries but fails to explain consciousness, or accepts a physical-experiential identity that it cannot make intelligible. Hutto's absolute idealism tells us that reality can be described (so far as it can be at all) only through one or another partial conceptual scheme and that all our remarks, whether about brains or experiences, are remarks about the one, underlying, undifferentiated reality. This is no comfort, since we will still want to ask how statements in the conceptual scheme of

physicalism relate to statements in the conceptual scheme of consciousness. It may be that all statements are in some way incomplete, or conceptual-scheme relative, but we will still want to know why we have a sense of mystery about the relation between consciousness and neurons when we do not have that kind of puzzlement about, say, the relation between nation states and atoms. Hutto has not reduced the mystery that is commonly indicated by references to the explanatory gap or the Hard Problem; he has merely given us a recommendation for a different way of stating these difficulties" (Robinson 2006: 162–3). The fact is that I had hoped to do more than simply recommend a new way of 'stating the difficulties': my ambition was to offer a diagnosis of why we cannot solve these problems (showing that the same conceptual impasse afflicts other domains too) and to advocate a strategy for quelling that temptation to try. Robinson seems to want something still more such as reason why experiences but not everything resists capture in the object based schema. I think enactivist thinking can help with this.

2. Batthyany summarizes my strategy well: "How does consciousness relate to the physical world? Hutto believes that within the framework of physicalism all attempts to answer this question must flounder. He isolates the two alternatives: Either we adhere to reductive physicalism and thus sacrifice consciousness from the outset, or else we adhere to non-reductive physicalism which may do more justice to consciousness, but on the other hand systematically abuses the notion of physicalism… Hutto argues that the inability to solve the metaphysical problem has its roots in the way the problem is usually defined: If consciousness researchers are determined to find an intelligible relation between the mental and the physical, then they have said too much too early" (Batthyany 2001: 94).

3. I do not deny that with greater technical advances we might learn more about the causes and mechanics of experiencing. But to think that this constitutes an explanation of the phenomenal character of conscious experience is a mistake. In aiming to 'explain consciousness' or to provide a 'science of consciousness' it may be that some researchers have in mind nothing more than having better accounts of mechanics of experiences, enabling better prediction and control. But this is a significantly weaker and quite distinct ambition from that of seeking to explain consciousness by making it 'intelligible' in 'other' terms. Solving the metaphysical problem depends on achieving the latter, thus it would be false advertising to claim that 'consciousness can be explained someday' with only the weaker aim in mind. I say more about this in my reply to Salucci (Hutto 2001).

4. This goes against a certain dominant trend in current thinking. Ever since the time of Jackson's famous thought-experiment about Mary there has been widespread acceptance of the idea that knowledge about the character of experience can be stated and fully captured propositionally.

5. Batthyany, who gave an otherwise sympathetic review of *Beyond Physicalism*, expressed surprise that after succeeding in doing away with unworkable physicalist accounts, the book took a 'surprising turn' – never returning to address its central question. Putting this complaint gently and politely, he wrote "it would still be interesting to get more information on the part of reality this book mainly deals with, namely consciousness" (Batthyany 2001: 95). Quite so.

6. In *Beyond Physicalism*, I wrote: "The fact is that what-it-is-like to be a bat is unbridgeablely distant from what-it-is-like to be a human. Even if we can appreciate and understand what-it-is-like to experience nonconceptually in some general sense, there are clear limits to what we can know about the quality of the specific experiences of many other, presumably conscious, animals. Our problem in understanding the character of some other minds is barred because

of the differences in our makeup. We cannot successfully simulate what-it-is-like to be them because we are not like them. For this reason, understanding the experiential lives of animals is not a puzzle which the intellect alone can solve (cf. Wittgenstein 1980: § 659–663 cf. also § 644)" (Hutto 2000: 50).

7. This ensures that we cannot understand experience in merely dispositional terms. For clearly, on the SMC account, there is something 'between' the inputs and outputs – the knowledge that enables the systems to mediate the inputs according to particular laws.

8. O'Regan, at least, does not shy away from the classical 'rules and representational' approach. He openly embraced it in his public responses at the Enactive Perception Symposium, organised by Centre for Research in Cognitive Science, Sussex and the Consciousness and Experimental section of the British Psychological Society, March 2004.

9. Myin and O'Regan talk in places as if this were a kind of second-order knowledge. They write "With any exploratory movement the perceiver makes, she has *knowledge about how* input will change, and this knowledge is never disconfirmed during her exploration" (Myin and O'Regan 2002: 34, emphases added). I find the implications of the claim that such 'knowledge is never disconfirmed' to be puzzling.

10. It would be tricky business for a philosopher of action to unpack the sense in which 'I' do these things – but they are certainly not automated responses.

11. It is important that the authors are minimally advancing a claim about constitution (although sometimes they appear to be making one about identity) and not just dependence, which is a considerably weaker relation (see Baker 2000: ch. 2 for an excellent discussion of these differences). Construed as a claim about dependence the SMC thesis is reduced to one about what underwrites visual experience. The danger here is that if visual experience only *depends upon* or *involves* skill-based activity it is easier to imagine that 'it' might be 'carved off' or put to one side when certain aspects of 'seeing' are studied. Since the authors deny that there is any explanatory gap and that experience involves nothing extra they must be presenting us with either an identity or constitution thesis. A general worry about this strategy might be that the relevant 'explanatory gap' can always be recast at the level of sense rather than that of ontology – thus it is possible to describe a given activity, just as we might an object, event or process, using only the language of physics and/or physiological, without mention of the subjective character of 'experiences' at all. Given that the authors do not deny that there are legitimate questions that can be asked about the character of experiences there will always be an issue about how these different levels of description relate.

References

Baker, L.R. 2000. *Persons and Bodies: A Constitution View*. Cambridge: Cambridge University Press.

Batthyany, A. 2001. "Review of Beyond Physicalism." *Journal of Consciousness Studies* 8: 94–5.

Bickle, J. 1998. *Psychoneural Reduction: The New Wave*. Cambridge, MA: MIT Press.

Churchland, P.M. 1989. *A Neurocomputational Perspective: The Nature of Mind and the Structure of Science*. Cambridge, MA: MIT Press.

Churchland P. S. 1986. *Neurophilosophy: Toward a Unified Science of the Mind-Brain*. Cambridge, MA: MIT Press.

Crick, F. 1994. *The Astonishing Hypothesis: The Scientific Search for the Soul.* New York: Simon and Schuster.

Dennett, D.C. 1991. *Consciousness Explained.* New York: Penguin Books.

Dretske, F. 1995. *Naturalizing the Mind.* Cambridge, MA: MIT Press.

Humphrey, N. 2000. "How to Solve the Mind-Body Problem." *Journal of Consciousness Studies* 7 (4): 5–20.

Hutto, D.D. 1998a. "An Ideal Solution to the Problems of Consciousness." *Journal of Consciousness Studies* 5(3): 328–43.

Hutto, D.D. 1998b. "Davidson's Identity Crisis." *Dialectica* 52(1): 45–61.

Hutto, D.D. 1999. *The Presence of Mind.* Amsterdam: John Benjamins.

Hutto, D.D. 2000. *Beyond Physicalism.* Amsterdam: John Benjamins.

Hutto, D.D. 2001. "Appropriate Quietism: Reply to Salucci." *SWIF book forum, http://www.swif.uniba.it/lei/mind/forums.html*

Hutto, D.D. 2003/2006. *Wittgenstein and the End of Philosophy: Neither Theory nor Therapy.* Basingstoke: Palgrave Macmillan.

Hutto, D.D. 2005. "Knowing What?: Radical versus Conservative Enactivism." *Phenomenology and the Cognitive Sciences* 4 (4): 389–405.

Hutto, D.D. 2006. "Turning Hard Problems on Their Heads." *Phenomenology and the Cognitive Sciences* 5: 75–88.

Kitcher, P. 1993. *The Advancement of Science: Science without Legend, Objectivity without Illusions.* Oxford: Oxford University Press.

Lowe, E.J. 1996. *Subjects of Experience.* Cambridge: Cambridge University Press.

Lycan, W. 1996. *Consciousness and Experience.* Cambridge, MA: MIT Press.

Mills, E. 1997. "Interactionism and Physicality" *Ratio* 10(2): 169–183.

Myin, E. and O'Regan, J.K. 2002. "A Way to Naturalize Phenomenology?" *Journal of Consciousness Studies* 9: 27–46.

O'Regan, J.K., Myin, E. and Noë, A. 2005. "Sensory Consciousness Explained (Better) In Terms of 'Corporality' and 'Alterting Capacity'." *Phenomenology and the Cognitive Sciences* 4 (4): 369–387.

O'Regan, J.K. and Noë, A. 2001. "A Sensorimotor Account of Vision and Visual Consciousness." *Behavioural and Brain Sciences* 24: 939–1031.

Penrose, R. 1994. *Shadows of the Mind.* Oxford: Oxford University Press.

Putnam, H. 1988. *Representation and Reality.* Cambridge, MA: MIT Press.

Rowlands, M. 2005. "Understanding the 'Active' in 'Enactive'." *Phenomenology and the Cognitive Sciences,* S. Torrance (ed).

Robinson, W. 2006. "Review of Beyond Physicalism." *Mind* 115: 159–163.

Ryle, G. 1949. *The Concept of Mind.* London: Hutchinson.

Tye, M. 1996. *Ten Problems of Consciousness: A Representational Theory of the Phenomenal Mind.* Cambridge, MA: MIT Press.

Van Gulick, R. 2000. "Closing the Gap?" *Journal of Consciousness Studies* 7 (4): 93–7.

Wittgenstein, L. 1980. *Remarks on the Philosophy of Psychology, Volume 1.* Oxford: Basil Blackwell.

Unnatural feelings

A non-naturalistic perspective on the emotions

Anthony Rudd

1. Introduction

Dan Hutto's interesting paper, 'Unprincipled Engagements' is a sort of prolegomenon to the philosophical understanding of the emotions; its concern is to clear away confusions which are rife in psychology and philosophy of mind more generally, and which are liable to distort our understanding of the emotions. I have a lot of sympathy with this project and Hutto does an excellent job of exposing various influential but deeply muddled views. But while I share his desire to avoid such evils as the "hard problem" of consciousness, and the "avocado pear" conception of the emotions, I am worried that his own assumptions are still too close to those which generate these confusions. In particular, I shall be criticising two main stances that Hutto takes; firstly, his commitment to a dualistic account of the relation of conceptual and non-conceptual factors, and secondly, his willingness to take a certain kind of evolutionary naturalism as having an important role to play in our understanding of the emotions.

There are significant connections between these two positions, and, of course, they both raise very large issues, which ramify much further than I can deal with fully here. Moreover, Hutto's paper is itself a broad sketch of a programme for making progress in exploring a large and complex territory, and I must admit that I'm not sure that I understand all of his argumentative strategy. So I will not be trying to present any simple knock-down argument against Hutto's approach. What I do want to do is to get a clearer grip on what is at issue here. I will do this by considering what seems to me a tension running through his paper between what he wants to achieve, and the means by which he wants to achieve it. I shall go on, for the sake of comparison and contrast, to sketch out an alternative approach to realizing some of Hutto's objectives, which is however, both less dualistic than what he proposes, and frankly anti-naturalistic. This will inevitably be very sketchy; my hope is that this account will at least serve as a triangulation point which will assist with the surveying of the conceptual landscape, and of the route that Hutto is attempting to take though it.

2. Limits to the conceptual? Some questions for Hutto

It is at first a bit surprising that, although the official topic of the paper is the emotions, much of it is devoted to a discussion of perception. But I think Hutto is right to see an important parallel here. Emotions seem to be at once intentional – I am angry with someone, happy about something –and to essentially involve feelings, perhaps even bodily sensations. Hence thinking about the emotions has to navigate between accounts that reduce emotions to "mere" irrational feelings and those which over-intellectualise them by treating them simply as a species of judgement. And there is a similar difficulty in thinking about perception, where we have to find our way between accounts that reduce it to the mere having of sensations, and those which take perceptual experience to be merely the acquisition of beliefs. So if we can understand how to do this, it may provide a model for understanding – or at least for avoiding some ways of misunderstanding – the emotions.

One way to formulate this issue has been in terms of the "hard problem" of consciousness. Though more commonly raised in discussions of perceptual experience, it applies as much (or as little) to the emotions. Physicalist and/or functionalist accounts of experience, it is said, may account for everything to do with information-processing, language, intentionality, behaviour, but they don't explain qualia, raw feels etc; that is, they don't explain why all this cognitive activity doesn't go on "in the dark", as it were (see Chalmers 1995, 1996). However, putting it this way seems to force us to choose between a reductive physicalism which insists that nothing is left over when all the objective data are in, and a kind of minimal dualism which adds "epiphenomenal qualia" (Jackson 1982) to the otherwise completely objective picture. And neither option looks attractive. Plainly, this problem arises as much for the emotions as for perception; once everything about behaviour, intentional directedness etc has been said, isn't there still the sheer subjective feel of rage or joy? But what is left of this mere feel when it is detached from everything else?

I agree with Hutto that we need to dissolve the hard problem by rejecting the assumptions it rests on, rather than trying to solve it on its own terms. His suggestion, referring to previous important work of his, is that the hard problem (along with the problem(s) of other minds) is generated by a commitment to understanding experience within "an object-based schema". (2) I think there is an important insight here, and in his previous writings Hutto has done a lot to show how we can and should avoid falling into the assumptions which lead both to materialist theories of mind, and to epiphenomenalist responses to them like Jackson's and Chalmers' (Hutto 1998, 2000). My main reservation about these earlier writings had to do with Hutto's commitment to a two-stage model, in which conceptualization is added onto a more basic level of non-conceptual experience.[1] In the current paper, he rejects the idea of non-conceptual content, on the ground that "talk of content is appropriate only in characterizing the conceptual aspects of experiential modes" (7). However, he remains committed to supposing that "the basic capacities for experience are non-conceptual" (7). Consequently, he rejects talk of content "when it comes to understanding feeling towards, at least in the most basic cases involving non-conceptual responses" (7). Hence his complaint against Crane; that he ties "intentionality and phenomenality too tightly together" (8).

By keeping intentionality and phenomenality at arms' length, however, Hutto risks staying too close to the assumptions that generate the hard problem. And, more specifically, this seems, despite his intentions, to keep drawing him back to what Goldie stigmatises as the "avocado pear model" of the emotions, according to which a "hard" core of basic biological emotions is surrounded by a "soft" layer of sophisticated but malleable cultural emotions (see Goldie 2000: 99) (5). And it seems significant that the paper repeatedly mentions "basic" or "primitive" emotions, which are supposedly explained – like our "basic", nonconceptual perceptual experiences – in the same way as the experiences of other animals; leaving an extra layer of culture (or conceptualisation) to be added to something that would have been complete in itself without it. So we have talk of "the most basic cases, involving nonconceptual responses" (7); "the basic character of our perceptual experiences" being determined by the nature of our sensory modalities and their objects (15); "our natural history" accounting for "our primitive reactions to others", and then of how these basic responses can "be encultured" (17); and of the doing away of a strong 1st/3rd person divide "at least with respect to our basic emotional responses and expressions" (19). Hutto does recognize that the "basic" emotions are open to modification in particular cases (17), so he doesn't accept the full avocado pear model – his view suggests rather the image of a (genetically modified?) avocado whose core is itself somewhat malleable. But I suspect we need to make a more radical break with this whole way of thinking, rather than starting from it and making modifications.

This distinction between the biological basics and what culture adds on is needed to make plausible the naturalistic, evolutionary account which Hutto considers in Sec 3. He provides an excellent critique of O'Regan and Noe's anthropomorphic talk about the brain making inferences and following rules, insisting quite rightly that neither bees nor brains follow rules, although we can describe their activities "for our benefit" (13) as if they did. But he nevertheless accepts "the basic message" of their Sensorimotor Contingency (SMC) account (10), which he supplements with some reference to Millikan on proper functioning. And so, Hutto says:

> …if different perceptual modalities developed to permit organisms to respond to salient features of their environments, then sensorimotor contingencies too will have been shaped in this way over the ages, as constrained by the nature of other 'internal' devices. Why do we experience certain features as 'green' rather than as 'red'? Or why do we experience these as 'green' rather than as [sic] not experiencing them at all? Ultimately we should answer with reference to facts concerning our natural history (13).

This looks as though it's meant to be an answer to the "hard problem". Why should there be experience at all? Why should it be like anything for an organism to be attuned to certain features of its environment? But I am doubly puzzled by this. Given his commitment to dissolving the hard problem, rather than answering it on its own terms, it would be surprising if Hutto was wanting us to take this as a "straight" answer. And, given his criticisms elsewhere of materialist attempts to get around the problem of experience, it would be surprising if Hutto really was subscribing to the explanatory "ultimacy" of natural history (see Hutto 1998, 2000). If, however, we do take the text at what seems to be its face value, I have to admit that I'm baffled as to how "natural history", and "proper function", together with references to honey bees and hoverflies, are supposed to shed any light on the hard problem. But if Hutto does not suppose that they do, then I really don't understand what is being claimed in the passage quoted above.

Hutto starts Sec 4 with the reassuring words:

> It should now be clear how the above framework [from Sec. 3] can help to understand the connection between intentionality and the phenomenal character of basic forms of experience, so as to make sense of emotional capacities for feeling towards while doing away with many of the assumptions that give life to some of the hard problems of consciousness (16).

Maybe it should be clear, but I'm afraid it isn't yet to me. The "phenomenal character" of experience simply wasn't mentioned in the Sec 3 discussion, and Hutto's own arguments there seem to me to establish the conclusion that there is nothing worth calling "intentionality" either in the cases he discusses. (We may find it useful to say that the bee dance is about the nectar, but it isn't about anything to the bees.) So I think Hutto is quite right that we shouldn't ascribe "content" to insects, but I think the moral we should draw from that is that the study of hoverflies is going to tell us precious little about human perceptual and emotional experience, permeated by content as that is.

3. Naturalism: initial worries

This isn't the place to develop a detailed argument against the avocado pear or two-level model of either perception or the emotions. Hutto doesn't want to wholly endorse that model, but he doesn't want to depart too far from it either. I want to try to clarify exactly where and how much Hutto and I do differ, and so, for the sake of contrast I will now sketch out the holistic and non-naturalistic view of both perception and emotion which I hold. According to this model, sensations and concepts in perception, and feelings and judgements in emotion, are inextricably tied together. There is no "basic" level of mere nonconceptual sensation/feeling that we share with nonconceptualising animals, and to which our more distinctive abilities add an extra layer. But if this is right, then appealing to naturalistic evolutionary accounts is not going to help us to understand human experience, either perceptual or emotional. (Following a hint from the very end of Hutto's paper, I shall also suggest that we cannot ultimately make a sharp distinction between the perceptual and the emotional anyway.)

I will start by going back to the "hard problem". That it seems to present us with a forced choice between reductive or eliminative materialism on the one hand, and epiphenomenalism on the other should itself be a reason for thinking that something has gone badly wrong in the posing of the problem. In fact the problem only arises if we start with two assumptions, both of which I think are false. Firstly, that we can clearly distinguish between the issues of intentionality, rationality and representation on the one hand, and phenomenal consciousness on the other; and secondly, that (given the first assumption) the former problems are actually amenable to being treated in a physicalist/functionalist fashion. But (taking the second assumption first) I can see no reason to think that the normativity that is essential to intentionality and representation can be dealt with adequately in a naturalistic framework.[2] And nor, in any case, do I think the first assumption should be granted; these issues cannot be adequately dealt with apart from phenomenal consciousness. My ability to think about the world, to represent states of affairs to myself, is bound up with the sensory experience I have of the world – how it looks, feels, tastes to me (Lowe 1995, Eilan 1998 and Rudd 1998). For the world to be represented to a subject is for that subject to experience the world in a certain way. And that sensory experience is itself already intentional and conceptual – it is experience of a world with such and such characteristics.

To fully escape from the assumptions that lead to the impasse of the hard problem (and to the stand-off between coherentism and appeals to "the Given" in epistemology – McDowell 1994, Lecture 1 and passim). We need to take very seriously Kant's dictum that "concepts without intuitions are empty, thoughts without contents are blind" (Kant 1933, A51, B75). And this, I think, means recognizing that the conceptual and sensory elements in experience can only be distinguished notionally from one another, but are inextricably commingled in experience. As McDowell says, "Conceptual capacities are already operative in the deliverances of sensibility themselves" (McDowell, 1994: 39). But if this is correct, then there is no basic level of mere sensory experience that we share with nonconceptualising animals, since all of our experience is permeated with conceptuality. This does not mean that we should regard animals as mere stimulus-response machines; certainly they experience the world, they are aware of things – and (at least some of them) have emotions. But their experience, lacking the conceptual articulation of ours', is something radically different from ours' and, for that reason, probably always will be enigmatic to us.[3] (It isn't just bats whose experience is opaque to us.) So the contribution of conceptuality (language, culture etc) to the animal level of sensibility is not like placing a layer of icing on a cake; it is more like adding a coloured dye to water, which then becomes permeated through and through by the added element.

Applying this model to the emotions, we would have to say that the supposedly "basic" level of mere feeling is, in humans, permeated by intentionality, so that it cannot be separated out as something distinct which we simply share with other animals. This should not lead us to fall into the opposite error of supposing that emotions just are judgements, when judgements are themselves thought of as cool, affectless notings of fact. My emotional states are intentional and evaluative – they are ways of recognising and responding to situations in terms of their significance for me, my values and projects. There have been various attempts in the literature to develop an understanding of the emotions in this "Kantian" way (by which I don't specifically mean Kant's own way, but one modelled on the broadly Kantian account of perceptual experience mentioned above). These include Goldie's account of "feeling towards"; Robert Roberts' account of emotions as "concern-based construals", which he explicates in part by reference to cases of "seeing-as"; and Nussbaum's view that emotions are essentially evaluative judgements about what is significant for me, and which are therefore necessarily intensely felt (Goldie 2000: 18–19, 58–83, Roberts 1988, Nussbaum 2001, esp. Part I).[4] All of these views – which overlap in large part – are trying to do justice to the peculiar mixture of feeling and of rationality in our emotional lives. For all of them the aim is an account which recognizes that reason and emotion are not just closely related, but that feeling itself is rational/intentional, and reason something that is felt.

Such accounts are, in some sense of that admittedly vague term, non-naturalistic. They stress the uniqueness of human emotional experience, its discontinuity with the experience of other animals, its difference from the subject matter of natural science. They thus stand at the opposite end of the spectrum from the efforts of "Evolutionary Psychology" to explain or debunk our emotional lives by claiming that the only really effective motivations must be basic biological imperatives that could have been selected as adaptive for our Neolithic ancestors. This non-naturalism makes many contemporary thinkers uncomfortable; it seems, after all, plausible to think that we should be able to tell a story about ourselves and about the development of our mental life that is continuous with the stories we can tell about the rest of organic nature.[5] But there is a dilemma here. Evolutionary Psychology manages to tell such a continuous story, but only at the cost of giving an utterly implausible, reductive account of human mental and emotional life.[6] If, on the other hand, we insist on descriptions of human emotions that are phenomenologically adequate – as Goldie, Nussbaum and Roberts all do – these turn out to be qualitatively different from descriptions of anything else in nature; the gap, the discontinuity is real.[7] Not seeing a third option here, I am happy to choose adequacy over continuity.

There certainly is a strong temptation to think that we must be able to distinguish between more "basic" emotions, closer to the biological bottom line, and more complex cultural ones. So we might think that fear is more basic than, say, embarrassment. After all, other animals may feel fear, but not embarrassment. But what about the fear of being embarrassed? To avoid such problems, we would have to specify that it is particular kinds of fear that are to be taken as basic, say fear of physical harm. But my fear of physical injury may include the fear that it will prevent me from playing a sport, or the piano; that it might make it impossible for me to hold my job, that it might make me a burden to my family… Phenomenologically, it seems artificial to suppose that these can be separated out from my "basic" animal feeling of fear. Goldie contrasts the fear of redundancy with the more immediate or basic fear of a rapidly approaching bus (Goldie 2000: 46–7, 115). But even in the bus case, although both I and the rabbit next to me might be said to feel fear, my fear will be fear for the person I am; that I, with all these projects, relationships, sorrows, joys, am being threatened with death or injury. And my fear may well be mixed with anger at the idiot driver, or with myself for not looking out carefully…If there is anything at work in this case that is purely 'animal', uncontaminated with personal and cultural complexity, it is probably just an impulse to run, to avoid; and that isn't in itself an emotion at all.

Part of what is crucial to see here is that the person who feels the emotions is ontologically prior to the emotions themselves. It is not the case that there is something called "fear", a universal which may enter into the lives of different individuals while retaining its own identity as fear. Rather, I, you, he and she feel fear at times; but the fear is not a quale which is independent of the rest of my mental life. My fear is fear for the person I am, or for the people or things I care about; it is the fear of someone who has these projects and attachments, who has these character traits, who is also feeling these other emotions, who is thinking these thoughts…All of this comes together in my total state of consciousness at any one moment, and in any such moment I carry with me an implicit sense of my past and of the future which I am moving towards. (As Goldie says, emotions have a narrative structure[8]; and this is because they fit into the narrative structure of my life as a whole, and they are inexplicable apart from that.) Given all of this, I don't think that trying to understand "basic" animal emotions and then work up to human ones, or to appeal to evolution to help us understand human emotion, is going to be very helpful.

4. Naturalism: deeper problems

There is, though, a deeper reason why appealing to evolutionary considerations is unlikely to help much. Orthodox evolutionary theory is firmly naturalistic in character. But, as I noted above, there are deep problems in giving naturalistic accounts of the characteristic powers of the mind – rationality, intentionality etc – or even bare sentience. That we have no adequate naturalistic account of consciousness is in effect conceded by reductive and eliminative materialists. Their rejection of consciousness as we normally understand it, is motivated precisely by the (accurate) perception that it cannot be fitted into an otherwise objective, naturalistic picture of the universe. But even less radical materialist thinkers, who want to stay closer to our intuitive sense of ourselves as conscious, have admitted their embarrassment about finding a place for consciousness in their wider world-view. Thus Fodor:

> Nobody has the slightest idea how anything material could be conscious.
> Nobody even knows what it would be like to have the slightest idea how anything material could be conscious.
> So much for the philosophy of consciousness (Fodor 1992).

That we don't have a naturalistic explanation for consciousness doesn't, of course, mean there couldn't be one. McGinn admits that consciousness is (even in principle) inexplicable by us, but claims that it is nevertheless a straightforwardly naturalistic phenomenon. There is a true theory, inaccessible to us, which would "describe the link between consciousness and the brain in a way that is no more remarkable (or alarming) than the way we now describe the link between the liver and bile" (McGinn 1989/2003: 449).[9] However, his own arguments show that consciousness is utterly, qualitatively, unlike bile or "other" biological phenomena; it's not that we can't see how the brain-consciousness link is no more mysterious than the liver-bile link; we can in fact see very clearly that it is far more mysterious. Consciousness plainly is not a naturalistic phenomenon in anything even remotely like the way that bile is, and to say that it is nevertheless naturalistic and unmysterious in some other way that we simply can't comprehend is to say precisely nothing.[10]

I have put the argument simply in terms of consciousness. But, given my response to the "hard problem", I do not think that it is merely consciousness in the sense of "qualia", bare sentience, that can't be explained naturalistically; what naturalism cannot explain is human rational, conceptually permeated consciousness – and human emotions are phenomena of such consciousness. (It is worth noting, however, that while McGinn and Fodor are wrong to think that problems of consciousness and rationality can be treated separately in humans, they are still right about the inability of naturalism to explain even the "bare" sentience that we do not have, but which some other animals presumably do. If this is right, then naturalism can't even fully explain the evolution of sub-human animal life, or the emotions of such animals.)

The point is this: an orthodox evolutionary account couched in purely naturalistic terms cannot explain consciousness. If one takes emotions to be conscious phenomena (and this is not to dismiss the notion of unconscious emotions, but to treat that as a necessarily secondary and parasitic notion) then one has to accept that naturalism cannot give a complete account of the emotions. And this means that attempts to understand our emotional life in terms that might be adequate for – or even continuous with those that might be adequate for – the study of bee dances and the like is bound to be seriously misleading. One response would be to opt for epiphenomenalism, allowing for evolutionary theory to give a naturalistic explanation, not, admittedly, of everything to do with the emotions, but at least of everything connected with behaviour. I think epiphenomenalism is untenable[11]; and Hutto certainly doesn't want to embrace it. But if we are to allow consciousness a significant causal role – if we are e.g. to assume that our behaviour is influenced by the conscious feel of our emotions – then we are committed to asserting that something that has not been, and it seems in principle cannot be, explained in naturalistic terms, has causal efficacy. In which case consciousness cannot even be safely ring-fenced; if naturalism can't account for consciousness, then it can't account for our behaviour. In which case, the evolutionary process itself cannot be fully understood in a merely naturalistic fashion.

This is a conclusion that clearly makes many philosophers uncomfortable; it goes against a metaphysical picture that is deeply entrenched in contemporary culture. But if one does take a robustly non-reductive account of human rational consciousness, it is decidedly difficult to see how it could have emerged from a non-rational, mechanistic natural world simply via familiar Darwinian mechanisms (Nagel 1997, ch. 7). I am in sympathy, then, with Nagel, when he asks "Why not take the development of the human intellect as a probable counterexample to the law that natural selection explains everything, instead of forcing it under the law with improbable speculations unsupported by evidence?" (Nagel 1986: 81). McDowell, whose account of perception I have largely followed so far, recognizes that there is a problem in explaining "how [it has] come about that there are animals that posses the spontaneity of understanding" (McDowell 1994: 123). However, in accordance with his quietist, therapeutic view of philosophy, this is a problem that he refuses to further engage with. But it can't really be evaded. While rejecting "bald naturalism", McDowell insists that we must not "regress into a pre-scientific superstition, a crazily nostalgic attempt to re-enchant the natural world" (McDowell 1994: 72). However, if we can't explain how creatures capable of rational thought could have emerged from a disenchanted nature by purely natural processes, and if we don't want to deny the unique character of our rational consciousness, then it seems that the only option left is to revise our account of what nature itself is.[12]

This may seem metaphysically extravagant; however, I am not suggesting that we need to develop a full-blown non-naturalistic metaphysics before we can do an adequate phenomenology of our rational-and-emotional consciousness. Nagel is right, I think, to reject the demand that we should stick with naturalism unless we can provide a better alternative: "What, I will be asked, is my alternative? Creationism? The answer is that I don't have one, and I don't need one in order to reject all existing proposals as improbable" (Nagel 1986: 81). Indeed, in line with the generally Kantian position I'm following here, I am quite sceptical about our capacity to produce any adequate metaphysics. To that extent, I am in sympathy with McGinn; we may be in principle unable to understand the relation of mind and world. However, I think we can see that, whatever it is, it can't be a straightforwardly naturalistic one. It follows that it is one which is not fully explicable through orthodox evolutionary theory. And given the prevalence of vague evolutionary hand-waving in contemporary intellectual life, this is a negative result of some importance.[13]

This is a line of thought to which I hope Hutto might be quite sympathetic. In the earlier works I referred to above, he argued against Physicalism and for a form of Bradleyian Absolute Idealism (Hutto 1998, 2000). It should be said that Hutto interprets Bradley as a less ambitious metaphysician than many have supposed,[14] but if this sceptical Bradley is closer to Kantian agnosticism than to Hegelian metaphysical exuberance, then so much the better, from my perspective. But it would be highly interesting to see Hutto spelling out in more detail what the evolutionary considerations that he mentions in this paper would look like when placed in the context of a Bradleyian metaphysics, rather than in the Physicalist framework that is usually taken for granted by those who appeal to such considerations. In any case, if evolutionary theory is going to tell us anything very helpful about our coming to be, it will need to be placed in some metaphysical context that is more adequate than that of contemporary Physicalism.[15]

5. Perception, action and emotion

I have tried to sketch a frankly non-naturalistic account of the emotions and of the mind in general, which can serve as a point of contrast and comparison to Hutto's account. Since Hutto seems to stand somewhere between my position and the straightforward naturalism of, say, Millikan, I hope this will be helpful to him in clarifying his position for us. I want to conclude by saying something to expand on the tantalizing remark with which he concludes his paper. Having noted Hurley's suggestion that action and perception cannot be treated as radically distinct, he goes on to suggest that "it is but a small step to add affect to this equation" and that therefore "it may be a mistake to think that acts of perception are ever truly emotionless or value-free" (21). I think this is correct. Perhaps it will be helpful if I explain why from my perspective this seems right.

All our perceptual experience of the world is conceptually informed. But our concepts are not (at least not in the first place) of Platonic/Aristotelian essences, which give the inherent conceptual structure of the world as it is in itself. They have, rather, essential reference to how the world seems to us – finite creatures within it, who approach it with urgent practical (but also aesthetic, ritual, social etc) needs. Our concepts then, pick out things and group them together on the basis of their perceived salience for us. So when I look around the world, I see it in terms of what is near or far, what can be helpful to me, what poses an obstacle, what is familiar, unknown etc. (Also, perhaps, what is sacred or profane, beautiful or ugly, good or evil, loveable or repugnant. Such concerns can be as immediate, or "basic" as any more obviously "practical", utilitarian concerns.) And even the apparently neutral, descriptive concepts I use – house, lake, car, hammer, sun – pick things out primarily in terms of the usefulness or relevance they have for us in our various activities. So we live in a perceived world not simply of neutral stuff, or facts, but of meanings; and meanings which are related to our possibilities as agents within that world.[16]

Thinking in this way enables us to see not only the link between perception and action, but between both of them and emotion. Whatever the differences between them, theorists like Roberts, Goldie and Nussbaum agree in seeing emotions as ways in which we recognise things, facts, situations, persons etc as having particular significance for us. For Nussbaum, "emotions always involve thought of an object, combined with thought of an object's salience or importance: in that sense they always involve appraisal or evaluation" (Nussbaum 2001: 23). When I feel emotionally about something, I am recognising it as significant for me, given the concerns, projects, relationships, values, beliefs etc that I have.[17] Nussbaum is careful to insist that such appraisal is often immediate; I just see this thing as horrifying, this person as lovable etc, without pausing to reflect. And I can be in an emotional state where I see everything around me in terms of the joy or sorrow I feel, though those things are not the objects or causes of my emotion, and even if the actual objects are absent. (And, of course, I can also have emotions about things which I am not currently perceiving, or which can't be literally perceived at all, like the state of the economy. So emotions are not just ways of (literally) perceiving things.) If all perception involves judgement, then the judgements which our emotions are, or involve[18], may be as much a part of our perceptual experience of the world as any other judgements.

This raises the question, though; are all perceptual experiences, as Hutto suggested, imbued with some sort of emotion, or just some? Roberts takes emotions to be "construals", that is, ways of "reading" or interpreting a situation, seeing it as something (scary, challenging, intimidating etc). Construal, in this sense, is pervasive. "Most of our experiences… are a hard-to-specify structure of percept, concept, image and thought…All such…are construals; only some of these however, are emotions. My formula is that emotions are…serious concern-based construals…" (Roberts 1988: 191). Clearly there is a difference between construing someone as a middle-aged man, or even as a rather odd-looking middle aged man who is sweating a lot and is in rather a hurry, and construing him as a loathsome villain whose depravity fills me with impotent rage. I'm inclined, though, to think these are points on a continuum. All perception is in some way "concern-based" in that it is, as I claimed above, implicitly structured by the concerns and possibilities of the perceiver; and even the basic concepts we use have their basis in common human concerns. The kinds of concern that we call emotional may have a particular intensity, a relation to what I take (consciously or not) to be really important, but their "seriousness" does not mark a distinction in kind from calmer construals.

We do also need to distinguish between cases where I am perceiving something as frightening, delightful or whatever, and those where I am not looking at anything in particular in that way, but am nevertheless approaching the world in a state of mind or mood, so that everything shows up for me as bright or as dreary etc.[19] And in such moods, I will be attuned to things differently; if I am feeling irritable, then the annoying aspects of things will stand out more perspicuously for me, if I'm happy, they won't feel so bad. (Of course, in cases where I am feeling a strong emotion about some specific thing I'm perceiving, that also affects the way I see everything else. If I see the approaching tiger as terrifying, I see the rest of my perceived world in terms of escape routes, traps, potential fellow-victims etc. And there are also cases where I am feeling a strong emotion about a particular thing (person, situation…) and this affects the way I perceive everything else, even though the object of the emotion is absent.[20]) Clearly I am not always looking at things with a strong emotional reaction to that thing as such; but it is much more plausible to suggest that I always approach the world in some mood or other, in accordance with which the world will have a subtlely or blatantly different 'feel' for me. I suspect the right thing to say here is that all perception is concern-based, and that there is a continuum of cases in which the concern is more or less intense or immediately affectively present to us, and also a continuum on which it is more or less focused on a specific object.

As for the value-ladenness of perception/action, which Hutto also mentions; if Nussbaum is right that all emotion is evaluative, and if it is right to say that all perception is in some measure emotional, then we have a nice syllogism to support the value-ladeness thesis. Of course, this would not necessarily involve valuation in any very sophisticated sense; my immediate repugnance for someone can properly be called an "evaluation" of him or her, but it may be one that I do not reflectively endorse. ("She's really a very good person; there's just something about me that makes me dislike her.") We may reluctantly endorse value-judgements which we are unable to feel deeply. Does that mean that, while all emotions are evaluational, not all evaluations are emotional? I suspect that isn't the right thing to say. Normally if I evaluate something as good or evil[21] I am evaluating it as something which we ought to feel positively or negatively towards. If I don't feel as I should, this may be a sign that I am losing faith in a value-system to which I still pay lip-service (even on the level of what I say to myself); or it may be a stage in a process in which I'm coming to adopt new moral beliefs, which I sincerely accept as true, but which haven't yet worked their way into the structure of my emotional life (as in the standard example of the reformed racist who still feels racial hostility while sincerely believing that it's wrong to). [22]

This account of perception and emotion is of course worked out within the framework of the generally Kantian position I have been outlining here. I will look forward to seeing how Hutto elaborates on those tantalizing programmatic remarks at the end of his paper, and to see how they can be developed within the general framework which he has sketched there.

Notes

1. See for instance, the following expression of commitment to a two-stage model: "experience is non-conceptual in nature…non-conceptual experience is a necessary platform for conceptual development" (Hutto 2000: 12).

2. I don't have space to argue for this here, but it has been extensively argued elsewhere – see, for instance, Putnam 1983 and 1992, Nagel 1997 passim; Robinson 1993, essays 1–6.

3. Note, however, that this is not the same as saying that animal experience lacks any kind of conceptual or proto-conceptual articulation.

4. See also Roberts 2004, though this has appeared too late for me to make use of it here.

5. There may well be other, less creditable, reasons why so many contemporary intellectuals feel the need to make at least a ritual bow in the direction of Darwin (rather like the ritual bows to Marx that were de rigour for so many post-war French intellectuals) even when Darwinian theory has nothing significant to contribute to the topic under discussion. But that is a matter for sociologists of knowledge, or for the intellectual historians of the future.

6. For an excellent – and justifiably acerbic – critique of Evolutionary Psychology, see John Dupré 2001.

7. Both Goldie and Nussbaum do make efforts to connect their accounts with evolutionary theorizing (see Goldie 2000, Ch 4; and Nussbaum 2001, Ch 2). But neither really adds anything substantial by so doing, or shows that evolutionary theorizing really helps us to understand human emotions.

8. See Goldie 2000: 12–16, 41–5, 69–72, 181–9.

9. Searle uses similar analogies (see Searle 1992: 90) – though in an attempt to argue that we do all really understand that and how consciousness is a naturalistic phenomenon. But my comments on McGinn's use of the analogies applies just as much to Searle; they would only really work as analogies if he were offering a reductive account of consciousness of the kind which he has explicitly repudiated.

10. This point is (almost) recognized by Galen Strawson, who notes that to call mental phenomena "physical" –if this is intended in a non-reductive sense – is to extend the concept of the physical so far that we really don't know what we are doing with it. Nevertheless, he still recommends that we do just that (See Strawson 1994: 47, 81–2, 104–5)

11. See Rudd 2000.

12. This idea is not a new one. As Frederick Beiser says, discussing Schelling: "Rightly, Schelling saw that the problem of dualism would be surmountable only if philosophers rethought the nature of matter itself. If matter is only bare extension, and if mechanism is the paradigm of explanation, then the only options are dualism and materialism. But neither is satisfactory." (Beiser 2002: 466). Given Hutto's critique of the object-based schema and his sympathies with (some forms of) Absolute Idealism, I suspect he may be quite sympathetic to this line of thought.

13. So my objection to McDowell is not that he fails to explain how beings with spontaneity came to exist, but that he doesn't reflect on the significance of our inability to answer that question. Forcing us to recognize the existence of inescapable but unanswerable questions is, to my mind, one of the vital functions of philosophy.

14. See Hutto 1998b.

15. Just in case it needs saying: this is not meant to justify metaphysicians in second-guessing or prejudging the results of empirical enquires.

16. This account is largely derived from Heidegger's description of our 'being-in-the-world' (Heidegger 1962: Div. 1).

17. "Significant for me", does not of course just mean, for the pursuit of my self-interested projects.

18. I'm deliberately suspending judgement here on the question of whether emotions are judgements (Nussbaum) and the weaker view that they essentially involve judgements. The points I want to make can be made on either view. (Given the qualifications that Nussbaum makes, or,

one might say, the way she understands what a judgement is, the difference seems to be at most one of emphasis, anyway.)

19. Goldie distinguishes moods and emotions; see Goldie 2000: 17–18 and Ch 6. But, as he is careful to note, the distinction is "a matter of degree" (Goldie 2000: 17).

20. As in Sartre's famous example – I can perceive the absence of the person who isn't there to meet me (Sartre 1956: 9–11).

21. I'm not sure if it could really make sense to say that I could recognise something 'objectively' as, say, disgusting or charming while having no propensity to actually experience it as such. It does seem more plausible to make such a distinction with respect to moral judgements. But here, too, there may be no sharp cut-off points.

22. See e.g. Roberts 1998: 195–7, Nussbaum 2001: 35. Roberts uses such examples to argue against the claim that emotions are judgements, for what I feel in such cases is contrary to what I judge. However, Nussbaum's response – that we can, after all, have conflicting judgements about something (Nussbaum 2001: 35–6) – seems convincing. Again, my suspicion is that the difference between them here is more terminological than substantive.

References

Beiser, F. 2002. *German Idealism: The Struggle against Subjectivism 1781–1801*. Cambridge, MA: Harvard University Press.

Chalmers, D. 1995. "Facing up to the Problem of Consciousness." *Journal of Consciousness Studies* 2(3): 200–19.

Chalmers, D. 1996. *The Conscious Mind*. Oxford: Oxford University Press.

Dupré, J. 2001. *Human Nature and the Limits of Science*. Oxford: Oxford University Press.

Eilan, N. 1998. "Perceptual Intentionality, Attention and Consciousness." *Current Issues in Philosophy of Mind*, A. O'Hear (ed.), 181–202. Cambridge: Cambridge University Press.

Fodor, J. 1992. "The Big Idea". *The London Times Literary Supplement*, July 3rd.

Goldie, P. 2000. *The Emotions: A Philosophical Exploration*. Oxford: Clarendon Press.

Heidegger, M. 1962. *Being and Time*. Translated by J. Robinson and J. Macquarrie. Oxford: Blackwell.

Hutto, D.D. 1998. "An Ideal Solution to the Problem of Consciousness". *Journal of Consciousness Studies* 5(3), 328–43.

Hutto, D.D. 1998b. "Bradleyian Metaphysics: a Healthy Scepticism." *Bradley Studies* 4 (1): 82–96.

Hutto, D.D. 2000. *Beyond Physicalism*. Amsterdam: John Benjamins.

Jackson, F. 1982. "Epiphenomenal Qualia." *Philosophical Quarterly* 32: 127–36.

Kant, I. 1933. *Critique of Pure Reason*. Translated by N. Kemp Smith. London: Macmillan.

Lowe, E.J. 1995. "There are no easy Problems of Consciousness." *Journal of Consciousness Studies* 2(3): 266–71.

McDowell, J. 1994. *Mind and World*. Cambridge, MA: Harvard University Press.

McGinn, C. 1989/2003. "Can we Solve the Mind-Body Problem?" In *Philosophy of Mind*, T. O'Connor and D. Robb (eds). London: Routledge.

Nagel, T. 1986. *The View from Nowhere*. Oxford: Oxford University Press.

Nagel, T. 1997. *The last Word*. Oxford: Oxford University Press.

Nussbaum, M. 2001. *Upheavals of Thought: the Intelligence of Emotions*. Cambridge: Cambridge University Press.
Putnam, H. 1983. "Why Reason can't be Naturalised." In *Realism and Reason: Philosophical Papers Vol 3*. Cambridge: Cambridge University Press.
Putnam, H. 1992. *Renewing Philosophy*. Cambridge, MA: Harvard University Press.
Roberts, R. 1988. "What an Emotion is: a Sketch." *Philosophical Review* (97): 183–209.
Roberts, R. 2004. *The Emotions*. Cambridge: Cambridge University Press.
Robinson, H. (ed.) 1993. *Objections to Physicalism*. Oxford: Oxford University Press.
Rudd, A. 1998. "What it's like and what's really wrong with Physicalism: a Wittgensteinian Perspective." *Journal of Consciousness Studies* 5 (4): 454–63.
Rudd, A. 2000. "Phenomenal Judgement and Mental Causation." *Journal of Consciousness Studies* 7 (6): 53–66.
Sartre, J-P. 1956. *Being and Nothingness*. Translated by H. Barnes. London: Methuen.
Searle, J. 1992. *The Rediscovery of the Mind*. Cambridge, MA: MIT Press.
Strawson, G. 1994. *Mental Reality*. Cambridge, MA: MIT Press.

Both Bradley and biology

Reply to Rudd

Daniel D. Hutto

1. Avocados and pears: The case for modesty

Rudd is right to observe that it is, "significant that the paper repeatedly mentions "basic" or "primitive" emotions" (Rudd: this volume). And he is sensitive enough to note that, "Hutto does recognize that the "basic" emotions are open to modification in particular cases (17), so he doesn't accept the full avocado pear model – his view suggests rather the image of a (genetically modified?) avocado whose core is itself somewhat malleable" (Rudd: this volume). This too is right, only I see the avocado core as being modified culturally or through individual experience, not genetically. My view is that some of our interpersonal response patterns are *re-tied* through enculturation. We gain new, norm-governed habits of response when we take on a second nature, as it were. In this process, at least *some* of our patterns of emotional expression and reactions are transformed. It is important to stress that, when this happens, the result is transformative, not merely additive. Coming in line with others, through imitation, learning and education alters the manner of our emotional expression and response, and indeed its character, quite radically.

So, there are two things to notice here. Number one, we have a *first* nature (I also call it an 'inherited' nature to avoid the unhelpful language of 'innateness'). For me this is *primitive* in the precise sense of being 'primary' – it comes first in the order of things. It is also *basic* or foundational in the developmental sense too – it serves as a *base* from which we build. Number two, it is possible for some creatures, human beings at least, to forge new perception-response ties, in *some* but not all cases. Thus I want to defend a quite modest line on the possibilities in this domain, holding that human psychology is quite a mixed bag – some of our emotional expressions and responses are relatively fixed automatic and unthinking, and nonverbal, others are more flexible – having been shaped by individual experience and various kinds of socio-cultural norms, those fostered by our attuning to others by participating in mimetic and narrative activities. Although I too want to avoid talk of levels and layers, in other respects I therefore stand opposed to Rudd's more radical suggestion that "sensations and concepts in perception, and feelings and judgements in emotion, are inextricably tied together. There is no "basic" level of mere nonconceptual sensation/feeling that we share with nonconceptualising animals, and to which our more distinctive abilities add an extra layer" (Rudd: this volume).[1]

To adopt this kind of line on this issue is, I think, demonstrably mistaken. Denying the existence of such a level in the human case would make it difficult to account for our reactions to certain perceptual illusions. The Müller-Lyer case is perhaps the best known of these (a version of which is reproduced in Figure 6.1. See also Crane 1992: 150–151, Jacob 1997: 67–69). When confronted with this visual illusion what we see is that the lines look to be different lengths, but in fact they are the same length. Interestingly, the effect persists even after we know this: despite what we know, one of them still *looks* to be longer. Unavoidably, our judgement must express a propositional content, such as, 'The lines are the same length'. The content of this proposition is captured in terms of its canonical concepts. In contrast, the purely perceptual response is distinguished, by my lights, by its not 'having' any such content. It has a certain experiential character which is bound up with its potential to guide actions in certain ways – indeed it may be that the illusion works so well because it appeals to our basic edge-detecting, perceptual mechanisms.[2] My claim is that the way humans respond to such illusions belies a more general capacity for nonconceptual perceptual responding that is quite basic to the way we navigate with respect to worldly offerings perceptually. My motto is that basic perceptual responding is neither content nor concept involving.

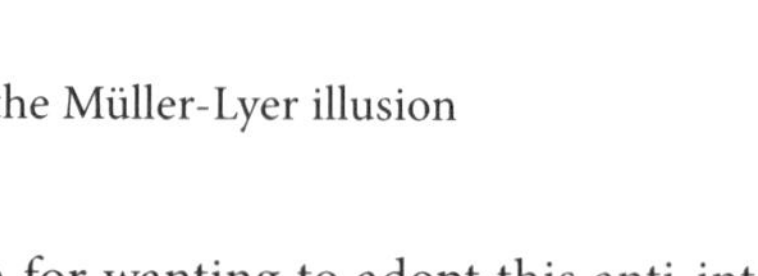

Figure 6.1 A version of the Müller-Lyer illusion

For yet another reason for wanting to adopt this anti-intellectualist view, we can focus on a favourite topic that causes trouble for McDowellians – the fact that we can discriminate many, many shades of colours even though we lack corresponding substantive concepts for these. For example, when choosing from a range of possible colours for the cover of my first book I used a Patone Matching System (or PMS) colour card. This enabled me to choose from an incredible array of colour shades, because each one was uniquely coded. The PMS card allowed me to identify the subtle differences in shade in that way. Without it I would have been unable to tell the closer shades apart and I would certainly have been unable to re-identify them using my own native resources.[3] This is important, if we consider that even McDowell accepts that the minimum criterion for having a 'concept' is that one has a natural ability to re-identify something as an instance of a re-occurring particular or kind. I think that there is more to having a concept than that; but let's not quibble. The point is that in making everyday colour discriminations, using unaided perception, we are surely not exercising our conceptual capacities for re-identification, even as minimally conceived. And yet, such discriminations can be vital to our worldly navigation and indeed they have a characteristically distinct phenomenology – I see and respond to a great many colours in the course of my day, even though I'd be at a loss to re-identify them.

It looks *ad hoc* to respond to this fact by trying to salvage the claim that such discriminations are conceptual after all, for example, by insisting that, "What is in play here is a recognitional capacity, possibly quite short-lived, that sets in with experience" (McDowell 1994: 57).[4] Certainly, it is explanatorily hollow to note only that some creatures, the linguistically competent ones, can attach demonstrative tags such as '*that* shade' to any and all of their discriminations. Such after-the-fact labelling gives us no reason to suppose that our primary modes of experiential responding are at root 'conceptual' even on a very minimal understanding of concept possession.

I do not even think that basic re-identificational abilities are conceptual based (or demonstrate conceptual understanding). Millikan has done more than most to enable us to understand the nature of this non-verbal ability to re-identify of individuals, stuffs and kinds within circumscribed historical domains (She uses the umbrella term 'substances' to cover all the items so tracked). Essentially, this requires a capacity (not a disposition) to keep track of what is the same through differences – a capacity to recognise some thing or things as being the 'same again' by imperfect but reliably enough means (Millikan 2000). To explicate the nature of such capacities would require an understanding of how organisms systematically 'mark' a given substance as being the 'same again' despite their using multiple, disparate means of identifying it: what we want therefore is an account of what such 'sameness marking' involves. In abstract, what this involves can be best captured graphically: *in effect*, we place what Millikan calls a Strawsonian dot for each distinct substance to be identified (or re-identified) on our 'mental map' and each of the various methods and procedures we have of identifying a substance can be thought of as different ways of causing that dot to light up.

Now, there are various ways of understanding how this process works in detail. But importantly, sameness marking *cannot* be achieved just by having the same passive representation tokened in one's 'mind' repeatedly (such as 'x is F' popping up, over and over again in the presence of X). Indeed – and this is the crux – it is a mistake to try to explicate re-identificational abilities in terms of the making of identity *judgements*: recognising something as being the same again does not reduce to noting repeatedly that the thing in question has a certain property. Re-identification does not reduce to a kind of predication; it is a basic ability, but it is one that neither requires nor involves being able to classify or categorise substances *as such* – or to group them under particular headings. For this reason, it is a mistake to think of basic recognitional capacities in terms of the making of indexical judgements, such as noting of something that it is '*that* shade' or even '*that* shade again'. The recognitional abilities in question are not based on a prior capacity for classification or categorization. There is no reason to think that our native perceptual abilities to discriminate certain features or to re-identify certain particulars (and kinds) rest on the having of or a capacity to use concepts or intensional predicates – not even 'low level' ones (for more details, see my reply to Crane). My nonconceptualist proposal is that, even in the case of human perceptual responding (or at least a great proportion of it), the various sensory modalities that underwrite our discrimination and identification procedures operate, each in their own characteristic way, by being informational sensitive to the natural signs that signal the presence of various worldly offering of importance to organisms. A great deal of 'cognitive' activity therefore takes place without, and prior to, the formation of intensional propositional attitudes or judgements (see my reply to Goldie). In sum, even the re-identification of particulars and recurring environmental kinds can be achieved by purely non-referential, non-propositional and non-inferential means.[5]

For example, making contentful judgements about the sameness of identity is not required, for example, to explain or understand the mechanisms by which we keep track of a thrown object's spatio-temporal movements over time. Such abilities require that the organism attends to certain perceptually salient attributes of the objects in question. The moving object might be detected by sensory means, by sensitivity to an appropriate mix of its tell-tale properties using multiple channels that detect – e.g. a characteristic colour, trajectory, manner of movement, unique composition, and so on. In certain contexts, spotting and tracking something for the purpose of guidance and coordination can be achieved using quite simple identifiers – specific colours, shapes, odours that are reliably associated with particular things or kinds. The general principle can be illustrated with a mundane example: if you are the only person who carries a full length umbrella to class then this can be used as an easy way of picking you out (even if it is not utterly foolproof). Or consider the ways in which I re-identify the milkman, again fallibly, by hearing the distinctive sounds he makes when opening the gate and clinking the milk bottles at a particular *time* each morning. In my usual setting, these are reliable enough sensory indicators that serve my coordination needs. My point is that my ability to re-identify substances in this way is the *basis for*, not the product *of*, judgements of the sort "There's the milkman", or "It's the milkman again" (or 'More milkman!'). In my own case and that of other linguistically competent humans, *but not that of non-verbals*, I can use concepts to make and express judgements about the very same situation. This is a powerfully different way of responding to such cases; one that involves habits of interpretation through which we *learn* to experience the world in conceptually mediated ways. This opens up a range of new possibilities for us: In forming content-involving beliefs and desires I can reason practically about what I ought to do, perhaps even adopting longstanding policies to do certain things regularly, such as ensuring that I get my weekly subscription out to the milkman on certain days, and so on. That is not a possibility for those without language. We can form judgements, but our basic perceptual responses, like those of other animals, do not involve them – I do not form content-involving 'thoughts' about the milkman in order to re-identify him by sensory means. Unlike Rudd, I claim that, for beings like us, both nonconceptual sensory responding and conceptually interpreted, perceptual based judgements are always ready options as ways of getting around in the world. The former is not removed from our repertoire with the arrival of the latter, at least not in all cases. And, although it is true that the latter has formed the dominant focus of much recent 'phenemonological' reflection (at least when this is attempted by analytic philosophers), I think it is possible, though not easy, to reveal just how greatly we continue to rely on our more animalistic modes of response in daily life and to demonstrate that these do in fact ground a great deal of our conscious experience of things (obviously, the animalistic responses in question would be those peculiar to *human* animals).[6]

In *Beyond Physicalism*, I was tempted to say that in such cases the milkman was presented under an *experiential* mode of presentation (or MoP), i.e. as opposed to an intensional one. I imagined that experiential MoPs might be construed as the distinct ways that particular objects are experienced (by means of the haptic, olfactory, visual and other senses, whether separately or fused together in some unison). At the time, the important thing I wanted to stress was that such MoPs were *not* to be identified with Fregean thoughts, intensions, 'senses' or *Sinn*. Even then I wanted to steer clear of a Neo-Fregean analysis of what is involved in basic acts of re-identification. Specifically, I object to the idea that we must 'represent' worldly offerings in order to respond to them appropriately and that this involves doing so intensionally – i.e. under a content-involving MoP. The worldly offerings (objects and states of affairs) to which we and other creatures are informationally sensitive – thus at which we are end-directed in our primitive responses – are not presented to, or apprehended by us under intensional MoPs, 'descriptions', or the like. My thought was that experiential MoPs better captured what was needed, for although these would be debars from entering into *inferential* liaisons (for obvious reasons) they would not be ruled out from interfacing with one another in other non-logical ways in perceptual processing.

The basic thought still seems right to me. But I must confess that it is not entirely clear what I was imagining experiential MoPs to be: Does each individual perceptible signal require a distinct MoP? Or, do *all* of the means that I have at my disposal for identifying the milkman – somehow bound together as a whole – collectively comprise a single conglomerate MoP? Or is there some way of carving up smaller subsets of these, as in cases in which we attend to just one feature of a complex visual scene? I am not sure how one might even begin to answer these questions in a principled way. Nor do I think they should be answered, for I now think that to talk of MoPs at all is to take a step on the road to confusion about the *role* and *character* of sensory stimuli (see my replies to Crane and Myin and De Nul).

And at all costs, we must guard against the idea that our means of identifying movements, sounds, looks, smells or feels could be the focus of one's attention or concern during basic acts of re-identification. Such our responses to natural signs are focused on what they point to; the signs themselves are merely pointers – mediating indicators – of the presence of something else. And the danger is that even if one is very careful to talk of MoPs it opens up a risk of conflating what is being responded to with the modes of response (see my reply to Crane). I have come to think that metaphors invoking the language of 'presentation' encourage this. We are less likely to go wrong by focusing on what-it-is-like to act and be acted upon when making such responses. This is how we can explicate their experiential character. In a different kind of inquiry, we might focus instead on their mechanics. Both are compatible possibilities (see my replies to Myin and De Nul and Goldie).

In all, I hold that it is crucial that we recognise that basic responding – even for humans – is nonconceptual. If we deny this we will be unable to make best sense of such phenomena as perceptual illusions, aspect-dawning, mental imagery and the fine-grainedness of experience (for more details see Hutto 2000: ch. 1). And there is yet another reason for taking this line. For, unless we are prepared to posit the existence of (at least some) innate concepts, there appears to be no alternative but to hold that concepts *develop* from more basic nonconceptual capacities of some kind or other. This is a simple point of logic. If concepts are not somehow 'given' then they must be acquired. Therefore, perhaps the most compelling reason for wanting to presuppose robust capacities for nonconceptual experiencing – which, for some creatures, can be shared – is that doing so gives us the necessary apparatus for understanding how concepts *arise* and *develop* (see my reply to Hobson). This idea has the status of a basic tenet for me. Thus:

> it is precisely when we try to identify the key aspects of [conceptual] development that the postulation of nonconceptual experience becomes crucial. Experience is a major platform for conceptual development. I made a structurally similar case when discussing the question of intentionality in chapters four and five of *The Presence of Mind*. I now want to consider its form relative to experience. The form of argument I have been advancing relies on an acceptance of Bermúdez's Acquisition Constraint which states:
>
> If a given cognitive capacity is psychologically real, then there must be an explanation of how it is possible for an individual in the normal course of human development to acquire that cognitive capacity (Bermúdez 1998: 19).
>
> By appeal to this constraint, if we suppose that the concepts of experience are not innate or *a priori*, then nonconceptual capacities must exist to enable us to acquire concepts. Consideration of the links between simulation, triangulation and the learning of concepts gives us ground for thinking that, at least with respect to learning experiential concepts human beings must have specific prior capacities involving the relevant nonconceptual experiences. In contrast, mere informational sensitivity, no matter how complex, is insufficient to ground this kind of concept learning. And if we think that more advanced concepts are acquired on the back of these, then it follows that experience is vital for learning any concepts at all (Hutto 2000: 43).

In contrast, to postulate the existence of *non-linguistic concepts* is tantamount to postulating the existence of some kind of substantive conceptual knowledge – declarative knowledge of essentially that same sort that at least we humans enjoy, yet knowledge which is prior to any truths that are learnt in social contexts. There are different ways of trying to make good on this sort of claim; Jerry Fodor's language of thought hypothesis is one such, but I assume that path is not attractive to Rudd (certainly not to McDowellians generally). But if this option is rejected too, then we are surely owed more details about the nature and origin of this special class of concepts, how they are evoked and the form of knowledge they provide. It would help if there was some successful argument to show that we really have no choice but to presuppose the existence of such concepts (i.e. even if no account of their origins is forthcoming). With that in hand, one might reject the Acquisition Constraint as an illegitimate demand (I take it this would be the line that Rudd would pursue). Yet without the imagined argument such a rejection is question-begging, on the supposition that the non-conceptualist option has not been shown to be incoherent or nonsensical.

The fact is that nonconceptualism holds out much more explanatory promise than either the empty offerings of Language of Thought theorists or the quietism of McDowellians (see Hutto 1999 122–4 and Hutto 2007). It does not level the playing field to claim that talk of nonconceptual triangulation "smacks of magic" (McDowell 1998: 410). For:

> treating nonconceptual capacities as a necessary condition for the development of concepts is not an attempt to reductively explain the emergence of concepts. Furthermore, if we explain the development of concepts by appeal to the training of individuals this account need not end in an explanatory regress. If triangulation is magical it is still possible to understand how the trick is pulled off. For, in order to understand the ultimate origin of the concepts deployed by the teachers we would have but to look to social and linguistic development of *Homo sapiens sapiens*. And here again, in providing such an account, the fact that we have similarly directed, inherited nonconceptual capacities has a vital foundational role to play, even if it cannot provide the whole story (Hutto 1999: 124).

I say a bit more, albeit in sketch, of what this development looks like in my reply to Hobson. But it is worth noting that anyone who adopts the line that 'basic' concepts exist (whether they harbour explanatory ambitions or not) faces a situation far more embarrassing than that faced by the advocates of non-conceptualism. In the primitive learning situation, when a child first enters into the world of public language and its norms, how can we say – prior to its mastery of such norms– that the teacher and the student agree in how they 'identify' things? What would it be to say that they agree in their deployment of non-linguistic 'concepts' or 'rudimentary notions'? How, we might wonder, are these acquired or activated?

To this it will be rightly objected that some common ground must be presupposed if we are to co-ordinate the very activity of teaching concepts. True enough. But invoking 'implicit but shared concepts' is precisely the wrong move when it comes to understanding the kinds of 'agreement' that are the basis of language learning (and subsequent development of language games). Our common ground with others is *nonconceptual*. Thus when veteran language users say of novices in training that they 'think *this* or *that*', they are charitably extending a conceptual schema to these early learners for the purposes of more easily describing their responses. It does not follow from this that pre-verbal infants are able to make content-involving conceptual identifications for themselves any more than it follows from the fact that we can ascribe 'propositional' attitudes to cats and mice that they believe and desire such things intensionally, i.e. under *any* description (see my reply to Hobson). And, if one did think that children were using non-linguistic 'theories' or 'concepts' at this point in their careers, then there is ample evidence to suggest that their concepts would not be 'shared' with those of their adult teachers in any case! (see Gopnik & Meltzoff 1997).

2. Whys and wherefores

Rudd is not sure about my 'argumentative strategy'. In particular, he is sure why I should want to appeal to evolutionary biology in order to help us to understand (1) the nature of intentional directedness and (2) the origins of experience. This seems especially baffling to him given that I steadfastly reject any and all attempts to solve the 'hard problem' of consciousness.[7] But this is only confusing because Rudd fails to distinguish between two, quite different formulations of that problem – what I have long called the *how*-formulation and the *why*-formulation (see Hutto 2000: Introduction). Trying to solve the *how*-variant is, I claim, hopeless. But I have always held there to be much brighter prospects for dealing with the second.

Chalmers, who gave the 'hard problem' its name typically presents it as a problem about explanation, asking: Why should there be conscious experience at all? (Chalmers 1996: 4). But unlike the question of how consciousness could be made intelligible in terms of something else, I do not think his why-question is all that difficult. Or rather, to be precise, when it is asked in a general way it comes to the same thing as asking: Why is there anything rather than nothing at all? I don't think we can or should try to answer *that* question (see Hutto 2003/2006: 83–4, 2000: 141). But, if Chalmers' why-question is formulated in a more specific way it can be answered by appeal to our natural history. Following Dretske, I hold that behaviour:

> can be identified with the whole series of events that lead up to, and result in, the production of a given bodily movement in particular circumstances. To think of behaviour in this way is to treat it as a process as opposed to a product. It is, therefore, distinct from a form of bodily movement. In this light, when we ask *why* a bodily movement occurred, as opposed to *how* it occurred, we can interpret this question as asking about what put the whole causal process in place. Or more precisely, we can inquire into the conditions that set it up such that the causal process would produce a result of X kind (as opposed to one of Y kind). With this distinction between the two understandings of behaviour in hand, Dretske respectively labels the target of these different inquiries 'triggering causes' and 'structuring causes' (Dretske 1988: ch. 1 & 2).
>
> The difference is easily demonstrated by considering the questions we can ask about the way in which a bi-metallic strip enables a thermostat to control the level of a room's heat. Such strips are assigned to this job because they are naturally responsive to changes of temperature. Yet it is easy to imagine that they could be given a different control function if they were tied to some other output mechanism. For example, the strip could be enlisted to control the opening and closing of a garage door. In such a case when the room-temperature falls below 18° Celsius instead of switching on the boiler, the garage door would be rigged to open (Dretske 1988: 41, 1991: 212–213). The triggering cause is the drop in room temperature but the structuring cause is the practical joker who has tied the thermostat to

> the garage door mechanism. Another of Dretske's examples involves a situation in which the triggering cause of a bomb exploding is a car's reaching a speed of more than sixty-five miles per hour. In this case, the structuring cause is the terrorist's wiring up a semtex device to the speedometer (Hutto 1999: 106).

According to the biosemeiotic approach I favour, natural selection plays the same sort of role as the practical joker or the terrorist in these stories (see my reply to Crane). Normal explanations in terms of selection pressures can be seen as specifying structuring causes by outlining the historical conditions in which certain stimulus-response routines were selected. I defended this distinction (and our need to call on it) against detractors in *The Presence of Mind*, chapter 4. And I have tried elsewhere to show how an account along these lines could be pressed into service in order to answer the modest *why*-question. I quote at length from chapter three of *Beyond Physicalism*, where I argued that:

> homuncular teleofunctionalism provides some insight into the possible origins of experience. It is able to give the right line of reply to Chalmers' why-formulation of the hard question, which asks: Why is there conscious experience at all? Yet, despite this, I baulk at endorsing the doctrine in its standard form because it is a special instance of the [explanatory] psycho-physical identity theory.
>
> ...one must countenance the real possibility that two systems might be functionally equivalent at the level of outward responsiveness to stimuli and yet differ with respect to how they manage to be so. It is possible that there is no detectable difference in their outward ability to perform in a range of tasks despite this internal difference – *ex hypothesi*, they produce their performances by different means. But to accept this is to endorse conscious inessentialism. Flanagan defines it as follows:
>
> [Conscious inessentialism]...is the view that for any mental activity M, performed in any cognitive domain D, even if we do M with conscious accompaniments, M can in principle be done without these conscious accompaniments (Flanagan 1991: 309).
>
> Naturalists ought to accept this doctrine. Yet Chalmers thinks that anyone who endorses conscious inessentialism cannot possibly answer the why-formulation of the hard question, which asks: "Why should there be conscious experience at all?" (Chalmers 1996: 4). Lurking in the background is the question: Why isn't mere informational sensitivity sufficient to co-ordinate an organism's response to its environment? Thus he claims that in order for consciousness to have "arisen during the evolutionary process....it [must] serve a function that could not be achieved without it" (Chalmers 1996: 120). This is simply false. All that is required is that having experiences conferred an edge at some stage in the cognitive arms race between two or more sorts of naturally evolved creatures – ones capable of experiencing, Ψs, and ones without this capacity, Φs.
>
> Flanagan considers this to be exactly what happened in our own natural history. He suggests that our Ψ-ancestors had greater biological fitness in activities

such as fleeing, fighting, food gathering and sex. Still it might be wondered why subjects of experience, "might have won – or should have been expected to win – an evolutionary battle against very intelligent zombie-like informationally sensitive organisms" (Flanagan & Polger 1995: 321). Yet we have evidence, here and now, that experience does make a difference to the performance of many general tasks. For example, Weiskrantz's studies of various neurological deficits in *Consciousness: Lost and Found* provides a whole catalogue of cases which advertise the advantages of being experientially aware. Consider that even a self-prompting super-blindsighter would be no match for a consciously aware subject in the majority of everyday tasks. Although it is amazing that blindsighted subjects are as sensitive as they are, despite their reported lack of experience, we must not forget that people with this affliction, "cannot avoid bumping into lampposts, even if they can guess their presence or absence in a forced-choice situation" (Dretske 1995: 121, cf. Van Gulick 1989: 218–220, Marcel 1988). For although information about their environment can play a role in their voluntary actions, even self-prompting super-blindsighters would be employing a comparatively slower and more roundabout means of accessing such information than conscious subjects employ (cf. Van Gulick 1989: 220).

An earlier Flanagan answered this query by pointing out that "one might think that neither group would be favoured over the other. But if speed of processing mattered, and it almost certainly did and does, then the [Ψ] group would have been favoured" (Flanagan 1991: 321, cf. also 319–322). Of course, it is also logically possible that the Φs might have been faster. But it is just these kinds of might-have-beens that the naturalist has no time for. If something like this story is correct, and experience has an evolutionary origin, then the Ψs simply were faster. In this light it becomes clear that Chalmers' why-question is badly formulated. It cannot be asked in logical vacuum. We need to consider a real context of a possible competition.

Moreover, since natural selection operates by means of variation, we should suspect that even if Ψs and Φs performed equally well across a specifiable set of parameters (by some spectacular chance), at some later point differences would emerge in their performances. Variation ensures that level-pegging does not occur for long. If Ψs and Φs were in competition and there was a real difference between them which Mother Nature could exploit, it would have. If this kind of evolutionary hypothesis is even roughly the right story to tell about our natural history then the fact that we and our hominid competitors would have hailed from a common stock would also go some distance in explaining why our older systems of response, such as those of our hormonal systems and our autonomic and central nervous systems, provide unconscious informational sensitivities that far outstrip the range of our experiential sensitivities (cf. Flanagan 1991: 330, Dennett 1997: 103–106). For example, it is well known that we can be, and frequently are, subliminally influenced by all sorts of informationally loaded cues of which we are wholly unaware.

> To return to the main point, all we need in order to explain why consciousness emerged is that it conferred a competitive advantage and, *contra* Chalmers, there is every reason to think it did. In context, the why-question about consciousness is no more worrying than any other question about why evolution chose one path rather than another….
>
> In light of this discussion the right move appears to be that, rather than abandon or ignore experience because it resists capture in an abstract functionalist framework, we should adopt a more meaty version of functionalism – specifically homuncular teleofunctionalism. (Hutto 2000: 72, 83–5).

I can get away with this precisely because I endorse a very particular kind of non-explanatory identity theory, the nature of which I outlined in my response to Myin and De Nul. By this means it is possible to avoid epiphenomenalism – 'to allow consciousness a significant causal role' – precisely because there are grounds for believing in causally efficacious conscious events or occurrences even though such efficacy cannot 'in principle … be explained in naturalistic terms' (Rudd: this volume). My so-called 'Davidsonian Neo-Bradleyianism' permits me to accept just this.[8] And taking this line is entirely consistent with the remarks I have made about how evolutionary biology can help us to understand the directedness of intentionality (for more details see my reply to Crane) and the origins of responses with an experiential character (in the modest sense described above).

This is the result if you try to answer the why-formulation in the way I do above while denying that the how-formulation can be overcome. For any functionalist who takes experience seriously, be they of the abstract or homuncular persuasion, can only address the how-question in a straight way by endorsing some form of *explanatory* materialism or physicalism. Although I think one is inevitably led to endorse some version of identity theory (to explain the causal efficacy of experience, if for no other reason), I reject *explanatory* physicalism in all its forms. I will not rehearse all my reasons for doing so, but let me sketch just one.

Barring practical quibbles about which level of functional analysis is appropriate in order to satisfy our questions about any given capacity, it is always possible to seek more basic explanations at a yet deeper level, presumably we can keep going until we hit rock bottom. We can go progressively lower and lower down levels, rather like opening a set of Russian dolls. It is generally supposed that we hit explanatory pay dirt when we reach the level of fundamental physics – that of an ideal physics. But this is not so, for in fact:

> our understanding of physical-physical interaction is ultimately no better than our understanding, or lack thereof, of psychophysical interaction (Lowe 1996, Mills 1997). If this is right, and we are not bothered about the first case, then why should we be bothered about the second? But, is this right? It would seem so: for even in cases of causal interaction between events of the same kind or same sub-

> stance, we ultimately lack an explanatory account of *how* one thing causes another. Consider the explanation of *how* one billiard ball causes another to move. No matter how detailed the reductive explanation one gets in mechanics, even those given in terms of microphysics will eventually run out of steam (cf. G. Strawson 1994: 32–36). And at every progressive stage there will be some point at which we will simply need to say, for example, that we know *that* this x causes that y, but we don't know how or don't yet know how. Simply stated, there is always a practical limit to how well we can understand causal interaction, even between physical events. We would ultimately need to appeal to the laws of physics. But even if we can describe or predict what happens in terms of laws, it doesn't follow that we can understand or explain this interaction (cf. Lowe 1996: 52). For, at base, such laws are merely descriptive they are not explanatory. As Hill notes, "physics itself countenances a range of primitive causal interactions – it must do so if it is to avoid postulating an infinite number of levels of explanation" (Hill 1991: 42). When we hit ontological rock-bottom we find just the same problem in understanding causal interaction as we do in the psychophysical domain (Hutto 2000: 141).

Now, I don't deny that improved knowledge in the various sub-domains helps when it comes to making better predictions about and controlling psychophysical events (and indeed all other sorts of happenings). So this kind of 'explanatory' descent has its point and purpose. What I deny is that this activity will ever yield 'explanations' that equate to an intelligible understanding of psychophysical causation. Hence, for this reason, *inter alia*, my identity thesis is of a decidedly non-physicalist sort.

3. The virtues of incompleteness

Rudd wonders how it is possible to square my attempts to understand the origins of perceptual and emotional responding by appeal to evolutionary biology while nevertheless retaining a commitment to a Bradleyian, essentially quietist, metaphysics. He would like to see me spell, "out in more detail what the evolutionary considerations … would look like when placed in the context of a Bradleyian metaphysics" (Rudd, this volume). Before turning to that, it is worth noting that he is right to say that we have some common sympathies on this front: i.e. a shared scepticism about the possibility of a positive metaphysics. But to fully understand my account it is important to recognise two things.

First, what I find most attractive in Bradley's approach to metaphysics is his denial that a final unified view of reality is achievable. He demonstrates this by repeatedly exposing the confused offerings of reductionists in a great variety of domains. And, although he directed his efforts against the phenomenalists of his own day and in anticipation of the positivist programme of the twentieth century, I hold that the misguided ambitions of physicalists deserve exactly the same kind of exposé. They continue to pursue what is, in essence, a positivist and neo-positivist project for a unified science (and they do so with a similar zeal). The only important difference is that contemporary physicalism is recast in terms of hoped for inter-theoretical reductions to the statements of a basic science, rather than a reduction of meaningful statements to a sensory foundation.

Second, inspired by Bradley, my *a priori* argument against explanatory physicalism (as explicated in the reply to Myin and De Nul) is that given the parochial and special-purpose nature of our inherited response systems (and the conceptual schemata that built from them) we can know in advance that certain reductions are not possible or will never satisfy us intellectually. For this reason we do not have to wait for the results of some proposed future science of consciousness in order to know that 'experience' will not successfully reduce to the 'physical' (or some other base). This is the basis of my 'intelligibility' argument against physicalism.

Importantly, it allows however that *within* specific domains, contextual – or what the pragmatists call provisional – 'truths' are surely achievable (see Hutto 2000: ch. 7). Keeping this in mind, Rudd need not worry that I have adopted certain assumptions of explanatory naturalists, despite myself. I emphatically do not think the natural sciences – and evolutionary biology in particular – can "give a *complete* account of the emotions" (Rudd, this volume, emphasis added). But I do think they can give a *partial* account – in particular, I think evolutionary biology can help us understand the intentional directedness and origins of experiences (in terms of structuring causes) and, I think, neuroscience can provide more detail about the triggering and processing mechanisms. So, I reject Rudd's claim that in studying the emotions, "the study of bee dances and the like is bound to be seriously misleading" (Rudd: this volume).

As I think humans have a mixed nature, my attitude on this matter is decidedly Aristotelian: "We proceed to treat of animals, without omitting, to the best of our ability, any member of the kingdom, however ignoble... Every realm of nature is marvellous... we should venture to study every kind of animal without distaste; for each and all will reveal to us something natural and something beautiful...if any person thinks the examination of the rest of the animal kingdom an unworthy task, he must hold in like disesteem the study of man" (Aristotle, *De Partibus Animalium*, I 645a6–8). I do not, of course, say that the *basic* perceptual and emotional responses of humans are *the same* as other animals, only that they have the same sort of origin and that they all operate on the same nonconceptual level – they are not content-involving. Social intelligence takes different forms in different species, our own included. This follows from the fact that each species has it is own set of inherited and learned routines of response (see my reply to Goldie).

Rudd's worry – that I will be forced to fall in with a more thoroughgoing naturalism – can be set against its obverse of worry, originally raised by McHenry

– that my Bradleyian account necessarily fails to give science its proper due. I think these opposing forces can be shown to cancel each other out. But achieving the right balance is not easy.[9] To do so I must answer Rudd in exactly the same way that I answered McHenry. Of the latter, I claimed that:

> [he reveals] his true colours when he suggests that science remains the best guide to metaphysics because of its ability "to deliver results" (McHenry 1998: 101). But if this is just a remark about its practical achievements, then it fails to offer succour to the naturalised metaphysician, since accepting this is consistent with endorsing the approaches of both Bradley and Dupré. If by 'results' he means something else then he needs to spell it out.
>
> Lastly, McHenry's objection to my approach crucially highlights the need to distinguish between what Kitcher calls 'legend bashers' [those who think science can tell the *complete* true story of reality] and 'science bashers'. I am one of the former, not the latter. But this is not transparent from the way in which [McHenry] presents my views. He says "in his emphasis of the negative cases, Hutto fails to note the amazing strides of modern science" (McHenry 1998: 99). My first reaction is to wonder why the cited cases are regarded as negative. In their own contexts each of the theories I discuss are examples of good science in action. It is *only* in the context of binding them together in a principled unified metaphysical framework that they are cast in a problematic or negative light. In my view, just as Davidson regards science as a suburb of our everyday language rather than a substitute for it, so I regard the various branches of sciences as equally suburban in character (cf. Davidson 1985: 172). To surrender this metaphysical ambition is to tow the Bradleyian line.
>
> The only other way to retain a principled unity would be to endorse some form of regulative eliminativism toward any unruly elements within theories or towards whole theories which resist incorporation into the grand whole. Indeed McHenry comes close to endorsing this position when he reminds us of the distinction between modest Quinean and ambitious, Whiteheadean versions of naturalised metaphysics. Quine's allegedly modest version of naturalism does "not recognise any picture of the universe beyond what the sciences provide, i.e. physicalism" (McHenry 1998: 100). But such a sparse physicalism is a non-starter, minimally, because it cannot coherently account for content or consciousness. Of course, eliminative physicalists, like Quine, will simply deny that any such attempt is necessary, but as these are non-optional features of reality, they need accounting for [i.e. Don't you believe it!] (Hutto 2000: 185).

My pragmatic partiality might be summed up with the motto: 'everything in its place'.[10] But it is true that like Bradley, I am – in a crucial respect – a kind of sceptic. Thus, my attempts to expose the failure of physicalism as an adequate metaphysics (in all its forms) was not the prelude to advocating its replacement with a *positive*, absolute idealist *account* of reality. Indeed, even my polemical manoeuvres against the pluralism of physicalism in favour of a more thoroughgoing monism only called on aesthetic considerations – and a demand that these should be applied consistently. My point was that appeals for metaphysical simplicity and unity are what ousted dualism, so the same rules should apply to physicalism. Put more simply, what is good for the goose is good for the gander. Since dualism is rejected primarily on the grounds of metaphysical extravagance and inelegance, when cast in the same light pluralism looks ugly as compared to a more thoroughgoing monism (see Hutto 2000: 159–161).

But – and the point is – it would be a mistake to think that such arguments were a softening up exercise, the prelude to an attempt to characterise reality as it-is-in-itself. I have stressed this before in response to McHenry, who wrote:

> Hutto would be wrong, I think, to infer from [the] recognition of the limitations of science that there is another discipline that succeeds in providing the true nature of reality (McHenry 1998: 99, 100).
>
> Indeed I would be wrong to infer this – but I never have. Thus, at least as I read Bradley, it is precisely because he is content not to make any positive offer that his approach is attractive. As I noted in the original paper to which McHenry replied, absolute idealism would be worrying, indeed confused, if it were making positive claims about the nature of reality. We must remember that Bradley is, in an important sense, a sceptical (or better an agnostic) philosopher. Still, in light of arguments of earlier chapters, his brand of scepticism is not as unhealthy as it might first appear. Thus it is the wrong tack to attempt to press him by asking, "But can Bradley's metaphysics deliver on its promise of a satisfactory theory of ultimate reality even if the aim is to provide only a view of Reality in broad outline?" (McHenry 1998: 98) (Hutto 2000: 183–4).

So, I fully agree with Rudd that, "consciousness plainly is not a naturalistic phenomenon in anything even remotely like the way that bile is, and to say that it is nevertheless naturalistic and unmysterious in some other way that we simply can't comprehend is to say precisely nothing" (Rudd: this volume). Again, I hope to have made my commitments on this score evident in *Beyond Physicalism*. Here is yet another salient reminder:

> McGinn appeals to the idea that there is a hidden structure of consciousness which explains the psychophysical link. The problem is that this missing link cannot be characterised as being either physical or mental. Thus he suggests, the hidden structure must, "exhibit both [the mental and the material] as aspects of a deeper reality" (McGinn 1991: 82). Given our limitations, we will never be able to make the relation between experience and its material substrate perfectly intelligible. In support of his aspectualism, he is therefore led to postulate a noumenal reality which he identifies with the natural.

Ignoring some of the contentious details of McGinn's views on perception-based epistemology, I have some sympathy with the structure of his position. Nevertheless it is hobbled by its allegiance to physicalism. For despite telling us that the noumenal is natural, he also tells us that, "Naturalism in the philosophy of mind is the thesis that every property of mind can be explained in broadly physical terms" (McGinn 1991: 23). Given this, we wind up with the idea that the noumenal, the natural and the physical are all one and the same. In order to understand how he hopes to pull off this, *prima facie*, nonsensical identification we must consider the passage in which he tells us that, "cognitive closure with respect to P [the property that explains the nature of the psychophysical link] does not imply irrealism about P. That P is (as we might say) noumenal for M [our type of mind] does not show that P does not occur in some naturalistic scientific theory T" (McGinn 1991: 4). Putting this together, we get the result that some physical theory does explain the nature of the psychophysical nexus but that this physical link theory is forever cognitively closed to us. This is why McGinn is a non-constructive naturalist who sees the mind-body relation as epistemically, but not metaphysically, problematic.

Flanagan reaches the same result, and in a similar way. He too tells us, "The wise naturalist is not a reductionist" (Flanagan 1993: 92). But in order to avoid the obvious difficulties in this position he proposes a distinction between what he calls linguistic physicalism and metaphysical physicalism, and suggests that non-reductive naturalists ought only endorse the latter. He describes these two options in the following fashion:

Metaphysical physicalism simply asserts that what there is, and all there is, is physical stuff and its relations. Linguistic physicalism is the thesis that everything physical can be expressed or captured in the languages of the basic sciences (Flanagan 1993: 98).

Despite other disagreements, both McGinn and Flanagan use the same tools in order to make sense of their brands of naturalism. Thus McGinn distinguishes between effective and existential naturalism. Effective naturalism concerns our ability to construct naturalistic accounts of any phenomenon, while existential naturalism is just a metaphysical thesis that nothing that happens in nature is inherently anomalous (cf. McGinn 1991: 87). But both of these brands of non-reductive naturalism are quite bizarre because, in endorsing them, one literally does not know what it means to be a physicalist. The problem here is Searle's problem all over again. The physical is robbed of any possible meaning as there are no principled boundaries, such as those established by the reductionists, by which to decide which phenomena are genuinely physical.

The all-too-convenient distinction between the epistemic and the metaphysical makes metaphysical physicalism or existential naturalism unintelligible. Furthermore we might ask: What warrants McGinn's staunch faith in the truth of physicalism? What justifies the idea that there exists a physical theory, that is, in principle, beyond our grasp, which explains the facts of psychophysical connec-

> tion? The answer, which he gives himself, is that nothing justifies the view. Rather it must be accepted as an, "article of metaphysical faith" (McGinn 1991: 87). On this point I am content to be a heretic (Hutto 2000: 107–8).

Why engage in any kind of metaphysics at all? Why not remain utterly quietist? As Bradley put it, "it seems desirable that there should be such a refuge for the man who burns to think consistently, and yet is too good to become a slave, either to stupid fanaticism or dishonest sophistry. That is one reason why I think that metaphysics, even if it ends in total scepticism, should be studied by a certain number of persons" (Bradley 1983/1930: 4–5). I would add that it is by seeing how to avoid certain 'problems' and dealing with others – such as understanding how mental causation is so much as possible but without succumbing to providing a philosophical explanatory account – is justification enough for continuing to think about these issues.

4. Import and care

Rudd both approves of and is intrigued by my remarks about the relation between perception, emotion and value that appear towards the end of my target paper. Perception, at least of the basic variety, is always "in some way 'concern-based'" because it is action-guiding and end-directed. It reveals a creature's selective interest, as it were: what it finds important or significant. I fully agree that the actions in question are "implicitly structured by the concerns and possibilities of the perceiver… If I see the approaching tiger as terrifying, I see the rest of my perceived world in terms of escape routes, traps, potential fellow-victims etc." (Rudd: this volume). Or better, we might say an organism's concerns and values are *revealed* in its responses. So, in this sense, it is surely true that not only we humans but all responsive creatures, "live in a perceived world not simply of neutral stuff, or facts, but of meanings; and meanings which are related to our possibilities as agents within that world" (Rudd: this volume).

We do not passively experience a meaningless world, as certain empiricists, under the sway of the myth of the given, might suggest. We are not mere recipients of unconnected and unrelated images, perceptions, and the like of which we must make sense. We are, by our nature, always engaged with our surroundings in embodied ways. We respond to, notice, focus on and remember that which we find interesting or important. The very possibility of human discourse – *logos* – depends on our ability to engage the attention of others concerning what we notice and value in this way.

I do not however say that *all* perceptual experiences are, "imbued with some sort of emotion" – but rather that perceptual responding in certain contexts *reveals* what matters to organisms. It does not follow that the organism in question is in a position to know that such things matter to it. That would require it to have certain reflective abilities. So, like Taylor, I hold that:

> while a prelinguistic animal can learn to respond to some object appropriately in light of its purposes, only the being with language can identify the object of a certain kind, can, as we might put it, attribute such and such a property to it. An animal, in other terms, can give the right response to an object – fleeing a predator, say, or going after food where 'right' means 'appropriate to its (nonlinguistic) purposes'. But language involves us in another kind of rightness... We cannot give an account of this rightness in terms of extra-linguistic purposes (Taylor 1985: 103).

If we can take seriously the idea of a well scripted pre-linguistic and, more interestingly, a pre-narrative level of experience then we can also take seriously the idea that the lives of living creatures are both dramatic in-themselves and ripe for narration in terms of certain kinds of stories; those with beginnings, middles and ends (see my reply to Gallagher). Yet while the drama of life has a biological basis, it is not restricted to it; at least not for us. Although we share with animals a concern for certain things and not others – i.e. our valuing certain 'big features of existence' – in line with our particular natural history, we don socio-cultural second natures that significantly modify our ways of responding and the range of our interests. Still, I think many deeply emotional modes of responding remain rooted in our basic, 'first natures' and that it is a real achievement that humans have developed the capacity to respond to things neutrally, by means of linguistic mediation (see my reply to Goldie).

Ultimately, our capacity to acting for reasons of our own, directing our actions at what we find meaningful and significant involves linguistically grounded representation and reflection – this, plus a certain narrative ability, allows us to make choices in the light of our wider ambitions, aspirations and historically established projects. I fully agree with Rudd that 'acting for a reason' need not be a cold and emotionless business. This is especially so in ethical cases. For, as Aristotle would have it, we become virtuous *when* our emotional responses have been properly cultivated and educated: transformed in important ways. The connection is made at the beginning of Book II of the *Nicomachean Ethics*, where he sets out the relation between habits, character, and virtue. He writes, "moral virtue comes about as a result of habit, whence also is the name *ethike* one that is formed by a slight variation from the word ethos (habit)" (*EN*, II, 1103a 16–18).

My account runs along similar lines. We start life with certain embodied habits and traits; but ones that can and typically are re-shaped. Our characters are not something merely created by us; they are developed, sculpted and fashioned in line with local norms. There is some flexibility about which habits we adopt and precisely how they develop – i.e. which and how our basic ways of responding, our actional and emotionally tendencies, are re-tied. And if we are to develop virtuously this is not achieved through blind drill, but through moral education and reflection.

Acting virtuously is a choice that is rooted in our motivations. Thus moral excellence is unavoidably initially rooted in our emotional responses and our animal natures – our base tendencies to seek pleasure and avoid pain. We are told that it is in response to pleasures and pains that we become bad, by pursuing and avoiding: those they ought not; when they ought not; and as they ought not.[11] Against this, "excellence tends to do what is best with regard to pleasures and pains" (*EN* 1104^b 26–8). This is why Aristotle stresses that, "our whole inquiry must be about these – to feel delight and pain rightly or wrongly has no small affect on our actions" (*EN* 1105^a 5–7).[12] It is also why, in discussing virtues such as bravery, he emphasizes the connection between virtue and proper emotion, saying, "he who stands his ground against things that are terrible and delights in this (or at least is not pained) is brave, while a man who is pained is a coward" (*EN* 1104^a 19–22). On his account, we become virtuous by habituating ourselves with respect to our passions so as, "to feel them at the right times, with reference to the right objects, towards the right people, with the right aim, and in the right way, is what is both intermediate and best, and this is characteristic of excellence" (*EN* 1106^b 21–4).[13]

Our capacity to choose freely stems in large part from fostering the right habits and acting virtuously involves, *inter alia*, performing the act with the right spirit or emotion. It is only by appeal to a person's steadfast character (bound up with their cultivated emotional responses) that we can understand the distinction between performing an act of a just character and acting justly. But – and this is the point – this sort of story about how we adopt new values remains firmly rooted in a view of psychology and biology according to which living beings are already thought of as 'end-directed' creatures (not merely as complex causal mechanisms). Some are barely sensitive, some are social and emotional, and some have cognitive abilities too. We are of the later kind.

I hold that our unique narrative abilities play *a* major part in enabling us to embody new values and to develop ethically – for it is through the use of self-narratives and attending to them (whether authored by ourselves or others) that we become able to state, reflect upon and transform our values and thereby ourselves (cf. Taylor 1985, Kerby 1993: 48–52).[14] Indeed, I hold that it is through encounters with certain kinds of narratives that we come by to understand reasons for acting in the first place (see my reply to Gallagher, this volume). Therefore although our uniquely human way of being in the world and with others is in part an expression of our pre-linguistic 'form of life', and this never leaves us, it is because we have linguistic and narrative abilities that enable us to represent and reflect on our actions and life episodes, that our ways of responding cannot be reduced to or understood in terms of our pre-linguistic responding.

On the whole, I would seek to restore some form of broadly Aristotelian psychology which respects the idea that living beings and their projects are a natural part of the world while at the same time recognising the important differences that certain abilities and opportunities bring. Ultimately, this is the way to make best sense of the complex nature of human persons (this requires more than merely being a member of the species *homo sapiens sapiens*). Persons, those who act for reasons of their own and who are responsible for their actions – the proper subjects of folk psychological narratives – are also real, flesh and blood, historical and biological beings; beings whose exploits lend themselves to narration. By my lights, they are not to be confused with extensionless points, logical linchpins, substances (neither egos nor brains) nor postmodern fictions.

Notes

1. Rudd here follows McDowell and it is instructive to recall the history of their common agenda. In his celebrated *Mind and World*, McDowell echoes Kant, in recognising a conflict between the idea that knowledge is constrained 'from the outside' and the idea that its basis is a matter of rational activity on our part (cf. McDowell 1994: 8). McDowell tells us that a, "genuine escape would require that we avoid the Myth of the Given without renouncing the claim that experience is a rational constraint on thinking" (McDowell 1994: 18). What is required to make such an escape, as McDowell puts it, is to see our knowledge-forming activities as a "result of a co-operation between receptivity and spontaneity" (McDowell 1994: 4). I object to the metaphor of 'receptivity' since I reject the idea that basic perception and judgement are logically linked. Certainly, these are not bound together in a kind of synchronic process as perceptual data become schematised (see my reply to Crane).

2. To take a simpler case, despite being wrong about many other things, Ayer was surely right to say "it is possible for a flower to look sky-blue to me without my having judged that this was so" (Ayer 1954: 101).

3. Indeed there is, "an overwhelming amount of empirical data which show that while our discriminatory capacities, with respect to shades – or, as psychologists find desirable to specify, hues – of colours, are quite fine-grained, our recognitional ones are pretty coarse" (Colive 1999: 7). For example, ordinary subjects can discriminate nearly ten million colours, even trained colour spotters are at best able to recognise thirty colours – and only then in very controlled conditions (Hardin 1988: 88–89).

4. Peacocke has identified another problem with McDowell's line on this topic. For, as he notes, it implies, "that the fine-grained representational content of experience of two people, neither of whom has the general concept 'shade', but one of whom has the concept 'scarlet', and the other who has only 'red' but not 'scarlet', would differ at the finest-grained level. This seems to me incor-

rect. Rather, there is a single shade (an analogously shape) that they both experience, and in the same ways. It is one which makes available various different demonstrative concepts to the two subjects, depending on the richness of the repertoire of general concepts" (Peacocke 1998: 382).

5. Creatures that can re-identify particular conspecifics, types of prey, mates, items or places will develop many useful but nevertheless fallible expectations about these and their hidden properties, as gleaned from previous encounters with tokens of their kinds or particular individuals encountered again and again over time. To echo Millikan, they will have the ability to mine the rich inductive potential of certain relatively stable, re-identifiable environmental kinds of importance. They will be capable of a kind of generalizing of sorts, but the means by which they do so does not involve the drawing of propositionally-based inferences.

6. I emphasise these points in order to make it clear exactly where Rudd and I disagree. In a series of exchanges that began after the initial version of this reply was forwarded to him, Rudd made it clear that his worries about the very idea of nonconceptual experience rested on two basic foundations. Thus: "My two main arguments for pan-conceptualism (or whatever you want to call it) are: a) Transcendental: If perception were not conceptual, it couldn't stand in any rational (as distinct from merely causal) relation to our judgements. But we do make judgements that are (rationally) based on, or in conflict with our perceptions, therefore… (essentially McDowell's argument b) Phenomenological: If we consider our experience of the world, we never just confront a non-conceptual Given; we always are aware of things as thus and such. This remains mostly implicit in that I am not constantly articulating "that's a chair, that's blue…" to myself, but it's not implicit in the sense of unconscious; I just am aware of the objects round me as blue chairs etc, and there is no more basic level of my conscious experience below this conceptual level (the fact that the implicit perceptual judgements can so easily become explicit if a question is raised, takes us back to a) above). I'm not concerned to claim anything more than these two arguments get us to" (personal correspondence, 8th February 2006). We do disagree fundamentally about both these points, and this means that we carry quite different burdens when it comes to explicating the relations between what is 'basic and nonconceptual' (in my case) or 'implicit and conceptual' (in Rudd's) and what is explicit and conceptual.

7. With reference to my remarks on these topics he writes, "This looks as though it's meant to be an answer to the "hard problem". Why should there be experience at all? Why should it be like anything for an organism to be attuned to certain features of its environment? But I am doubly puzzled by this. Given his commitment to dissolving the hard problem, rather than answering it on its own terms, it would be surprising if Hutto was wanting us to take this as a "straight" answer. And, given his criticisms elsewhere of materialist attempts to get around the problem of experience, it would be surprising if Hutto really was subscribing to the explanatory "ultimacy" of natural history. If, however, we do take the text at what seems to be its face value, I have to admit that I'm baffled as to how "natural history", and "proper function", together with references to honey bees and hoverflies, are supposed to shed any light on the hard problem" (Rudd: this volume).

8. The informative if inelegant title is bestowed, courtesy of Robinson. He writes: "Hutto's way out is absolute idealism, in a version for which I will coin the name 'Davidsonian Neo-Bradleyanism'. This view is stated (153–163) and then defended in the last two chapters. A leading consideration is that 'no ordinary statement manages to say anything complete because it is always contextual'. (154) 'The world... cannot be intelligibly characterised in entirety by any conceptual schema.' (160) …In defending absolute idealism, Hutto argues that it is compatible with a correct understanding of science. Problems in achieving unity of science that have been

raised by well known, analytic philosophers of science are discussed, and turned to advantage for Hutto's view. Likewise, well established criticisms of correspondence theories of truth are reviewed in the service of supporting an absolute idealist conception of truth. If the truth of single statements cannot be correspondence to single facts that make them true, if statements always depend on a background that cannot be bounded, then everything we say is but an incomplete description of Reality as it appears from some limited perspective. Analytic philosophers will find many points in Hutto's statement and defense of absolute idealism that they will wish to dispute – although which ones may differ for different readers. Nonetheless, they will find these sections of the book to be of special interest and value. Hutto's discussion will require them to look at many familiar ideas in a new light and it will challenge them to test their ideas on fundamental matters of meaning, truth, knowledge and conceptual schemes" (Robinson 2006).

9. In his review of *The Presence of Mind*, Wringe also picked up on my need to effect precisely this kind of balancing act. For although I argue that the directedness of intentional attitudes and the origins of experiences can be understood using the resources of evolutionary science, I also hold that propositional attitudes, "have an irreducibly normative dimension of a sort that cannot be naturalised. Given this two-tier account it might be open to Hutto to own up to the circularity by recognizing that all explanation hails from a conceptual perspective that must presuppose intentionality. Yet since he does not offer to naturalistically explain such conceptual content this does not make the circle vicious for his project [for] Hutto argues deftly that even if full-blown beliefs and desires cannot be understood by appeal to scientific theorising, this does not prevent them from being real, since in the words of Putnam (who he quotes), "there are whole domains of fact with respect to which science tells us nothing at all." This position is easier to state than defend and though much of what Hutto says here is plausible it would be interesting to see the anti-naturalistic metaphysical position, which he is committed to deal with at greater length" (Wringe 2001). *Beyond Physicalism* was my attempt to meet this very challenge.

10. Some have objected to my Bradleyean inspired 'pragmatic partiality' – the idea that 'we are never free from some limited perspective or other' (Hutto 2000: 157) – on other grounds. Fischer, for example, think this sort of approach to be 'inherently flawed' and hopes for a more progressive view of how we might develop our concepts, without any in-built restrictions. He wrote, "These objections are in the end Hegelian, and it may be that it is the Hegelian brand of idealism that I find preferable, both absolutely, and in the case of the mind/body problem. The denial of the god's-eye-perspective is, in the final analysis, not something that Hegel would find palatable for the above reasons" (Fischer 2000: 128). I respond to this, objecting to this form of Hegelianism in Hutto 2003/2006, ch. 6.

11. For example, as Burnyeat observes, Aristotle's approach allows us to make sense of how it is possible to take pleasure in something good but doing so in the wrong way. He gives these examples, "enjoying philosophy for the sense of power it can give, enjoying a trip abroad because of the splendid photographs you are taking, enjoying a party because you are meeting important people" (Burnyeat 1980: 76).

12. Kosman tells us, "Aristotle's more detailed discussions of the virtues make it clear that it is with respect to how one feels and not simply how one acts in light of one's feelings that one is said to be virtuous" (Kosman 1980: 108).

13. This is yet another reason why we are not simply seeking theoretical knowledge when making enquiries into ethics. We must develop a practical desire – a taste – for acting virtuously, but this involves more than merely a theoretical understanding of the pleasures this involves, as

in the contrast between learning that "skiing is enjoyable" by hearsay as opposed to learning this by engaging in the activity itself (cf. Burnyeat 1980: 76).

14. I stop short of saying that our reasons or emotions, "fit into the narrative structure of my life as a whole, and they are inexplicable apart from that" (Rudd: this volume). Like others I am sceptical about the idea of narrating a life as a whole.

References

Aristotle. 1984. *The Complete Works of Aristotle: The Revised Oxford Translation.* New Jersey: Princeton University Press.

Ayer, A.J. 1954. *Philosophical Essays.* London: Macmillan.

Bermúdez, J. 1998. *The Paradox of Self-Consciousness.* Cambridge, MA: MIT Press.

Bradley, F.H. 1893/1930. *Appearance and Reality.* Oxford: Oxford University Press.

Burnyeat, M.F. 1980. "Aristotle on Learning to be Good." In *Essays on Aristotle's Ethics*, A.O. Rorty (ed.), 69–92. Berkeley and Los Angeles: University of California Press.

Chalmers, D. 1996. *The Conscious Mind.* Oxford: Oxford University Press.

Colive, A. 1999. "The Finer-Grained Content of Experience." Unpublished manuscript.

Crane, T. 1992. "The Nonconceptual Content of Experience." In *The Contents of Experience*, T. Crane (ed.), 136–157. Cambridge: Cambridge University Press.

Davidson, D. 1985. "Reply to Quine on Events." In *Actions and Events: Perspectives on the Philosophy of Donald Davidson*", E. LePore and B. MacLaughlin (eds), 172–176. Oxford: Basil Blackwell.

Dennett, D.C. 1997. *Kinds of Mind.* London: Phoenix.

Dretske, F. 1988. *Explaining Behaviour: Reasons in a World of Causes.* Cambridge, MA: MIT Press.

Dretske, F. 1995. *Naturalizing the Mind.* Cambridge, MA: MIT Press.

Fischer, N. 2000. "Review of Beyond Physicalism." *Consciousness and Emotion* 1(2): 318–23.

Flanagan, O. 1991. *The Science of the Mind.* Cambridge, MA: MIT Press.

Flanagan, O. 1993. *Consciousness Reconsidered.* Cambridge, MA: MIT Press.

Flanagan, O. 1996. *Self Expressions: Mind, Morals and the Meaning of Life.* Oxford: Oxford University Press.

Flanagan, O. and Polger, T. 1995. "Zombies and the Function of Consciousness." *Journal of Consciousness Studies* 2: 313–21.

Gopnik, A. and Meltzoff, A.N. 1997. *Words, Thoughts, and Theories.* Cambridge, MA: MIT Press.

Hardin, C.L. 1988. *Color for Philosophers: Unweaving the Rainbow.* Indianapolis: Hackett.

Hill, C. 1991. *Sensations: A Defense of Type Materialism.* Cambridge: Cambridge University Press.

Hutto, D.D. 1999. *The Presence of Mind.* Amsterdam: John Benjamins.

Hutto, D.D. 2000. *Beyond Physicalism.* Amsterdam: John Benjamins.

Hutto, D.D. 2001. "Appropriate Quietism: Reply to Salucci." *SWIF book forum, http://www.swif.uniba.it/lei/mind/forums.html.*

Hutto, D.D. 2002. "Have you heard any Good Transcendental Arguments Lately?: Reply to Praetorious." *SWIF book forum, http://www.swif.uniba.it/lei/mind/forums.html.*

Hutto, D.D. 2003/2006. *Wittgenstein and the End of Philosophy: Neither Theory nor Therapy*. Basingstoke: Palgrave Macmillan.
Hutto, D.D. 2004. "Questing for Happiness: Augmenting Aristotle with Davidson." *South African Journal of Philosophy* 32 (4): 383–93.
Hutto, D.D. 2007. *Folk Psychological Narratives: The Socio-Cultural Basis of Understanding Reasons*. Cambridge, MA: MIT Press.
Jacob, P. 1997. *What Minds Can Do*. Cambridge: Cambridge University Press.
Kerby, P. 1993. *Narrative and the Self*. Indiana: Indiana University Press.
Kosman, L.A. 1980. "Being Properly Affected: Virtues and Feelings in Aristotle's Ethics." In *Essays on Aristotle's Ethics*, A.O. Rorty (ed.), 103–116. Berkeley and Los Angeles: University of California Press.
Lowe, E.J. 1996. *Subjects of Experience*. Cambridge: Cambridge University Press.
McDowell, J. 1994. *Mind and World*. Cambridge, MA: Harvard University Press.
McDowell, J. 1998. "Précis of Mind and World." *Philosophy and Phenomenological Research* 58: 365–8.
Marcel, A. 1988. "Phenomenal Experience and Functionalism." In *Consciousness and Contemporary Science*, A.J. Marcel and E. Bisiach (eds), 121–58. Oxford: Clarendon Press.
McGinn, C. 1989. *Mental Content*. Oxford: Basil Blackwell.
McGinn, C. 1991. *The Problem of Consciousness*. Oxford: Basil Blackwell.
McHenry, L. 1998. "Naturalized and Pure Metaphysics: A Reply to Hutto." *Bradley Studies* 4: 97–101.
Millikan, R.G. 2000. *On Clear and Confused Ideas*. Cambridge: Cambridge University Press.
Mills, E. 1997. "Interactionism and Physicality." *Ratio* 10(2): 169–183.
Peacocke, C. 1998. "Nonconceptual Content Defended." *Philosophy and Phenomenological Research* 58: 381–8.
Robinson, W. 2006. "Review of *Beyond Physicalism*." *Mind* 115: 159–163.
Strawson, G. 1994. *Mental Reality*. Cambridge, MA: MIT Press.
Taylor, C. 1985. "Self-Interpreting Animals." In *Human Agency and Language: Philosophical Papers 1*, 45–76. Cambridge: Cambridge University Press.
Van Gulick, R. 1989. "What Difference Does Consciousness Make?" *Philosophical Topics* 17: 211–30.
Weiskrantz, L. 1997. *Consciousness Lost and Found*. Oxford: Oxford University Press.
Wringe, W.G. 2001. "Review of *The Presence of Mind*." *Metapsychology* 5 (43).

Intentionality and emotion

Comment on Hutto

Tim Crane

1. Introduction

I am very sympathetic to Dan Hutto's view that in our experience of the emotions of others "we do not neutrally observe the outward behaviour of another and infer coldly, but on less than certain grounds, that they are in such and such an inner state, as justified by analogy with our own case. Rather we react and feel as we do because it is natural for us to see and be moved by specific expressions of emotion in others" (Hutto section 4). This seems to me to be a good starting point for any account of the ascription and epistemology of emotions, an excellent description of data that any theory of the emotions has to take into account.

What I find puzzling is that Hutto seems to believe that this view is in opposition to certain widely accepted metaphysical assumptions about mental phenomena, and that these assumptions must be dispensed with if we are to give a proper account of emotion and avoid the problems which philosophy has traditionally had with the emotions.[1] This collection of assumptions about the mental is what Hutto calls the 'object-based schema.' The details of these assumptions will be discussed below; but the points I want to make in this note are (a) that Hutto is wrong in thinking that the plausible claims he makes about emotion (quoted above) require us to deny the object-based schema; and (b) that he is wrong in his claim that the object-based schema is entirely mistaken. Having established this, I will then make some remarks about Hutto's attack on my view of intentionality.

2. The object-based schema

Hutto introduces the object-based schema as follows:

> The hard problem of consciousness, conceived of as a problem about intelligibility, and the explanatory gap stem directly from our tendency to employ an object-based schema when characterising experience... We tend to think of experiences as inner objects (states, processes or events – or more commonly, determinable properties of these).

He then says:

> This whole way of thinking about experience is encouraged by and reinforces the common idea that our experiential concepts grasp (or pick out) determinate objects or determinable objective features.

The object-based schema therefore seems to be the view that our concepts of experience pick out or refer to determinate inner entities, which may be objects in a narrower sense (i.e. persisting concrete particulars), or events, or processes or properties.[2]

It is clear that Hutto does not deny the existence of experiences. He talks later of his "insistence that we recognise both that experiences exist and that they matter", and we should all share this insistence. But he goes on, mysteriously, to say that "what we must not do is to think of [experiences] as existents or model them as inner objects, properties, and so on." The claim seems to be that experiences *exist* but they are not *existents*. But how can this be? Since Hutto does not tell us what he means by 'existent', we are somewhat left in the dark about how to answer this question. We must assume that Hutto cannot mean by 'existent' *something which exists*. So let's consider instead a number of other possible ways, suggested by other parts of his paper, in which things which exist might not be existents.

(1) *Reification*: At a number of points in the paper, Hutto talks as if the mistake in the object-based schema is that it 'reifies' experiences. There are experiences, to be sure, but they should not be reified. What does this really mean? The trouble with talk of reifying experiences is that it suggests that reifying is something that is *done* to already existing experiences. (After all, no-one here is denying that experiences exist.) It's as if the idea is: 'of course, there *are* experiences, but beware of reifying them! Say that experiences exist, by all means; but do not say that they are *things*!' But it is plain that an experience is a thing in the broadest sense of that word and so it doesn't need to *be* reified: it already is there. For this reason, I am sceptical whether the charge of 'reification' really makes much sense.

(2) *Reference*: Hutto later says that experiences are 'not referents.' Presumably he is employing the standard post-Fregean terminology according to which a refer-

ent is something which is referred to by a term.[3] Hence what he is saying is that we cannot refer to experiences. I cannot, for example, refer to my first experience of eating pigs' brains by using the words 'my first experience of eating pigs' brains.'

Taken literally, this view is quite incredible. For it cannot be seriously denied that the concepts and words we use to describe experience refer to their referents. These referents are 'entities.' And as noted above, in one clear sense of 'thing', they are things. In which sense? The obvious answer in the case of experiences is that they are things that happen, or events.

An example will help. Suppose Cortes really did gaze at the Pacific from a peak in Darien. Then it is true that a certain thing happened – Cortes gazed at the Pacific – and my description 'Cortes' gazing at the Pacific' refers to that thing which happened. These things are what philosophers and others call events. To say that there was such an event is simply to say that such a thing happened. What reason can there be to deny that this event is the *referent* of the words in question – that we can *refer* to this event – once we accept that there was such an event?[4]

(3) *Innerness:* Perhaps the problem with the object-based schema is not so much that experiences are supposed to be referents or that they are events or entities, but that they are *inner* events. So let's apply this to our example: was Cortes' experience an 'inner' event? This all depends on what 'inner' means. If it means 'in or inside Cortes' then it is not plausible that this particular event is inner. For if Cortes gazed at the Pacific, then he saw the Pacific, but if he saw the Pacific then he stood in some kind of relation to the Pacific. And since the Pacific is not inside Cortes, nor is this relation in which he stands to the Pacific. Yet the event referred to by the phrase 'Cortes's gazing at the Pacific' is an experience for all that. So there is no reason to think that all experiences, as normally understood, are inner in the above sense. Some are, however: a feeling of nausea is undeniably something which is felt to occur inside the body. Further discussion of this question must depend on what important philosophical issues turn on calling something 'inner', and this leads us into more substantial theorising. But the obvious intuitive point is that there is nothing in the ordinary idea of experiences as events which implies that they are inner, and nothing that implies that they are not.

(4) *Determinateness*: Perhaps instead the problem with the object-based schema is that experiences are supposed to be determinate. I take determinate to mean: not vague. Are experiences vague entities? This is a difficult question which everyone has to address; but it does not seem to identify the central issue between Hutto and his opponents. This is partly because the question of vague or determinate entities is not something which arises only in the case of experiences, but arises elsewhere too. We might wonder how determinate Cortes's experience of the Pacific is: how much does it involve? How little? Yet the same questions could be raised about the Pacific Ocean itself: how far does it extend? What are

its boundaries? The question about the Pacific is as good (or bad) as the question about the experience of the Pacific. This suggests that if there is a problem about determinacy, it has nothing to do with the mental or with experience as such.

So if the object-based schema simply is the claim that experiences are entities ('reified'), or the referents of experience-terms, then it does not seem to involve any especially problematic ideas. If it is the claim that experiences are inner and determinate, then it is debatable but not obviously absurd.

But the object-based schema comes in many forms. Sometimes it is simply the view that there are mental *states* or *properties*. Later on in Hutto's paper I myself am described as failing to 'free myself' from the 'schema':

> For by endorsing intentionalism, the idea that experiences are in fact intentional states, [Crane] continues to accept that, "Pain is a state of consciousness, or an event in consciousness …" (Crane 2003: 31). For example, while he denies that pains are a kind of qualia – which would make them higher-order properties of intentional states – he nevertheless falls in line with the standard idea that, "states are normally understood as instances of properties…" (Crane 2003: 45).

But the idea of mental properties should be accepted by anyone who accepts that there are kinds of mental state or event. The word 'anger' is an abstract general term for a kind of property, the property predicated of someone when we say that they are angry. To say then that I am angry with my father, is (in part) to predicate this property of me. My anger is an instance of a property in the same sense that my being heavier than my father is an instance of a property – a relational property I have which depends on certain intrinsic properties of mine and my father. These instances of properties – of my father and me – are called *states*, since it is a state or condition of me that I weigh what I do, and a state or condition of my father that he weighs what he does. Moreover, these are states (like my anger) which may also be had by others (others may weigh what I do, others may be angry in the same way as I am). This is all that is meant by saying that mental states are instances of mental properties, and Hutto has told me nothing which makes this way of talking in the least mysterious or confusing.

So far I have found little to object to in the object-based schema, and no argument against it. But the protean nature of the model allows Hutto to incorporate into it even more implausible and incoherent ideas. For example, when introducing what is supposed to be the 'standard view', Hutto quotes Max Velmans:

> As with any term that refers to something that one can observe or experience, it is useful, if possible, to begin with an ostensive definition – that is to point to or pick out the phenomena to which the term refers and, by implication, what is excluded (Velmans 2000: 6).

If Velmans is really talking about referring to experiences here, then his remark seems to be off-target, since experiences themselves (as Hutto himself emphasises), are not something 'one can observe or experience.' But this has nothing to do with the idea that experiences are objects, events or properties – unless it is insisted that the only objects, events and properties there are are those we can observe or experience. But surely no participant in this debate will say that.[5]

A further controversial component of the object-based schema is its claim that our terms for experiences are based or 'grounded' on 'ostensive definitions': one's understanding an experiential term is based on experiencing its referent. Hence if I understand the phrase 'the experience of tasting pigs' brains' that is because I can ostensively refer to this experience of mine. This obviously raises the question of how I can understand someone else's utterance of the sentence 'I first had the experience of tasting pigs' brains when I was seventeen', since according to the model I understand the expression 'the experience of tasting pigs' brains' only by reference to my own experience. Hence, on Hutto's view, the model gives rise to questions about the basis on which we can judge that others have the same experience. If experiences are private objects, referred to ostensively, and if terms for experiences can only be learned by these 'ostensive definitions' then how can I ever reasonably judge that others experience as I do?

I agree with Hutto that this is a hopeless situation to get into. But it has little to do with the view that there are inner mental states or properties, or even that these states or properties are (in a certain innocuous sense) private. Saying that there are mental states or properties (inner or not) does not imply that terms for these states or properties have to be applied on the basis of an 'ostensive definition.' I myself think that when one has had an experience for the first time, one can refer ostensively or demonstratively to the object of the experience in a way in which one could not before one had the experience. One might say, having eaten pigs' brains, 'So *this* is what pigs' brains taste like!' But the 'this' arguably refers to the taste of the dish, and not to the experience. And in no sense is the 'this' part of a *definition* of the phrase 'the taste of pigs' brains.'

As for the much-discussed privacy of mental states, I think it should now be clear what to say, after decades of Wittgensteinian reminders. If saying that a mental state is private means that no-one can ever know what someone else's mental states are, then it is clear that mental states are not private. But if the thesis that mental states are private is simply the thesis that necessarily, each person's mental states are their own and no-one else's, then it is an indisputable truth that mental states are private. Hutto writes as if there is an unavoidable trap contained in orthodox philosophy of mind, the trap of being committed to private objects and unknowable mental states, and that the only way to avoid this trap is to say things like 'experiences exist but are not existents.' But once the relevant sense of 'private' is clarified, and once we are in possession of a good epistemology of the mind, then it is clear that there is no such trap.

A further problematic idea which Hutto identifies as contained within the object-based schema concerns the behavioural basis of the application of mental concepts. The problem here is that if we think of mental phenomena on the object-based schema, then we will be led either towards the view that we can only infer someone's inner life from their behaviour, or (even worse) towards a behaviouristic view of the inner life in general. The object-based schema "supposes that we [attribute emotions to others] in purely spectatorial contexts – ones in which we are at a necessary remove from others since the only access we have to the 'inner' life of others is through their outward behaviour." A further idea is that according to the schema, we only have access to behaviour construed 'coldly' or without interpretation. Thus there is a problem how we get from this cold conception of the mental to anything like the reality of an inner life. There is supposed to be an unbridgeable gap even in the *application* of a concept – for example of a concept of an emotion like anger – between the behavioural basis of that application and the emotion itself.

Again, this is certainly a bad picture of emotions and emotion-concepts (indeed, of all mental concepts). But once again I don't see why it is supposed to follow from the views about mental states and properties which seem to be the plausible heart of the object-based schema. There is no inconsistency in saying that anger is a mental property – that property of people which is predicated of them when we say that they are angry – and that we can simply know that someone is angry by observing them. Indeed, it seems very plausible to me that one can literally see that someone is angry, and not simply infer their anger from an 'uninterpreted' behaviour (see McDowell 1978). The mere idea that there are mental properties encounters no difficulty with this kind of application of mental concepts.

To sum up so far: Hutto has persuaded me *neither* that there is anything confused or misleading in thinking of mental phenomena as 'entities'/'referents' (or in 'reifying' them) *nor* that thinking of them like this implies that they are the kind of problematic 'private' entities he and other followers of Wittgenstein worry about. The reason is that there are at least two ideas contained in what Hutto calls the 'object-based schema' – one innocuous and one implausible. There is the innocuous claim that there are mental events, processes, properties etc. – i.e. that these things *exist*, that they are *entities*. Then there is the implausible claim that if there were such entities, they would have to be 'private' entities which we could only refer to by observing them and which would therefore be impossible to attribute to others. The latter is an unacceptable idea, for sure (and the 'therefore…' is a non-sequitur). But it is not a consequence of the existence of mental properties, processes and events. Moreover, the existence of mental properties, events and processes is entirely consistent with the plausible claims Hutto makes about emotions later in the paper. Therefore, there is no need for Hutto to deny the innocuous claim in order to defend the plausible views of emotion. His diagnosis of the problems to which emotions give rise is mistaken.

3. Intentionality

I now turn to intentionality, and to some of the criticisms Hutto makes of the views I expressed in my paper 'The intentional structure of consciousness' (2003) and in my book *Elements of Mind* (2001). I do this partly to set the record straight, since Hutto's paper contains a number of misunderstandings of my views. But I will also take this opportunity to clarify some fundamental points about intentionality; the matter may therefore be of some general interest.[6]

Hutto is sympathetic, as I am, to Peter Goldie's (2000) use of the notion of *feeling towards*. But unlike Goldie, Hutto has little sympathy for the things I say about intentionality. Independently of his criticism that I am committed to the 'object-based schema' model of the mind, then, Hutto has three criticisms of my account of intentionality. The first is that on my view, subjects are directed towards *intentional contents* in intentional experiences, and this is implausible for a number of reasons (for example, that many experiences are non-conceptual, and content is conceptual). The second is that the fact that our intentional experiences can 'miss their mark' does not imply that they are directed on contents rather than ordinary things. The third is that we are not *related* to the modes by which intentional objects are perceived (as my account is supposed to imply) and hence we do not *experience* these experiences (as my account is also supposed to imply).

Unfortunately, all three criticisms misconstrue my views. First, I never say that intentionality is directedness towards contents as opposed to objects. Rather, the idea of a relation (which I call a *mode*) to a content is supposed to be part of an explanation of what it is for a subject's mind to be directed towards an object. Also, since I do not equate *content* with *conceptual content* I am not committed to the claim that experience must be conceptual merely by saying that experience has a content. Second, since I do not say that we are directed towards contents, then *a fortiori* I do not say that we are directed towards contents because intentional experiences can miss their mark. Third, I do not say that we are related to intentional modes. Rather, modes are what relate us to intentional contents. If Hutto were right then I would be committed to the absurd view that someone who believes that *p* is related to *belief* as well as to *p*. But this obviously is not a consequence of my view.[7] So the reason Hutto gives for thinking that on my view we are aware of experiences disappears.

I have clearly failed to explain my conception of intentionality in anything like a satisfactory way. So I should have another try.

For me, the basic intentional (and therefore mental) notion is the notion of directedness towards an object – with 'object' interpreted in a very broad way. I include among objects in this sense material and abstract objects, properties, states of affairs, facts… anything which one can think about, or have one's mind directed towards in some other way. Following the tradition, I call these objects *intentional objects*. It is crucial to recognise that intentional objects are not entities of a certain kind. They cannot be, since some intentional objects do not exist. Yet all entities exist. In other words, to talk about an intentional object is to talk about *that on which one's mind is directed*, whether or not it exists. I take it for granted that our minds can be directed on the non-existent, although this is what gives rise to some of the hardest problems of intentionality. A conclusion I draw from this fact is that intentional states cannot, in general, be relations to their objects (Crane 2001, chapter 1).

To say that all states of mind must have an intentional object, then, is just to say that it is impossible for there to be a state of mind which is not *about* something, which is not *directed* on something. There are however different ways in which a state of mind may be directed on something: wanting something, disliking it and merely contemplating it are all intentional states, but different ways of being directed on that something. And in 'The intentional structure of consciousness' (2003) I also said that the way in which pain is directed on a part of the body is a form of intentional directedness. The way in which these intentional states differ need not be in their object, but in what I call their intentional *mode*. (The intentional mode is what Husserl in the *Logical Investigations* called the intentional *quality*; other philosophers, who think that all intentional states are propositional attitudes, would call it the *attitude*.)

Intentional states can, however, be identical in mode and intentional object, but nonetheless differ. This is because they may differ in the way in which they present their object – or, as I put it, in the *aspect* under which they present it. This kind of difference in intentionality I describe as a difference in intentional *content*. For a state to have intentional content is for it to have an (existing or non-existing) intentional object presented under a certain aspect. Since it is impossible, I claim, for an intentional state to have an object without presenting it under some aspect, then it follows that all intentional states have intentional content. I do not say that the intentional content of a state of mind is the way the world is represented as being, since some intentional states (e.g. desires, hopes) do not represent the world as actually *being* a certain way, but rather represent a non-actual condition of the world. Nor do I say that all content is propositional – that is, assessable as true or false – since there are many states of mind (notably object-directed emotions like love and hate) which do not have propositional contents. Many intentional states do have propositional content – these are the propositional attitudes. And finally, I do not say that all intentional content is conceptual, though what this precisely means should be left to another occasion (see Crane 1998; Gunther 2002).

I therefore understand intentionality in terms of the three central ideas of intentional object (where object is not understood as *thing* or *entity*), intentional mode (belief, desire, hope, fear etc.) and intentional content (that which characterises that on which the state is directed, and therefore incorporates the aspectual shape of that intentional state).

I hope it is clear from this brief description of my view of intentionality that it implies none of the things that Hutto says it does. First, intentional directedness is towards intentional objects. If I want a bottle of inexpensive burgundy, that is the object of my desire. On some views, desire is really a propositional attitude: what makes it the case that I desire a bottle of inexpensive burgundy is that I am related to a proposition (which may be represented as, for example, the set of all worlds in which I have a bottle of inexpensive burgundy). But what I want – the intentional object of my desire, what my desire is directed on – is not a proposition, but a bottle of inexpensive burgundy. (I don't myself endorse this view of desire, but it is uncontroversial and it illustrates well the difference between object and content on which I want to insist.)

Hutto writes that "introducing content into the equation is an unnecessary and potentially confusing extra step when it comes to understanding *feeling towards*, at least in the most basic cases involving nonconceptual responses." But if feeling towards is supposed to discriminate between different ways in which objects of emotions can be experienced (conceptually or nonconceptually), then introducing content is necessary. For differences in content are supposed to be differences in the aspects under which intentional objects are apprehended (again, conceptually or nonconceptually). To deny a role for content here is to accept the phenomenologically incredible idea that one can have a conscious intentional state directed at an object *as such*, as opposed to an object appearing in a certain way.

Hutto is sceptical about what I say about intentional modes and intentional contents, but I submit that the best way to read him is as misunderstanding what I mean by mode, object and content. In one particularly puzzling passage, he says that a proper account of the relation between experience and belief

> requires endorsing a position that Crane summarily dismisses when considering the options. He writes, "The second view, that the phenomenal character of the state of mind is *fixed purely by the mode*, has little to be said for it; obviously, any plausible intentionalist view must allow that the intentional object and content contribute to phenomenal character."

The quotation here from me describes a view which I reject, and Hutto claims to endorse. But if Hutto has understood what I mean by 'mode', then this is very puzzling. For the position he says he wants to endorse here implies that the phenomenal character of (e.g.) a visual experience is determined solely by the fact that it is a visual experience. And this cannot be true: two experiences can both be visual experiences and yet differ in their phenomenal character, on anyone's understanding of 'phenomenal character.' If Hutto has understood me here, he would be endorsing an incredible view. Since I don't think he means to endorse such a view, I must conclude that he has misunderstood what I mean by 'mode.'

Hutto takes exception to my description of content as what one would put into words (a phrase I borrow from J.J. Valberg). He seems to think that this description runs into problems in saying what the intentional states of non-verbal animals are. There isn't actually a problem here, but my use of this phrase has caused problems elsewhere so I should probably stop using it and say exactly what I originally meant. I did not mean: if a state of mind S has a content C, then C can be expressed in words regardless of whether the subject of S has a language at all. Rather, I meant: if you put your thoughts into words, then what you put into words is the content. This is consistent with there being aspects of content which cannot be put into words, and obviously implies nothing about non-verbal animals.

Just to labour the point: I do not mean that you cannot directly express what the *object* of your thought is. If I put my desire into words, when asked what I want, I might say 'a bottle of inexpensive burgundy.' What I have put into words is the (non-propositional) content of my desire; but by putting this into words, I have *ipso facto* given the intentional object of my desire. The fact that the phrase 'a bottle of inexpensive burgundy' can both *give* the intentional object of my desire and *put into words* its content is simply a reflection of the fact that (as Dummett says when discussing sense and reference) "in saying what the reference [of an expression] is, we have to choose a particular way of saying this" (Dummett 1975: 227).

Moving on to Hutto's second point: I, too, want to "retain the simpler idea that we are only ever directed at those items we are meant to be directed at": these items are intentional objects. This should be clear from what I said above in re-expounding my view. And I agree with Hutto too that "we normally account for straightforward perceptual error by invoking experiences that make sense of why such beliefs *seemed* justified, given how things *looked* to us at the time." I have explained above why it is that intentional states involve direction upon objects, not contents; we do not experience contents. If anything, contents are that by means of which we have experiences of objects. So Hutto and I ought to be in agreement here. But he thinks we are not. He says that on his view "object and content do not contribute to the phenomenal character by being part of what is experienced", implying that on my view they do. But this is not so: on my view an intentional object is not *part* of what is experienced; an intentional object of an experience is *what is experienced*. Content, although in some sense part of an experience, is not part of what is experienced. So on my view too "object and content do not contribute to the phenomenal character by being part of what is experienced."

Finally, to return to Hutto's third point against me, it should be clear by now that I never say or imply that experiences are experienced, I never say that consciousness is what is experienced, and I see nothing in my view which entails or even suggests that intentional contents appear 'before the mind's eye' as a kind of 'calling card.' These ideas do not follow from my view of intentionality.

4. Concluding remarks

Hutto's strategy in the first part of his paper is to identify a collection of assumptions about the mind, which he calls the object-based schema, and then to attribute these assumptions to what he supposes to be the orthodox philosophy of mind. The assumptions are a combination of the innocuous (there are mental properties) and the absurd (we experience experiences). Given this way of collecting ideas together, it is easy to see how the 'schema' both fits all current theories and also damns them all. Yet, as I have argued, there is no reason to think that all (or any) current theories are committed to all these assumptions, and hence to the model.

Hutto reads my views on intentionality in a similar kind of way. His remarks attempt to convict me of some obvious error, like the error of thinking that experiences are the sorts of things that can be seen or experienced. It has been a common charge of a certain style of philosophising, often inspired by Ryle and Wittgenstein, that 'Cartesian' or 'representational' views of the mind (like mine) imply the absurd idea that all we are aware of are representations.[8] This is the charge which Hutto brings against me too. But, as I hope to have shown, it is unfounded. The truth is rather that my views on intentionality are quite in sympathy with Hutto's views about emotions, but his procrustean tendency to force views into vague all inclusive 'schemas' does not allow him to see this.

Notes

1. "For if we ought to legitimately abandon certain assumptions about the "extensions" of experiential concepts and how they are acquired, we can put to rest certain of the concerns that give emotions a bad name" (Hutto section 1).

2. Hutto's claim that experiential properties are determinable seems to be a slip. Of course, there are determinable experience properties: *listening to Wagner*, for example, is a determinable

of which individual acts of listening are determinates. So any experience of listening to Wagner has the determinable property of being an experience of listening to Wagner. But no particular experience will be *simply* determinable; so it would be wrong to say that any view says that experiences only have determinable properties (as if one could listen to Wagner without listening to some particular performance of some particular work).

3. In the passage in question, he contrasts referents with modes of presentation. But the contrast, on Frege's view, is not exclusive: just because something is a mode of presentation does not mean that it cannot be a referent. The expression 'the sense of "Napoleon"', for example, refers to a mode of presentation of Napoleon; so the sense of 'Napoleon' is the referent of this expression.

4. Hutto later admits that "we can still refer to 'experiences'" so long as we are using phrases like 'she saw the yellow card' rather than 'she saw yellowness.' I doubt the significance of this distinction; nonetheless, I assume that Hutto is here taking back his earlier claim that experiences cannot be referents.

5. It is perhaps worth saying, though, that there is an ordinary sense in which one can be aware of being conscious: one can be aware *that* one is conscious. In this sense one can experience being conscious; but this does not imply that one is aware of one's consciousness as one is aware of its objects.

6. Hutto ends his discussion of intentionality with some remarks about David Lewis' 'ability hypothesis', which should not pass without comment, since they represent a common misunderstanding. Hutto says that if it is viewed as a reductive account (presumably of experience) then "the original 'ability hypothesis' is circular, since the notion of a particular sort of experience (e.g. recognising red, re-identifying red) must be invoked in order to characterise the abilities in question." He then endorses a non-reductive 'non-circular' understanding of the hypothesis. But the attribution of circularity misunderstands the nature of the ability hypothesis as endorsed by Lewis and others. The hypothesis is not meant to be a reductive explanation of consciousness. Rather it is supposed to be an account of our *knowledge* of consciousness. It is certainly related to the reductive account of consciousness given by Lewis and others – since it is employed in a *defence* of that account against the claim that our knowledge of consciousness shows that consciousness is not physical. But this is inessential to the hypothesis, as is shown by the fact that the hypothesis could be employed by someone who rejects reductionism (as it is, e.g., by Mellor 1992). Hence it cannot be an objection to the hypothesis that it invokes the notion of an experience (of red, say). These experiences are what it is that is supposed to be known. The ability hypothesis as such does not try and reduce these *experiences*; rather, it makes a claim about what it is to know them. Compare: the hypothesis that *knowing how to ride a bicycle irreducibly consists in the ability to ride a bicycle, and not in any propositional knowledge*, is not undermined by the fact that this statement of the hypothesis employs the phrase 'ride a bicycle.' And this would be true even if there were a true reductive account of what it is to ride a bicycle.

7. Unless a is related to the relation *R* whenever it is true that *aRb*. But I doubt that this is what Hutto has in mind: for then he would be committed to the equally absurd view that when *a* is bigger than *b*, *a* is related to the relation *bigger* than.

8. Vincent Descombes (2001) raises a similar charge against what he calls 'mental philosophy'; I criticise Descombes in my 2004.

References

Crane, T. 1998. "Content, Non-Conceptual." In *Routledge Encylopedia of Philosophy*, E.J. Craig (ed). London: Routledge.
Crane, T. 2001. *Elements of Mind*. Oxford: Oxford University Press.
Crane, T. 2003. "The intentional structure of consciousness." In *Consciousness: New Philosophical Essays*, A. Jokic and Q. Smith (eds), 33–56. Oxford and New York: Oxford University Press.
Crane, T. 2004. "Critical Notice of *The Mind's Provisions* by Vincent Descombes." *European Journal of Philosophy* 12: 404–411.
Dummett, M. 1973. *Frege: Philosophy of Language*. London: Duckworth.
Goldie, P. 2000. *The Emotions*. Oxford: Oxford University Press.
Gunther, Y. 2000. *Essays on Non-Conceptual Content*. Cambridge, MA: MIT Press.
Husserl, E. 1900/2001. *Logical Investigations*. English Translation by J.L. Findlay. London: Routledge.
McDowell, J. 1978. "On 'The Reality of the Past.'" In *Action and Interpretation*, C. Hookway and P. Pettit (eds), 127–144. Cambridge: Cambridge University Press.
Mellor, D.H. 1992. "Nothing like experience." *Proceedings of the Aristotelian Society* 93: 1–16.
Velmans, M. 2000. *Understanding Consciousness*. London: Routledge.

Against passive intellectualism

Reply to Crane

Daniel D. Hutto

1. Clarifications

Crane finds fault not with my positive conclusions, but with my description of the current lay of the land in the philosophy of mind. And, as he claims my assessment is false, he concomitantly rejects my diagnosis of its perceived troubled state.[1] By his lights, I am just wrong to suppose that there is a widespread (if only tacit) commitment to thinking of experiences as spatio-temporal objects: this is a commitment to what I call the object-based schema. More than this, he makes the stronger claim that even if this practice abounds, it would hardly matter since there is no good reason that philosophers and cognitive scientists ought not to engage in it in any case.

> Hutto has persuaded me neither that there is anything confused or misleading in thinking of mental phenomena as 'entities'/'referents' (or in 'reifying' them) nor that thinking of them like this implies that they are the kind of problematic 'private' entities he and other followers of Wittgenstein worry about (Crane: this volume).

Yet the reason Crane says all of this, I think, is because he has not properly understood what I am arguing against. Let me start by supplying a clarifying example in order to make clear (i) to whom the charge of 'reifying experiences' applies; (ii) to whom it does not and (iii) what form it actually takes.

Love exists – or so one hopes – but unless our imaginations are corrupted we are not tempted to try to understand it using the same schema that we employ when dealing with ordinary macrophysical objects. It may be true to say, without any explanatory agenda or deeper philosophical spin, that a loving relation takes this form: xRy. And again, unless someone (perhaps a diehard Russellian) puts a strong metaphysical interpretation on such an expression, it would be madness to deny that love is a relational property *of some sort* of the kind that exists between intimates. Surely, it is the case that X instantiates the property of loving Y, and Y instantiates the property of being loved by X. In observing that this is the state of play with love – and let's assume it is – we have not made any contentious philosophical moves. We can go further without risking much and say that X's act of loving Y is a locatable and dateable occurrence (or a series of such occurrences – which can be, perhaps with some difficulty, tracked over time and space by tracking X and noting X's loving proclivities). Following Crane let's call this the 'innocuous view'.

Do I think that someone who holds it is in the grip of a philosophical picture – in particular, that they have misapplied the object-based schema? Not at all. Falling prey to *that* sort of mistake is what happens when one goes on to make further sorts of claims about the nature of loving experiences. One, for example, might take seriously the idea that we can locate the relational properties in question either *within* oneself or *within* the other person (presumably, when we are talking about the experience of *loving* these will lie with the lover, just as the property of *being loved* will reside with the person loved). It might be further claimed that such 'experiences' play distinct causal roles within persons – making specific contributions to the production of action or at least influencing them in important ways. And if one thought this then, assuming that there can be no action at a distance, it might be inferred that these 'experiences' *must* be located somewhere *within* the lover's skin. In large part, it is seeking to find a causal role for experiences – seeking to *explain* the mechanics of how experiences move us to act – that encourages subscription to 'internalism'. Those who are attracted to this combination of ideas are typically in the grip of the object-based schema, for they are *compelled* to think of experiences as spatio-temporal objects of some sort (usually as phenomenal properties of brain states). For it is thought that 'experiences' had better be such if they are to have even a chance of making a causal difference – if they are to figure as an important link in the chain of occurrences (and, of course, this way of thinking leads to worries about whether such properties would in fact be the causally relevant ones). And this leads to debates about whether such properties are all on a level or whether they supervene in stronger or weaker ways on underlying properties that do make a difference, and so on.

'Love', so construed, would in some such way be thought of as a *portable* internal property of some state of X – a property whose nature is potentially amenable to further scientific investigation like any another. And if we could isolate its location more precisely in X, if say it appears somewhere in X's cranium as a property of a brain state then perhaps, if we were lucky (and could enforce appropriate controls on emerging brain imaging techniques, such as fMRI or TCS), we might find its identifiable neural *correlate* or we may discover the neural state or property with which it is identical. One might then go on from there to try to explain the nature of these psychophysical relations in various ways, depending on whether one leans towards reductionism or non-reductionism. Those who find these projects acceptable are in some way or another buying into the idea that experiences – here understood as 'phenomenal properties' – are a kind of object (broadly construed). And there seems to be, at least according to a quick head count, plenty of folk who think just this, despite what Crane says (see Hutto 1998a, 2000: ch. 3 & 4, 2001a, 2006a). Those who buy into this picture believe that a science of consciousness is either certainly on the cards or at least not beyond hope.

To think this is, by my lights, to have fallen into a philosophical trap. For such hope depends on having *reified* experience. Crane says that he is "sceptical whether the charge of 'reification' really makes much sense" (Crane, this volume). Let me be clear. This is not, as Crane quite correctly observes, like a process of pickling. One does not manipulate the phenomenon itself – it remains just as it is. 'Reification' is what one does in thought and imagination: in mistakenly *modelling experiences* as objects one draws a range of false analogies with physical objects, events and processes.[2] As a result it can look to one who does this *as if* a host of questions can be rightfully asked about experiences which can, at least in principle, be answered; in fact they cannot. Experiences themselves, which are not objects of this kind, remain untouched in the process.

By my lights, this kind of confusion is very serious. It is the source of the temptation to think that the so-called 'hard problem' of consciousness can be solved. Yet such activity turns out to be a mistaken attempt to apply certain concepts beyond their proprietary domain. This tendency is not unique to the way we tend to (mis)understand consciousness. As I argued in *Beyond Physicalism*, problems in understanding the metaphysics of quantum physics have precisely the same source and the standard offerings exhibit the same pattern of options. For me, commitment to the object-based schema, whether one endorses it explicitly or implicitly, encourages us, wrongly, to take certain philosophical problems seriously when we ought not. This is, for example, the case especially when one's thinking about consciousness is also bound up with certain explanatory projects familiar to naturalists. In his recent review of that book, Robinson captures this aspect of its programme in snapshot:

> Physicalism is rejected through an examination of many of its instances. Explanatory physicalisms fail to overcome the Hard Problem. In an especially cogent discussion (p. 98–100), Hutto shows that identity theories fail to make the proposed identifications intelligible, i.e., they do not explain how experiences and neural states could be identical. The root of this unintelligibility is that 'experience cannot be understood in terms of the object-based schema to which physicalism is implicitly committed' (p. 110), where an 'object-based schema' is one that locates objects in space and time. (Quantum physics is offered as another example of failure to fit the object-based schema.) It is not that experiences are to be thought of as objects in a non-spatial realm; instead, we should follow Wittgenstein in re-

> garding our talk of experiences as expressive rather than using an object and name model (Robinson 2006: 161).

It should be clear that, on my rendering, there are not – and have never been – "at least two ideas contained in what Hutto calls the 'object-based schema' – one innocuous and one implausible" (Crane: this volume). It is Crane, and not I, who claims that the "object-based schema comes in many forms" (Crane: this volume). My version does not therefore have a "protean nature". That this is a mistake should be evident from my reply to Myin and De Nul and by attending to my previous writings on this subject or the reviews of it (Hutto 2000, ch. 3 and 4, Hutto 2001a).[3] But to be fair, I did not explicate this in any detail in the target paper, I merely referred to my previous work.

All the same, in objecting to the use of the object-based schema as a means of understanding experience I have only ever targeted what Crane calls the implausible idea and not the innocuous view. I could hardly have advanced the version of the non-explanatory identity thesis, derived and adapted from Davidson, had I done otherwise (see Hutto 1998b, 2000: ch. 5). Thus I agree that in a sense 'experiences are objects' in that they are dateable happenings. And Crane is right that, as such, we can refer to them, as we certainly do when we talk of events such as 'My experience of eating pigs' brains on Tuesday the 5th of November, between the hours of 6 and 8 PM'. We can also, in much the same way, linguistically denote experiential 'properties' using noun phrases such as 'John's getting angry at the party'. But it must be understood that in both cases the usage trades on an utterly anodyne reading of 'object' or 'property' and that no further move is made by everyday speakers to understand these as part of a larger philosophical project. Daily life and talk does not harbour the kind of explanatory ambitions I described above. This is shown by the fact that the notion of 'object' in question is a cover-all, one loose enough to encompass not only spatio-temporal 'events' but anything that one refers to or thinks about. This is what Crane calls a schematic conception of object. Most philosophers would insist on something more refined as a basis for their ontology.

With this in mind, I perhaps should have been clearer to stress that when I say 'experiences exist but they are not existents' what I meant was that they are not existents 'in the sense' of being phenomenal objects – i.e. such things as qualia. Experiences exist – certainly – but not as experiential items of our acquaintance, rather they are embodied actions (or re-enactments). Since actions are dateable, locatable events, so too are experiences. Thus I agree with Crane that "in one clear sense of 'thing', [experiences] are things. In which sense? The obvious answer in the case of experiences is that they are things that happen, or events" (Crane, this volume). What I deny is a certain picture of experiences as referents, according to which they are phenomenal items of our direct acquaintance (or even fictional items of Joycean 'stream of consciousness' narratives). To treat them as referents in this way is to misunderstand their nature. I am not therefore advocating the 'quite incredible' idea that we cannot use concepts and words to refer to experiences. Nor do I deny that *in some sense* experiences are 'referents' or that *in some sense* they are 'entities'; but in both cases the qualifications matter greatly. And this is true for Crane as well. For in other places he, like most philosophers, is just as circumspect as I am in the target paper in his use of object talk: Thus he tells us "I can think about the First World War – but this is an event not an object" (Crane 2001: 14).[4]

My reason for rejecting the object-based schema is (in part) connected to my rejection of the idea that descriptions of 'how things seem to us' should be construed *as reports* of or about *inner phenomenal* or *mental objects*. To understand the true focus of my concern it is important to distinguish between quite different ways of referring to and characterising experiences and what these involve. Linguistically competent creatures can refer to experiences as *events* or *happenings* – I can do this with respect to either my experiences or yours. To deny this would be absurd, as Crane's examples make abundantly clear. But we must be careful in understanding what such acts of reference involve. There is, on the one hand, the having of an experience (by some creature) and the quite separate act of referring to such events. Only linguistically competent beings are able to make reference to experiences in this way. But, although familiarity with the concepts of experience is required, nothing else of any importance is needed that would distinguish such referential acts from those that involved designating any other public event or happening.

After appropriate training, it is also possible to describe what a particular experience is like *for me*. But this does not involve referring to experiential properties (e.g. qualia) in the sense of referring to inner mental objects or reporting on inner events. The capacity to describe the character of one's experiences requires a very special sort of intersubjective training, that of the kind that enables us to say what experiences are like by speaking *indirectly* about their worldly objects of focus (actually, I think this works in something like the way Crane describes in his commentary when he talks about how we might refer to the *taste* of pigs' brains – see Hutto 2000: 132). The point is that these second-order activities are parasitic, late-arriving developments – the unique province of those creatures that have acquired a public language and certain practices. One can only remark on 'how things appear' if one is in a position to conceptually distinguish 'how things in fact are' – and this requires first learning to make moves in an intersubjective social space (Hutto 2005a).

A basic capacity for experiencing worldly things or their features surely predates the capacity for describing the *character* of such experiences – and in some cases the latter ability never develops. It certainly does not follow from the fact that one is able to experience that one can automatically characterise one's experiences.

I don't expect that Crane would deny this; but he does hold that even in the basic cases, on first having an experience, that there is always something to which one could *refer* (at least potentially) – its content – and about this we strongly disagree, as will become clear shortly.

At one point Crane writes: "*If* the object-schema model simply is the claim that experiences are entities ('reified'), or the referents of experience-terms, *then* it does not seem to involve any especially problematic ideas" (Crane: this volume, emphasis added). As a whole this claim is true, but the antecedent is false. My complaint against the misapplication of the object-based schema is restrictively aimed at those who hope to use it in certain *explanatory* projects – of which explanatory physicalists of both the reductive and non-reductive stripes are prime culprits (see Hutto 1998a, 2000: ch. 3).[5] It has also helped to sponsor some deeply problematic views about the way in which we learn our concepts of experience and still does for *some* (those I mentioned in the target paper). Some, but of course, not all, contemporary thinkers in the philosophy of mind continue to promulgate these mistaken views. The fact is that free and easy talk of 'mental objects of experience', those which are essentially involved in having phenomenal states of consciousness, is still not unusual (for example, see Tye 1996: 10). And it is worth stressing that not everyone committed to the object-based schema wears this attachment on their sleeves. One may unwittingly promote it. Tacit support for this way of thinking is implied by the sorts of questions that one is prepared to take seriously about consciousness, the methods one thinks can be used in order to study it, and even the views one feels compelled to reject (and the reasons one has for doing so). This last point matters in assessing the positions of Dennett and the Churchlands, for instance.[6] Certainly, not everyone agrees that "experiences themselves (as Hutto himself emphasises), are not something 'one can observe or experience'" (Crane: this volume, emphases added).

It is pretty clear that Crane and I do not see the current state of play in contemporary philosophy of mind in the same way. But this may be, in part, because he has conflated two quite different claims and assumed that I am arguing against the more outrageous one. For he appends the following to his statement just quoted above: "This has nothing to do with the idea that experiences are objects, events or properties – unless it is insisted that *the only* objects, events and properties there are are those we can observe or experience. But surely *no participant in this debate will say that*" (Crane: this volume, emphases added). It is true that only diehard Berkeleyians, of which few remain, will say that *the only* objects, events and properties that exist are those which we can observe or experience. But that is beside the point, for there are many in the contemporary scene who are committed to the weaker idea, openly or not, that the having of an experience equates to being in mental/

brain states which have inner phenomenal properties (objects) – and indeed that these properties are directly experienced. This is the claim I target, not the former.

In truth, I don't understand why Crane dismisses my diagnosis of the trouble caused by the object-based schema. In other contexts he not only makes the very distinctions about objects I wish to draw, but he even does so in much the same way that I do. For example, he observes that our everyday talk of objects is polysemic, distinguishing between a *substantial* conception (according to which objects have a certain nature, e.g. as being existent in space-time, or as having qualitative experiential properties) and a *schematic* one (according to which objects are understood grammatically or functionally – from which it follows that they need have no common nature). And this distinction matters for Crane – for in talking about the 'objects' at which we can be intentionally directed he is not talking about 'objects in the ordinary sense' (or, if so, he is only talking about these on case-by-case basis or as Aristotle would say, incidentally).

And, on this basis, he rejects the idea that the objects of thoughts – what is thought about – can be rightly understood as 'ideas in our minds' or 'representations in our heads' (Crane 2001: 16). He also rejects the idea of qualia. But, in my book, this *just is* to reject the object-based schema! I trace the source of the metaphysical variant of the hard problem precisely to adherence to a specific sort of substantive conception of 'mental objects' (where these are imagined to be properties of either brain or mental states distinguished by their qualitative features and having spatio-temporal locations). Therefore I can only presume that it is because Crane has misunderstood my concerns about the object-based schema and its nature that he says that he "found little to object to in [it], and no argument against it" (Crane: this volume). Given what he writes elsewhere, he *ought* to object to certain common misuses of it. And as for the argument against it, it is true that I did not rehearse it in the target paper but it is detailed in my previous work and also, in sketch, in my reply to Myin and De Nul, this volume (Hutto 1998a, 2000: ch. 4).

Having clarified the true scope of my complaint against certain uses of the object-based schema, I wonder therefore if Crane would persist in claiming:

> a) that Hutto is wrong in thinking that the plausible claims he makes about emotion (quoted above) require us to deny the object-based schema; and (b) that he is wrong in his claim that the object-based schema is entirely mistaken (Crane, this volume).[7]

Crane's postulation of *intentional* objects is not at all in conflict with the object-based schema. His major ambition is to defend the strong view that "our conception of mind is unified by the idea of intentionality, the mind's directedness on its objects. Intentionality is the distinctive mark of all and only mental phenomena" (Crane 2001: 2, 6, 13). And in making the case for strong intentionalism he holds that a certain, standard 'conception of consciousness' is mistaken. Which one? The very one that those committed to applying the object-based schema when modelling experiences entertain: i.e. the conception of consciousness that Crane puts under fire is precisely that in which experiences are thought of as either qualia or inner representations. Thus, despite misunderstanding the scope, purpose and target of my diagnosis, Crane sees a potential point of agreement between us. He writes:

> Intentional states involve direction upon objects, not contents; we do not experience contents. If anything, contents are that by means of which we have experiences of objects. So Hutto and I ought to be in agreement here (Crane: this volume).

In advocating his strong intentionalism he also makes it clear that, "Directedness *is* the idea that intentional states have objects" (Crane 2001: 13, emphasis added). But these intentional objects are not, as he puts it, "shadowy intermediaries" (Crane 2001: 14). For, "it is crucial to recognise that intentional objects are not entities of a certain kind. They cannot be, since some *intentional objects do not exist*" (Crane: this volume, emphasis mine). So, in the end, Crane befriends me at least in rejecting those who model 'the having of experiences' as 'having an object in one's consciousness'.

2. Misattribution and reconciliation?

Given the above, why did I try to distinguish my views from those of Crane's in the first place? Crane holds that it was because I had misunderstood the use he makes of the core notions in his account of intentionality. These are:

A. Intentional object (where object is not understood as *thing* or *entity*);
B. Intentional mode (belief, desire, hope, fear etc.);
C. Intentional content (that which characterises that on which the state is directed, and therefore incorporates the aspectual shape of that intentional state).

Importantly, for Crane, 'content' is equivalent to *the aspect under which an intentional object of an intentional state is presented* (Crane 2003: 38). Contents are, therefore, both modes of presentations and real existents – they are what subjects are *related to* in acts of thinking, whereas intentional objects are that at which the subject's thoughts are *directed.* As a class, the latter do not exist. Accordingly, experiencers are *always* related *to* intentional contents and only sometimes to intentional objects (if the world obliges). And they are related 'by' psychological modes 'to' contents. For example, in having a thought about a unicorn I am *related to* a *content by* some *psychological mode* (believing, fearing, imagining, etc). But what my thought is *directed at* is a unicorn, here understood as an intentional object. As a result, in a very strong sense my thoughts cannot misfire with respect to what they are *about*. To be a thought *just* is to be directed at some intentional object or other.

As I said in the target paper, the reason I want to distance myself from this sort of account is that I doubt 'contents' ought to play any role in our understanding of basic experiential responding at all. My initial and continued concern is that, "whereas talk of being directed at an object is relatively straightforward, we might wonder what being related to contents consists in" (Hutto: 2006b). And it remains my view that "introducing content into the equation is an unnecessary and potentially confusing extra step when it comes to understanding *feeling towards*, at least in the most basic cases involving nonconceptual responses" (Hutto: 2006b). And to be precise, I have no issues with the idea that we need to make sense of linguistically mediated contents when it comes to understanding propositional attitudes. My worries about the content are restricted to basic cases of what we might call phenomenal responding.

Crane, however, took it that I was in fact objecting to the idea that we might be 'directed at' contents and that I had (wrongly) accused him of thinking that this was possible. Consequently, in his reply, he writes "I *never* say that intentionality is directedness *towards contents* as opposed to objects" (Crane: this volume, second emphasis mine). Very well, but that is not the true focus of my worry. I accept, however, that the confusion is entirely my fault. For in introducing the matter I wrote "I deny therefore that the possibility of misdirection, however frequent, gives us reason to think that we are *directed at* contents (propositional, conceptual or otherwise) rather than the objects or states of affairs that we are meant to be directed at when things are as they should be" (Hutto 2006b, emphasis added). This way of putting things caused us to talk past one another. With hindsight, it would have made things clearer if I had put my point disjunctively: basic intentional responding neither involves being *directed at* or being *related to* 'contents'. It cannot, *a fortiori*, if there are no such things as 'contents' at the level of basic experiencing.

Crane clearly believes that *contents* are objects. As a class, they exist as genuine *relata*. And it follows that if 'relations must relate what exists' then contents must exist. And if something exists it must be an existent (Crane 2003: 39). Thus Craneian contents are existents in the Quinean sense. They are *substantive* things and not merely *schematic* ones. I thought that Crane subscribed to the object-based schema because I thought that in addition to understanding contents as substantive objects he also regarded them as *phenomenal* objects. It is the role that Crane wants contents to play in enabling us to make sense of experience that encouraged this thought. I misunderstood what he meant to claim by saying that intentional contents are not just real *relata* but also 'how things seem to be'. For by his lights, intentional contents are not only entities, they are also 'modes of presentation'. I mistakenly took it to be the case that Crane understood them to be modes of presentation in phenomenal terms – i.e. as the 'way things seem' to subjects *experientially*.[8] I therefore imagined his attitudinal modes to be 'ways of being aware' of *phenomenal* objects: i.e. contents.[9] On this rendering, both mode and content together would constitute a complex, but thoroughly phenomenal mode of presentation of intentional objects.[10] It is with this in mind that I wrote:

> Interestingly, Crane accepts that the content of a sensation-state is a matter of its object being presented in a certain way. This content need not be propositional (Crane 2003: 44). Construed thus, it may be difficult to see what distinguishes mere modes and non-propositional contents, since modes are defined as a way of being aware (Crane 2003: 52).

In his commentary, Crane makes it abundantly clear that this is *not* his position. Thus he writes emphatically: "I never say or imply that experiences are experienced, I never say that consciousness is what is experienced" (Crane: this volume). He suggests that the source of my confusion was a misunderstanding of what he meant "by mode, object and content" (Crane: this volume). This is surely right. Terminological differences were at the root of my interpretative trouble. For example, it was with the notion of contents as 'modes of presentation' in mind that I wrote "we are not related to the modes by which such objects are perceived, as Crane's analysis implies" (Hutto 2006b: this volume). On the basis of our further correspondence I now see, and accept, that if we read 'mode' in the way that Crane uses the term, I had misrepresented his views. For him, contents are aspectual modes of presentation of intentional objects; they are substantive objects to which we are psychologically related *via* an attitudinal mode. Accordingly, only 'modes' of the first sort (modes of presentation, that is) are objects; those of the second are not. Yet although I misrepresented Crane's view in the target paper, this was not because of 'procrustean tendency' on my part manifesting itself in a drive "to force views into vague all inclusive 'schemas'" (Crane: this volume). Indeed, the object-based schema is neither vague nor all inclusive.

Yet even after clarifying all this, my complaint about Crane's proposals still hold. For these were always about the role he sees for 'contents' when it comes to understanding experiences. And if I have now understood Crane's account properly, then I have new questions about it. For if contents are not, as I wrongly supposed, 'phenomenal' modes of presentation then it is not obvious how they can do the required work Crane requires of them – i.e. of enabling us to understand the *character* of experience. Indeed, why when engaged in that project isn't it sufficient to simply focus on the *modes* in isolation (those psychological attitudes by which one is allegedly *related to* Craneian contents)? Certainly, it looks as if these are all that should interest us when it comes to understanding and classifying the purely *experiential* aspects of perceptual acts. For, to prosecute that project, it is quite inconsequential to know which intentional object is being 'thought of' and to which content a thinker is related. If one is interested in the character of phenomenal experiences it seems one should exclusively focus on Craneian *modes*. These alone reveal the relevant psychological similarities and differences between perceivers. For those interested in what-it-is-like questions the real issue is the *way* one is related to the world and not *what* it is to which one is related nor what it is that one's thought is directed at: the very mention of 'intentional contents' and 'intentional objects' is irrelevant to the project of characterising and classifying experiences in terms of their purely phenomenal aspects. And it is not at all clear from what Crane has said why such a project would be incoherent.

This can be so even if we agree with Crane that there is *always* an intentional aspect to experience. Of course, we can type individuate experiences (and thereby identify them) by appeal to the *ways* creatures respond to certain types of substantive *objects*. On my account these will not be contents, simply triggers of various sorts. As such, these will be real entities but *not* modes of presentation of any kind. I say more about this in the next section. Crane's strong intentionalism however requires him to take a different view. He claims that there is an essential role for content when it comes to understanding experiences. Indeed, for him, intentionality *is* the defining mark of the mental. He makes this clear in reviewing the main options for understanding phenomenal experience, saying that "the non-intentionalist says that it is a difference in *qualia*. The intentionalist says it is a difference in *how things seem to be*, that is, a difference in the intentional content" (Crane 2001: 147).

Yet, as we have established, for Craneian contents – *how things seem to be* – are not to be understood in phenomenal but only cognitive terms. But if contents (should we imagine them to exist) are understood as having only cognitive value then it is not obvious why they are *essential* for understanding experience. Answering this is Crane's burden. I take it that he would say that the 'subject-mode-content' structure is in fact a complex package, and that *all* of its parts are necessary for understanding experience (Crane 2001: 143). Strong intentionalists assume that modes *necessarily* relate subjects to contents. But, in light of the queries just raised, I do not see how, even if this were true, it could secure the result that Crane wants.

Moreover, at this point, I want to reiterate and re-emphasise my original worry – i.e. that talk of content 'introduces an unnecessary and potentially confusing' extra step when it comes to understanding basic experiences. They are asked to play a *pivotal* role in Crane's account (quite literally). They are real objects to which subjects are related and also the *way* intentional objects are presented. But in order to perform this double duty they seem to be pulled in opposing directions. In fact, it makes them rather peculiar things. As real *relata* they are surely things. But this is not their defining or most interesting feature. It is rather that they are aspectual shapes. So understood, they are *intrinsic* features of intentional objects.

So contents are *both* entities and aspectual shapes – as the latter they are presumably facets or presentations of intentional objects. Being an aspect of something is an internal relation – not an external or 'real' one. Thus the necessary relationships between intentional objects and contents must be internal at best, especially since not all intentional objects exist. It is playing both these roles that makes them peculiar. For puzzles arise if we think of contents both as entities in the sense of existing objects – entities that are *sometimes* identical with intentional objects – and also as aspectual shapes which are *intrinsic* features of their intentional objects.

Let me explain. As a class, intentional objects – being merely grammatical – do not exist. As a class, contents – being substantive objects – do. Sometimes the members of these classes overlap. In other words, some intentional objects of thoughts *happen* to exist, some do not. My *existence* as an object of your thought is therefore incidental. It does not exemplify what is *essential* for being an intentional object. (And clearly the converse holds: my existence as an intentional object is not essential to my existence as a substantive existent. I may exist unthought of). But, if I am to be the content (substantive object) of your thought, the object to which you are psychologically related, I *must* exist. At least one *essential* feature of being a content is being a genuine *relata*. Sometimes, but not always, the intentional objects of our thoughts (what they are *about* or *directed at*) and what we are *related to* (content understood as objects) co-incide or, better, they are *contingently* identical.

But when contents are understood as aspects – as the way things seem to subjects – they are thought of as standing in an internal relation to intentional objects.[11] So, in general, the kind of relation that holds between contents and intentional objects cannot be a merely *contingent* one – such as, incidental identity. Contents *just are* the way intentional objects are presented; they are their aspectual shapes. Contents are modes of presentation and as such they must be internally related to their intentional objects. This is just the flipside of the idea that every intentional object of thought must be presented in some way or another.

But, it may be wondered, how can something that merely happens to exist be an *aspect* of something that does not exist (as sometimes intentional objects do not)? How is it that non-existent intentional objects can possibly exhibit aspects – aspects which are also real entities? Contrawise, how can contents be aspectual shapes of intentional objects in those cases in which intentional objects do, as it happens, exist? For, in such cases, intentional objects are presumably contingently identical with their contents. If so, they would have to be, in some sense, *self-presenting* aspects.

The account raises other questions too. Crane tells us that "the intentional object of your thought is what is given in a (correct) answer to the question, 'what are you thinking about?" (Crane 2001: 17). This works fine in some cases – those in which intentional objects (grammatical) are also contingently identical with 'ordinary things' (substantive). But things do not always go so neatly. Thus modifying one of

Crane's examples, let us imagine that Cortes really didn't gaze at the Pacific from a peak of Darien. *Pace* Keats, let us say he gazed upon something that looked damned like it – what is now the Panama Canal (assume he was a bit misdirected).[12]

If so, how should we answer Crane's criterial question with respect to this variant? What is Cortes thinking about? He *thinks* he is thinking about the Pacific – ask him; that is what he says. However his thoughtful attitude (mode) relates him to the Panama Canal (content/object), as a matter of fact. What is he thinking *about* – i.e. directed at? Is it the Pacific (intentional object) as presented under the aspect (content) 'the Panama Canal'? Is it the Panama Canal (intentional object) presented under the aspect of 'the Pacific' (content/object)? Is it the Panama Canal (intentional object) presented under some more neutral aspect (content/object)?[13]

All told, Crane's account and mine are similar in *some* respects and fundamentally at odds in others. We agree that experiences ought not to be modelled on objects. We agree that experiential modes must be taken seriously, but not as 'substantive objects' and not as things seen (for further clarification about my views on this see my reply to Rudd).[14] We both hold that experiences are the *way* worldly offerings appear in acts of intentional directedness.

Yet there remains a fundamental difference: I deny, whereas Crane affirms, the existence of 'contents'. For him, contents are an *essential* ingredient in any adequate account of experience. For me, in understanding basic experiences postulating them yields only confusion. I have already raised some fresh worries about what Crane has to say about the pivotal role that contents are meant to play in making his strong intentionalism credible. Yet it is worth taking my complaint about contents further. In the next section, I go beyond Crane's somewhat idiosyncratic account to raise doubts about the very idea that basic experiences could be contentful. This is important for the idea that basic experiences are content involving has a widespread, deep and pernicious grip on philosophical and psychological imaginations – and it ought not.

3. Rejecting passive intellectualism

Crane holds that "all intentional states have intentional content" (Crane: this volume). But he qualifies this: "I am not committed to the claim that experience must be conceptual merely by saying that experience has content" (Crane: this volume). We must be clear; it is not that there are two *kinds* of intentional content, one conceptual, the other non-conceptual. The difference is rather in the *way* that content is, or rather is not expressed. Sometimes it is characterised (or accessible) using canonical concepts available to a subject, at other times, not. Thus it is possible for "subjects to be in a state with a content p, [even if] they do not possess the concepts which are canonical for p" (Crane 2001: 152). This is just what it is to be in a state with nonconceptual content. This explains why "the content of the experience is what you would put in words if you had the words in question (see Crane 2001: 144). He illustrates the difference as follows: "to believe that a certain pig is flying you have to have the concept of a pig, but that to *see* that this pig is flying you don't need to" (Crane 2001: 152–3).

In positing the existence of nonconceptual content Crane also makes it clear that he is not wedded to the idea that such content must be truth-conditional. He stresses "Nor do I say that *all content is propositional* – that is, assessable as true or false – since there are many states of mind (notably object-directed emotions like love and hate) which do not have propositional contents" (Crane: this volume, emphasis added). All the same, he begins with a truth-conditional formulation when explicating the nature of basic perceptual acts. And this is because, for him, like many others "Perception aims at truth… Perception *presents* the world as being a certain way, it 'aims' (as it were) to tell us how the perceptual world is" (Crane 2001: 151). It is the very function of perception to inform "us about the world" (Crane 2001: 150). What singles perceptual experience out as nonconceptual is not that its content is of a non-propositional variety, rather it is that "The content of perception is more detailed, more specific, containing more information than the contents of beliefs and other propositional attitudes" (Crane 2001: 151).

It is against this backdrop that we must make sense of his remarks about object-focused emotions. Presumably, the content of such states is purely referential and not propositional.[15] And it is precisely our 'terms of reference' that could be used to (potentially) put such contents into words. The point is that in making such translations we would not be seeking to capture a proposition, one using standard complement *that*-clauses. Nevertheless, on this view, whether truth-conditional or merely referential, basic perceptual and emotional modes of responding involve contents that are potentially linguistically expressible (in some very strong sense of 'potential'). Hence – once again – the claim that: "if you put your thoughts into words, then what you put into words is the content" (Crane, this volume).

To suppose that basic perceptual acts are content involving – be the content conceptual or nonconceptual, truth-conditional or referential – is to subscribe to a form of intellectualism.[16] I reject all such accounts. By my lights, intentional directedness of non-verbal responding does not involve having mental states relating to contents: *a fortiori* there is no content to be translated into words *at all.*

Furthermore, I reject the claims that the primary function of sense perception is the production of states with (or related to) veridical contents and the primary function of emotional responding is the production of states with (or related to) referential contents. In general, what goes on in both cases is that characteristic responses are prompted by an organism's sensitivity to particular natural signs; these in effect guide actions and coordinate interactions with specific objects and states of affairs. Such on-line informational sensitivity and responsiveness can be of graded complexity; sometimes making use of single cues or a variety of them. Typically, this will depend on the degree of 'hostility' of the organism's environment and how well equipped it is to deal with it (see Sterelny 2003, ch. 2 & 3).[17] Some organisms will get by with simple detection-response systems, others will need to use more 'robust' tracking systems because they face greater environmental challenges (for example, from mimics, parasites or cunning predators). Recognition and response routines may be hard-wired or learned – but the important point is that the informational sensitivity they exhibit does not involve being sensitive to or acquiring 'contents'. Organisms do not need to relate to, acquire or process contents of any kind in order for them to achieve their ends successfully. Radical enactivism about intentionality is committed to understanding perceptual and emotional responses in this way; indeed this is what makes the approach distinctive (see Hutto 2006b). Our primary engagements with the world are not made in terms of 'truth' or 'reference'; rather they are best understood in terms of informational sensitivity and the actions and interactions such sensitivity sponsors.

In thinking about this, we should take heed of Akins' astute critique of received philosophical wisdom about the nature and purposes of sense perception; specifically, the idea that the function of the senses is 'to tell us truly about the world'.[18] Her detailed neurophysiological investigations reveal not only *why* we ought, but also *how* we can replace this idea with a more narcissistic account – one that focuses on what such responding does for organisms. She illustrated this by focusing on the complex nature of thermoreception. It involves initiating certain characteristic routines of organismic response prompted by the firing of 'warm spots' and 'cold spots' and two pain receptors (nociceptors). Without repeating the details of her description, she makes it clear that the primary function of the thermoreceptors is to provoke differential responses when a creature is in extreme conditions of very high or very low temperature, as required by its vulnerabilities in certain parts of its body (see Akins 1996). Her analysis reveals that this is not achieved by *first* providing a 'thermometer-like' indication of the ambient environmental temperature which is then processed and re-formatted in particular ways so it can be further used by the organism.

This brings out that the traditional view of sensory perception is not simply wedded to intellectualism – it is wedded to intellectualism of a *passive* variety. Accordingly, the *primary* job of sensory and emotional responding is to *supply* 'contents' to 'mental structures' making them contentful mental states. Fodor has been the most forthright champion of this sort of idea. On his variant, once protoconceptual symbols become properly 'activated' they acquire content, and once this happens they can be manipulated and used for other purposes further down the line. This requires appropriate re-formatting. As such, perceptual and emotional 'contents' are not, in the first instance, integrally tied with actions and responses. They need to be processed first. It is, therefore, perhaps not surprising that those attracted to this sort of view are inclined to talk of 'presentations to subjects' and 'the reception of perceptual givens' supplied by the senses'.[19]

Traditional views about what sense perception supplies are generally, in important ways, bound up with accounts of informational content and the way it is processed. To understand the idea of informational content, as opposed to what I've been calling informational sensitivity, requires making sense of the notion of 'intrinsic indication'. To be sure, those who talk of informational content – like Dretske and Fodor – are explicit about the fact that it does not equate to representational content. Hence, Dretske says of it: "More is needed to be a representation. E.g. the only way… [information-carrying] natural signs can misrepresent is if… they fail to indicate something they are supposed to indicate" (Dretske 1988: 67). But this remark does not get to the root of the matter. For one might still imagine that informational content is somehow 'intrinsically' indicative and that it becomes representational content *proper* once it has been extracted and given a specific job. The very idea of naturally-occurring 'standing for' relations must be rejected. We are led to ask: just what is content such that signs or signals not only 'have' it but that it can be 'ported' into cognitive systems? What is kind of 'thing' is it imagined to be such that it can be extracted from signals, re-formatted and preserved during further processing?

Content of this kind cannot be understood wholly in terms of covariance. The idea that it can is doubtless promoted (and given a certain respectability) due to equivocation in the way we typically use the 'carrying information' metaphor. For it can be unpacked either solely in 'covariance' terms or in terms of a quite different notion of 'contained' or 'encoded' content. The latter way of speaking is common to engineers when they talk of encoding information in a signal. When it comes to basic perception, I take it that the first use is legitimate but the second is not. Let me explain. It is quite acceptable to say that:

> s's being F 'carries information about' t's being H if it has the property of standing in a covariance relation to that other state of affairs (and *vice versa*).

Philosophers often quibble about the precise nature, scope and strength of the covariance relations that would be required in order to engender a true 'information relation' – certainly, one can argue for stronger or more relaxed criteria (cf. Dretske 1981, Millikan 2004). I favour the softer option when it comes to understanding informational sensitivities of biological organisms, but for the moment that is a side issue. The important thing to notice is that if we are only thinking about carried information in terms of covariance, the informational relations in question, however strong, are symmetrical. Thus if the first state of affairs 'carries information' about the second then the second 'carries information' about the first (i.e. from the point of view of the universe – or, better, from no point of view at all). At bottom, everyone can agree that covariance relations of this type must hold between signs and worldly offerings if organismic actions are to succeed. Informational sensitivity introduces asymmetry into the story in that organisms are selectively responsive to signs in ways that suit their purposes. Yet from this fact alone no support at all is rendered to the claim that the signs (or signals) to which organisms are sensitive 'have content' or that they are used to '*tell* the creature about some external state of affairs' or that they are used to '*refer* to some worldly item'.

The idea that organisms rely on perceptually tracking certain natural signs and that successful coordination of their actions depends on certain environmental correspondences holding gives no support to the idea that their responses are content involving. To think otherwise is to try to attempt to milk the respectable idea of an informational relation for something more than one is legitimately entitled to. It is to be under the sway of what I call the 'containment metaphor' – this is the idea that our sensations or sensory inputs somehow already 'contain' information and that this information can be extracted and modified by certain processes. Such ideas are *extremely* familiar – indeed they are built into talk of 'data' and 'the given', and they stem from and promote a picture of the mind as something 'informed' by the world, something that receives contentful 'impressions' of it, from it. Although Sellars and others have subjected the notion of 'the given' to scathing critique, it still walks abroad in the imaginations and offerings of many of today philosophers. It is the beating heart of traditional cognitive science.

Equivocation in our understanding of 'carrying information' – sometimes to mean 'containment' and sometimes to mean 'covariance', sometimes both – is rife. It even occurs in the writings of those who openly oppose the received view of the function of the senses that gives life to standard talk of acquiring or picking up informational contents. For example, in explaining how bats track insects, Akins pens:

> …because the neuron responds to only particular aspects of a complex stimulus, its signal contains information about only those specific properties [containment]. For example, think of the response properties of neurons in the FM/FM areas of bat auditory cortex. These neurons will fire whenever there is a pair of stimuli with a distinct profile [covariance] – two stimuli separated by a certain time delay with a particular frequency 'mismatch' between a fundamental tone and its harmonic, each stimulus falling within a certain amplitude range… the response of an FM neuron does not tell us, say, how many harmonics each signal contained, or their pattern of frequency modulation, or the amplitude of the signals except at a certain point in the signal sweep and so on. Much information about the acoustic properties of the original stimuli… has simply been lost [containment] (Akins 1993: 149).

The trouble is that once these two senses of 'carrying information' get confused, an offending idea is wrongly enshrined. For example, we are told: "Typically, the sensory systems overload the information-handling capacity of our cognitive mechanisms so that *not all that is given to us in perception* can be digested" (Dretske 1981: 148). Consequently, "Until information is lost... an information-processing system... has failed to classify or categorise, failed to generalise, failed to recognise the input as being an instance (token) of a more general type" (Dretske 1981: 141, cf. Jacob 1997: 71). According to Dretske's influential account, 'informational content' is lost when it is reformatted – converted from analogue form to digital form. But the counterpoint to this is that certain property-specific information 'contained' in the signal is also *preserved*. Information is lost and gained. Digitalisation is just one proposal about the nature of the process that enables a cognitive system to re-format the information given to it by the senses so that it can represent a specific state of affairs as being *of this* kind rather than *of that* kind. It is possible to rewrite this proposal in terms of informational sensitivity, but rather than provide such details I want to focus on the idea that there could be something *supplied* in sensory encounters that needs re-formatting: something – some content – that is extracted and survives onward processing.

I reject the idea that signs or signals contain any such informational content and the attendant idea that there could be such things as natural indication, an intrinsic – 'standing to' – relation. In contrast to the passive intellectualism of content-based accounts, I hold that in order to 'indicate' at all, signals (or indices) have to be *used* in particular ways – e.g. in the re-identification of particular types of thing. The following formulations highlight the important differences between the standard 'intellectualist' as opposed to the radical enactivist position of the sort I am propounding.

> Experiences nonconceptually represent that there is a surface or an internal region having so-and-so features at such-and-such locations, and thereby they acquire their phenomenal character (Tye 1996: 139).
>
> Experiencings are organismic responses to certain triggers because in 'Normal' conditions responding thusly has in the past guided actions with respect to worldly offerings in a way that helped the ancestors of such organisms to proliferate (thereby ensuring the proliferation of their response systems) (Hutto 2000: 60–1).

In its first appearance, I called this view a kind of 'modest biosemantics'. With hindsight, I see that this was a misleading label given that I have always rejected the idea that it is possible to understand the relations in question as truth or referential relations. On this matter I disagree with biosemanticists such as McGinn (1989), Papineau (1987) and Millikan (1993). As I wrote some time ago:

> Millikan lists six fundamental differences between human and animal representations which are meant to "secure our superiority, [and] make us feel comfortably more endowed with mind" (Millikan 1989: 297). The most important one on her list is the fact that we are able to make logical inferences by means of propositional content. Thus only representations of the kind which respect the law of non-contradiction can be deemed to have propositional content. In a nutshell, she holds that there are distinct types and levels of representation and that not all representations have the kind of content appropriate to full-fledged beliefs or desires. What this means is that biosemanticists need not, and should not, hold that content of the frog's intentional icon is captured by the conceptual content of the English sentence "There is an edible bug" or any other near equivalent. Millikan is explicit about this. With reference to bees she writes:
>
>> Bee dances, though (as I will argue) these are intentional items, do not contain denotative elements, because interpreter bees (presumably) do not identify the referents of these devices but merely react to them appropriately (Millikan 1984: 71).
>
> What I take from this remark is that we identify the object that the bee is directed at as nectar using our own conceptual scheme. Indeed, we settle on this description because it is explanatorily relevant when giving a full, selectionist explanation of the proper function of bee dances.
>
> But if one is willing to concede this then it is difficult to see what could motivate thinking that basic representations have truth conditions … we might ask: What is true? How can we have a truth relation if one of the crucial *relata* is absent (Hutto 1999: 79–80)?

There is no such thing as a truth-conditional semantics without the resources of a complex language. In stressing this, it is probably best to understand my account of basic responding as a kind of biosemiotics in that – and *only* in that – in basic cases, organisms get by using effective non-verbal on-line signals (and off-line icons). These guide actions and interactions but cannot be understood in terms of reference or truth.[20]

To emphasise this, I talk of Local Indexical Guides and Local Iconic Guides (or LIGs) in contrast to Millikan's Pushme-Pullyu representations (see Hutto 2007). For, even though Millikan says that these representations are only to be thought of as representations in the way that 'zero is thought of as a number', I hold that even this is a bridge too far (Millikan 2004: 158). LIGs are not 'representations' at all – they have no 'content' of any kind, nonconceptual or otherwise. As the name implies, they guide actions in response to specific worldly offerings.

I am well aware that this goes against the grain: the received wisdom is that some kind of 'content' is *needed* to explain sophisticated worldly alignments. The notion of 'content' binds together several others that have a venerable pedigree

– those just discussed about the function of the senses; the nature of what they supply; and how that information is further processed. I reject this clutch of ideas. For once it is realised that the only legitimate notion that can be derived from 'information theory' is that of covariance relations – and not referential or truth relations – it becomes clear that the way actions and interactions are guided in perceptual and emotional responding only exploits purely indexical signs (and by using off-line icons which poach on these, see my reply to Goldie). So, not only do the standard claims made about 'content' and its source lack support, we can easily get by without postulating such things. Signals prompt routine responses that succeed in fulfilling their proper functions when certain conditions hold – i.e. if organisms are well-designed and in normal environments, these signals will guide their actions in relation to worldly offerings well enough. Local Indexical Guides prompt Action Coordination Routines of varied complexity.

In ridding ourselves of the idea of contentful attitudes (three-place relations) we can still speak of intentional attitudes (two-place relations). But without contents, at the nonverbal level, there is only the creature, the worldly offering and the way it is experienced. Once 'contents' are removed from the story, there is just the organism, object and mode – X's seeing Y *as round*. It follows that there can be no distinction between particular experiential 'ways of being aware' (seeing, hearing, hurting, etc.) and 'ways things seem' (the aspectual shape under which an object is 'presented'), as per Crane's distinction between modes and contents. The particular character of a given experience is determined by the sensorimotor contingencies of the particular sense modality in question. Of course only encounters with certain types of object will trigger these, and they need not be triggered by the sorts of objects at which the creature *ought* to be intentionally directed. The character of perceptual and emotional responding is fixed by the sensorimotor contingencies (which may be extended re-habituated response patterns – if they have been 're-tied'). Seeing X 'as round' is to be disposed to respond to X in certain characteristic ways, just as experiencing one's ankle 'as painful' is to be so disposed to respond to it in specific ways. Yet Crane has complained:

> the position [Hutto] says he wants to endorse here implies that the phenomenal character of (e.g.) a visual experience is determined solely by the fact that it is a visual experience. And this cannot be true: two experiences can both be visual experiences and yet differ in their phenomenal character, on anyone's understanding of 'phenomenal character' (Crane: this volume).

There can be no responding to things without implying a certain manner of response, and there can be no question that what one responds to makes a difference to the manner of that response. For me, talk of things 'appearing a certain way' needs to be unpacked in terms of actions and possible actions. Thus we can distinguish what is involved in visually experiencing an X as opposed to a Y (or a particular X as opposed to a particular Y). I am not therefore driven "to accept the phenomenologically incredible idea that one can have a conscious intentional state directed at an object *as such*, as opposed to an object appearing in a certain way" (Crane, this volume). Crane is right in thinking that we must account for such differences. It is his interpretation of what this involves that I reject. Specifically, I object to the attempt to do so by appeal to the 'content of appearances' to which we relate or that are somehow given to us by the world.

Saying that the character of experience 'is *fixed purely by the mode*' is just to say that we can type-individuate the character of experiences by the way they *feel* – in doing so, neither the objects *responded to* nor the objects that *ought to be responded to* enter into the equation as 'part of the experience'. This is not to say that the character of specific experiences can be understood simply by knowing which *type* of mode or modality (visual, auditory, etc.) is in operation. The character of particular experiencings is fixed by the *particular* mode of response (visual, auditory, etc.) in response to *specific* kinds of objects (existing triggers). Contra Crane, these objects are not 'contents'. To explain why such responding takes place at all and how the underlying mechanics came to be in place one has to look to the ends that such systems of response served in coordinating action with respect to certain historical objects and not others (at least often enough to have ensured the proliferation of such perceptual systems). In other words, by appeal to structuring causes it is at least possible to explain *why* experiences have the character they do, even when they are not *de facto* directed at their proprietary objects (see my reply to Rudd). Such structuring causes are responsible for putting systems of response in place that may be set off by a range of existing triggers – it may be that none of the objects to which they respond are type-identical to the original triggers.

In short, to say that we are 'meant to be intentionally directed at Xs' is shorthand for saying that that sort of response enabled our forerunners to track Xs (not Ys, Zs, etc.). Thus my biosemiotic proposal understands propriety triggers in terms of their proper functions – what a device is 'meant to be' directed at is determined by the ends it served. All the same, when it comes to understanding primary intentionality we are not interested in *the way* mechanisms respond or even *what* sort of things they may happen to respond to while attempting to carry out their proper functions. An understanding of *intentional directedness* cannot be achieved by focusing on the *mechanics* or *dispositions* of sensory detectors.

On this account what such systems are meant to be 'directed at' is quite independent of the range of things to which they are disposed to respond, i.e. those to which they will *in fact* respond and those to which they *would* respond to, counterfactually (i.e. in nearby possible worlds). Perceptual mechanisms do not always function as they 'ought to', even when they are not suffering from any mechanical upsets (here the 'ought' is unpacked historically and indexed to the kinds of response that were responsible for the original propagation of such mechanisms). Intentional directedness is *normative* in precisely the following sense (and no other): it aims at engendering certain types of organismic responses to certain things (or types of things) and not others.[21]

Understanding what it is that a perception-response system *ought* to respond to is a question about natural history (ancient or recent) – it is not to be answered by saying what would be best for the organism to do in some circumstance, in *abstracta* (see Hutto 1999: 64–65). Natural history ultimately explains why our perceptual systems have the characteristic response patterns that they do. Determining *actual* directedness is a matter of deciding which trigger – of the many possible triggers that *could* have prompted the response – is the one responsible for doing so in a particular case. It is to answer the question 'What is the organism directed at, *de facto*?' Determining *intentional* directedness is a question for an evolutionary biologist. It is to answer the question 'What ought the organism to be directed at?'

I stress this because, when it comes to understanding the *character* of experiences, both *actual* directedness and *intentional* directedness lie in the background. Investigations that seek to understand the phenomenal *character* of particular acts of experience must be focused on *how* organisms respond to particular objects (under another description one would be investigating the mechanics of the response). The focus must be on the *how* not the *what* (and certainly not whether the response is 'as it ought to be'). Hence, I reject Crane's strong intentionalism for the same reasons that I reject strong representationalism.

> It is here that we come to the crux of the matter, for it would appear that only if we think of representations as functionally or dispositionally defined creature-relative responses, is the strong representational thesis plausible. Yet, for this very reason, we can see why it must be false. This is because representations cannot be understood in purely functional or dispositional terms. For if experiences are functionally defined by appeal to how a creature is disposed to respond then they cannot be understood in terms of how the creature is supposed to respond. It is by accommodating this distinction that the [biosemiotic] theory enables us to solve the problem of normativity in a way that enables us to understand basic intentionality. But there is a price. It is that representations cannot be understood in purely mechano-functional or dispositional terms. Consequently, in so far as we must think of experience in such terms, even though they will be theoretically compatible with a [biosemiotic] approach to intentionality, they cannot be subsumed within it. The result is that if we want to avoid the problems of objectifying experience and instead maintain that experiences are creature-relative, or even subject-relative, responses which typically influence actions, then we are forced to distinguish intentionality and experience (Hutto 2000: 63–4, with changes).

The intentional directedness of our basic acts of perception is fixed by our natural history. But understanding this only helps in understanding *what* particular organisms (ought) to be directed at and *why* their systems function as they do. Understanding the *character* of experience cannot therefore be simply reduced to an understanding of intentional directedness (which is what I meant by warning against 'tying intentionality and phenomenology too tightly together').

Sometimes we respond to things in a characteristic, experiential way even when the 'normal' triggers that were initially meant to sponsor such responses are absent. This does not, of course, entail that in such cases one is *actually* or *intentionally* directed at non-existent objects (other than in the sense that one's systems were originally meant to guide responses to certain kinds of objects and that these are not currently triggering the response). It is for this reason that I can experience 'my arm as painful' even when I have no arm. In this case my sub-systems are set to respond by directing responses in a limb-focused way, but the triggers are abnormal: there is no limb. In engendering such a response my sensorimotor activity is functioning as it ought, mechanically speaking, even though the normal cause is missing.[22]

Triggering objects and the historical, structuring causes (some class of 'objects') make a difference to what experiences are 'like'. Yet neither contributes directly to the character of the experiences in the sense of being part of it. They lend only off-stage support or historical sponsorships: nothing more.[23] Classifying an experience as being of X-type as opposed to Y-type requires more than an understanding of its phenomenal character, and – of course – such classifications requires going beyond questions about phenomenality.

In the final analysis, I think a radically enactivist approach is best; holding that – with some very important qualifications and modifications – something like the sensorimotor contingency approach is along the right lines for understanding the *character* of experience (see my reply to Myin & De Nul).[24] Apart form enabling us to avoid certain misleading philosophical pictures of the nature of experience, one benefit of taking this line is that it suggests an answer to the question: Why are there experiences at all?[25] If experiences are understood as a kind of differential responsiveness to worldly offerings this would provide a way of explaining their origins (see my reply to Rudd). Most importantly, I argue that introducing content into the story is *only* necessary in order to understand the ways in which objects of perception and emotion are experienced in culturally and linguistically mediated ways (see my replies to Goldie and Hobson). Even in the human case, we act and interact in characteristically experiential ways long before we learn to refer or make claims about our experience.

Notes

1. In his words: "Hutto writes as if there is an unavoidable trap contained in orthodox philosophy of mind, the trap of being committed to private objects and unknowable mental states" (Crane: this volume). In denying this to be so he goes on to dismiss my "diagnosis of the problems to which emotions give rise [as] mistaken" (Crane: this volume).

2. There is a similar problem with talk of 'reduction' – that is, if one does not acknowledge that one is talking at the level of sense, not ontology. Some reductive physicalists talk as if they were interested in ontological reduction. But surely they don't mean this for then they would be engaged in the strange project of breaking up higher order phenomena into smaller parts. To borrow Crane's apt analogy, this would be equivalent to 'reducing a sauce'. Thus, it is potentially misleading for Moser and Trout to suggest that, "A primary goal of reduction is ontological unification" (Moser & Trout 1995: 191, Smith 1993: 228, cf. also Levine 1993: 134). But in fact both reductive and non-reductive physicalists are already agreed about what there is and what there is not; they differ only in their commitment to the project of reducing theories of putative higher-order phenomena to theories of lower level, more basic phenomena. Thus reductionists are committed to a project of ontological unification only in the sense that, unlike non-reductionists, they believe it is possible to demonstrate ontological unity. With some interpretative charity we can put this gloss on their words.

3. Chapter 4 of *Beyond Physicalism*, where I first set out the object-based schema, has been identified as "the philosophical heart of the book. First, [Hutto] identifies what is essential to physicalism by giving a definition of the physical; physicalism thereby becomes the assumption that reality is identifiable with spatio-temporal locatability, what Hutto calls in a Kantian manner the 'object-based' schema'. This is revealed to be an assumption inspired by classical physics. He then shows how the assumption of this schema is not even adequately applicable to the nature of 'physical' reality by a brief discussion of the findings of quantum physics, which creates an explanatory gap if one remains stuck in the assumptions of the object-based schema. Hutto then reasons analogically to the following question: If physicalist metaphysics cannot account for quantum physics and its entities, is it so wise to believe that the physicalist conceptual framework is able to account for consciousness as well? Does not an analogous explanatory gap exist? Formulating this question is to my mind the real virtue of this book" (Fischer 2000: 125).

4. Davidson, for example, once proposed that we individuate events by appeal to their paradigmatically causal characters (Davidson 1980: 179). But Quine observed that this method "purports to individuate events by quantifying over events themselves" (Quine 1985: 166). Davidson conceded this during an interchange and in reply suggested that events could be identified as the same if they coincide spatio-temporally (Davidson 1985: 175). This method of individuation was useful, he thought, because it allows us to distinguish events from objects, even when they spatio-temporally coincide. This is because events occur in space-time while objects occupy it (Davidson 1985: 176). If we use Davidson's criterion then events are not objects despite being existents, since they are not 'existing entities' – they are not occupiers but occurrences.

5. I have clarified this before. For example, in reply to Salucci I wrote "When I introduced the notion of an object-based schema I did not do so to support Crane and Mellor's style of attack on physicalism. My discussion of the objections and replies to their well-known argument was meant to provide a basis for recognising a stable core to the notion of the physical, both in its current and future uses. This was meant to demonstrate what remained constant in the concept

throughout historical developments and revisions of theoretical detail. I argued it is best to see the standard notion of the 'physical' as tied to an object-based schema; the concepts of physics, despite their abstract manifestations, developed from and could be applied to ordinary spatio-temporal objects. Introducing the idea of an object-based schema was a crucial step in my overall argument since it enables us to see why the 'mental' and the 'physical' are not intelligible within a common conceptual framework. It is the failure to provide such a framework that is physicalism's main failing as a philosophical doctrine" (Hutto 2001b). Or to put this in Crane's own terms, to be wedded to the object-based schema is therefore to think of experiences as substantive 'inner' objects in a very particular way – one wedded to a spatio-temporal schema.

6. Some, such as Chalmers, wear their commitment to the object-based schema openly on their sleeves. Others such as Dennett are attached to the idea in a negative way. For example, Dennett's scruples are born from a reactionary fear of becoming ontologically committed to 'inner objects, states and events', which can only be accessed first-personally. In my book, his 'fictionalism' about experience is driven by fear of becoming attached to an object-based schema. For a more detailed analysis of these two thinkers on this topic see Hutto 2006a.

7. I do not say the object-based schema is 'entirely mistaken'. It applies perfectly well in many domains, but not when it comes to understanding experience.

8. This is surely a possible view. Others have defined qualia as nothing more than "the way things seem to us" (Find 2001: 148–149, Flanagan 1993: 62–63).

9. I was partly encouraged in this by Crane's initial openness in characterising the nature of modes of presentation. He approves of Searle's introduction of the term 'aspectual shape' precisely because "it is not yet tied to a particular theory or account of intentionality and related phenomena, as some terms are (e.g. Frege's *Sinn or sense*). Aspectual shape, like directedness, is something that any theory needs to explain, not a theoretical posit" (Crane 2003: 38).

10. I had originally imagined Craneian *contents* to be something like Russellian 'sense-data' and Craneian 'modes' to be like Russellian sensations: "Let us give the name sense-data to the things that are immediately known in sensation: such things as colours, sounds, smells, hardness, roughness, and so on. We shall give the name sensation to the experience of being immediately aware of these things" (Russell 1912: 4).

11. To talk of aspectual shapes of objects is equivalent to saying that the objects are presented in a certain manner. Hence, the 'relation' between intentional objects and contents that Crane needs is rather like that of a name to its bearer. One refers to, the man, George Orwell by using the names 'George Orwell' or 'Eric Blair'. Names are logically tied to their objects – one cannot use a name and fail to refer, even if the object of reference is absent.

12. Cortes's situation here, despite his 'eagle eyes', is not entirely unlike that of the misbegotten frog of philosophical fame and his adventures with bee-bees, flies and black dots. For all intents and purposes, from his experiential 'point of view' the two 'objects' are indistinguishable – i.e. qualitatively so. To accept this we need not get embroiled in the debate about whether or not the imagined experiences of Cortes (or the frog) are in fact type-identical in *every respect*. Individuating them by using wide criteria they are surely not – experiences of the Pacific and experiences of the Panama Canal are not the same. But the *character* of these – as bound up with the responses they inspire – would be, *ex hypothesi*, type identical.

13. The point is that in many cases there will be more than one way to answer Crane's criterial question correctly. Typically, we must distinguish between two things: (i) what, on any given occasion, a person or organism is *de facto* directed at or 'thinking about' (e.g. the presence of

measles, scarlet fever, the Pacific ocean, the Panama Canal etc.); and (ii) what on any given occasion an organism is *supposed* to be directed at or what a person thinks he/she is thinking about (e.g. the Pacific Ocean but not the Panama Canal, measles but not scarlet fever).

14. I spell out my positive view concerning this more fully in my reply to Myin and De Nul. In one footnote Crane points out that Lewis' original ability hypothesis was not reductive. He is right. But it is sometimes viewed as such. For the record, what I said was that "viewed as a reductive account of what experiences are, the original ability hypothesis is circular" (Hutto 2006b).

15. This would certainly fit with what Crane says in his commentary about our being able to refer to experiences by referring to the *objects* of experience in ways in which one could not before one had the experience. I assume Crane would agree that only those with a command of language could do this, but he also supposes that there is something – some content already – involved in experience to which non-verbals could make reference if they only had the wherewithal. It is the latter idea that I find objectionable.

16. He gives the following example: "the content of the sensation is that one's ankle hurts, the object of the sensation is the ankle (apprehended as one's ankle) and the mode is the hurting" (Crane 2003: 53).

17. Sterelny divides informational environments into three main types: those that are transparent, translucent and opaque. Most organisms make their way in worlds that are of the second variety.

18. Or, on other variants – which we should also reject – what the "senses immediately tell us is not the truth about the object, as it is apart from us, but only the truth about certain sense data" (Russell 1912: 6). The problematic idea is that senses serve to *tell truths* about something or other.

19. The core idea is – of course – deeply Kantian: "The data which sensitivity gives us is brought under intellectual control by the understanding" (Bennett 1981: 16).

20. I thank Jordan Zaltev, Göran Sonesson and Jen Allwood for their helpful discussions in Lund and Sweden in December 2005, which encouraged this change of banner.

21. Looking to evolution provides a principled ground for the notion of 'normal', but it also allows us to remain silent on whether or not a response is in fact performing its historically conceived proper function. In principle, to decide this we would have to determine whether or not the current conditions matched those which actually advantaged the organism's ancestors when the response systems were first selected. My bet is that in most cases there would be no such match: most existing organisms traverse very different sorts of environments than those occupied by their evolutionary forerunners. For this reason it would be improbable to suppose that our attempts to say what constitutes a 'normal observer' or 'standard conditions' by appeal to our current conventions, as has been the practice of some philosophers, will neatly match those that are evolutionarily grounded.

22. We should reject the general formula that: "an intentional object of an experience is *what* is experienced" (Crane, this volume, emphasis original). Such talk is promoted by a failure to recognise that: "the verb 'to represent' is equivocal. Used as an achievement verb, to represent something requires that there be something to represent. Thus Brentano claims that representing something in thought requires that there exists something for the thought to represent. But 'represent' is also used as a try word. You can represent the golden mountain even if there is no golden mountain to represent. This is what confused Brentano. The verb 'to represent' collapses the distinction between succeeding and trying or seeming to succeed. The teleosemanticist, in order to speak most clearly, should refuse to equivocate in this way. He or she should simply

deny that you can see or think of or represent what doesn't exist, refusing to use the verbs 'to see', 'to think of', 'to represent', and so forth except as success words. This avoids the confusion that results in the reification of special 'intentional objects' … what the philosophical tradition has previously done is to confuse actually representing with merely being in a mental state turned out by cognitive equipment designed to produce representations. Such a mental state may, of course, cause the mind to churn as though it were representing, but that does not produce actual representing. Teleosemantics neatly disposes of Brentano's reified intentional contents" (Millikan 2004: 66).

23. Crane seems to agree on the general conclusion but we have very different accounts as to why this result holds. He writes "on my view an intentional object is not part of what is experienced; an intentional object of an experience is what is experienced. Content, although in some sense part of an experience, is not part of what is experienced. So on my view too, 'object and content do not contribute to the phenomenal character by being part of what is experienced'" (Crane: this volume).

24. I once proposed that we are better off understanding experiences as modes of presentation not as referents (this was part of my attempt to make a clean break with the object-based schema when it comes to understanding what experiences are). But I now see more clearly the difficulties and attendant risks of this proposal. The metaphor of 'modes of presentation' can encourage the passive view of experience and promote the idea that experiences must have their own particular kind of 'content'. Robinson rightly observes that in presenting this idea "Hutto struggles to make out a view in which experiences 'should be regarded as modes of presentation, rather than as referents' (131). Readers of this discussion (131–135) will have to make what they can of the idea of an 'elliptical conceptual means of indexing' experiences (135) and such claims as 'it is better to regard consciousness, not as what is experienced, but as how things are experienced' (135), and 'there are more phenomena than those over which we can existentially quantify, at least… [if] the entities in question must be modelled as some kind of object which has specific properties' (134)" (Robinson 2006).

25. Such an account may even provide a respectable way of unpacking the idea of an affordance (this is another idea toward which I have been attracted but against which I have harboured concern about standard characterisations).

References

Akins, K. 1993. "What is it like to be Boring and Myopic?" In *Dennett and His Critics*, B. Dahlbom (ed.), 124–160. Oxford: Basil Blackwell.

Akins, K. 1996. "Of Sensory Systems and the 'Aboutness' of Mental States." *Journal of Philosophy* 113: 337–72.

Bennett, J. 1981. *Kant's Dialectic*. Cambridge: Cambridge University Press.

Chalmers, D. 1996. *The Conscious Mind*. Oxford: Oxford University Press.

Crane, T. 2001. *Elements of Mind: An Introduction to the Philosophy of Mind*. Oxford: Oxford University Press.

Crane, T. 2003. "The Intentional Structure of Consciousness." In *Consciousness: New Philosophical Perspectives*, Q. Smith and A. Jokic (eds), 33–56. Oxford: Oxford University Press.

Davidson, D. 1980. *Essays on Actions and Events*. Oxford: Clarendon Press.

Davidson, D. 1985. "Reply to Quine on Events." In *Actions and Events: Perspectives on the Philosophy of Donald Davidson*, E. LePore and B. MacLaughlin (eds),172–176. Oxford: Basil Blackwell.
Dretske, F. 1981. *Knowledge and the Flow of Information*. Cambridge, MA: MIT Press.
Dretske, F. 1988. *Explaining Behaviour: Reasons in a World of Causes*. Cambridge, MA: MIT Press.
Find, A. 2001. "Qualia Realism." *Philosophical Studies* 104(2): 143–162.
Fischer, N. 2000. "Review of *Beyond Physicalism*." *Consciousness and Emotion* 1(2): 318–23.
Flanagan, O. 1993. *Consciousness Reconsidered*. Cambridge, MA: MIT Press.
Hutto, D.D. 1998a. "An Ideal Solution to the Problems of Consciousness." *Journal of Consciousness Studies* 5(3): 328–43.
Hutto, D.D. 1998b. "Davidson's Identity Crisis." *Dialectica* 52(1): 45–61.
Hutto, D.D. 1999. *The Presence of Mind*. Amsterdam: John Benjamins.
Hutto, D.D. 2000. *Beyond Physicalism*. Amsterdam: John Benjamins.
Hutto, D.D. 2001a. "Conceptual Schema and the Problem of Consciousness." In *Dimensions of Conscious Experience*, P. Pllykkänen (ed.), 15–43. Amsterdam/Philadelphia: John Benjamins.
Hutto, D.D. 2001b. "Appropriate Quietism: Reply to Salucci." *SWIF book forum, http://www.swif.uniba.it/lei/mind/forums.html.*
Hutto, D.D. 2006a. "Turning Hard Problems on Their Heads." *Phenomenology and the Cognitive Sciences* 5: 75–88.
Hutto, D.D. 2007. *Folk Psychological Narratives: The Socio-Cultural Basis of Understanding Reasons*. Cambridge, MA: MIT Press.
Jacob, P. 1997. *What Minds Can Do*. Cambridge: Cambridge University Press.
Levine, J. 1993. "On Leaving Out What It's Like." In *Consciousness*, M. Davies and G. Humphreys (eds), 121–36. Oxford: Blackwell.
McGinn, C. 1989. *Mental Content*. Oxford: Basil Blackwell.
Millikan, R.G. 1984. *Language, Thought and Other Biological Categories*. Cambridge, MA: MIT Press.
Millikan, R.G. 1989. "Biosemantics." *Journal of Philosophy* 86: 281–97.
Millikan, R.G. 1993. *White Queen Psychology and Other Essays for Alice*. Cambridge, MA: MIT Press.
Millikan, R.G. 2000. *On Clear and Confused Ideas*. Cambridge: Cambridge University Press.
Millikan, R.G. 2004. *Varieties of Meaning: The 2002 Jean Nicod Lectures*. Cambridge, MA: MIT Press.
Moser, P. and Trout, J.D. 1995. "Physicalism, Supervenience and Dependence." In *Supervenience: New Essays*, E. Savellos and Ü. Yalçin (eds), 187–217. Cambridge: Cambridge University Press.
Papineau, D. 1987. *Reality and Representation*. Oxford: Oxford University Press.
Quine, W.V. 1985. "Events and Reification." In *Actions and Events: Perspectives on the Philosophy of Donald Davidson*, E. LePore and B. MacLaughlin (eds), 172–176. Oxford: Basil Blackwell.
Robinson, W. 2006. "Review of *Beyond Physicalism*." *Mind* 115 (457): 159–163.
Russell, B. 1912. *The Problems of Philosophy*. Oxford: Oxford University Press.
Salucci, M. 2001. "Before Idealism." *SWIF book forum, http://www.swif.uniba.it/lei/mind/forums.html*

Smith, A.D. 1993. "Non-Reductive Physicalism?" In *Objections to Physicalism*, H. Robinson (ed.), 225–50. Oxford: Clarendon Press.

Tye, M. 1996. *Ten Problems of Consciousness: A Representational Theory of the Phenomenal Mind*. Cambridge, MA: MIT Press.

Emotional experience and understanding

Peter Goldie

1. A shared emotional experience

You and a friend are on a walk, and you each pick a berry off a bush. She puts her berry in her mouth. She looks at you, grimaces, wrinkles her nose and curls her lip. You throw your berry onto the ground and you both walk on.

What has happened here? It would seem that your friend has had an experience. You know as much from the expression on her face. But more than that, you know that her experience is concerned with the taste of the berry, and that the experience is, to put it mildly, one of dislike. And more than that: you have learned not only about her experience, but also something about the world that you and she share as social beings: by her facial expression you can tell not only that she feels dislike of the berry, but that she is indicating to you that you would dislike it too. You know that it is not edible, and that is why you throw yours away without first trying it.

This simple story illustrates what our everyday experience can be like: we have, in the words of Dan Hutto's title, emotional experience, expression, and response.

2. What sort of account might we give of it?

My simple story, and others like it, give rise to all sorts of profoundly difficult philosophical questions, and all sorts of possible answers. Hutto certainly wants to give an explanatory account of this sort of story. But what sort of account might one give? There are several possibilities. One possibility would be to give a quasi-scientific account of what happens (typical causes and effects) in physically embodied things like us, with brains – to say 'how it works'. It might begin with a rather programmatic functionalist account, which could ultimately go on to pick out the underlying neurology. Another possibility would be to explain how we are epistemically justified in our beliefs about other people's thoughts and feelings just on the basis of their behaviour or facial expression. A third possibility would be to give a philosophical descriptive account that is faithful to the phenomenology. And a fourth possibility (there are others too) would be to give an account of how our concepts of emotion and of other psychological states are applied to ourselves and to others, and whether they are applied univocally, in spite of asymmetries in the epistemology; this is, as Hutto points out, a conceptual problem.

My understanding is that Hutto is setting out to reject the 'how it works' kind of account. He thinks that the so-called hard problem of consciousness, the explanatory gap, and other difficulties, arise inevitably with 'how it works' accounts. At least, he thinks they arise inevitably if we are in the grip of the wrong model of experience – what he calls an 'object-based schema', which treats psychological phenomena as if they are 'determinate objects'. I myself do not think that the difficulties arise only if we are in the grip of this object-based model of experience; I think they arise naturally as part of the contrast between the impersonal explanatory perspective of the sciences and the personal perspective involved in capturing what is to be explained.

The point can be put in very familiar terms[1]. When scientists give a true and full account of a volcano's typical causes and effects, of how it works, then we know everything about it – we know what a volcano is. There is nothing more to be explained. In a similar way, scientists (and philosophers as part of the enterprise of cognitive science) might try to explain, in terms of their typical causes and effects, a wide variety of states and capacities that are, broadly speaking, psychological: consciousness, perception, thought, sensation, reason, reasoning, free will, intention, emotion, memory, imagination and so on. And yet, when we know all the causes and effects of these psychological states and capacities, there is always and inevitably going to be something that at least appears to be left unexplained, namely the phenomenal nature of experience – the famous 'what it is like'. How could such phenomenology arise from, or be correlated with, or be identical to, these physical causes and effects? This question (and others) presses on us just because the impersonal account provided by the scientist treats the human being as an object of study in just the same way as the volcano is treated: as something that can be explained merely in terms of causal processes. The force of the question does not depend on one's being persuaded to adopt the object-based schema, whatever its particular merits or demerits.

3. Hutto's 'non-reductive variant of the ability hypothesis': three worries

Hutto says that he endorses a 'non-reductive variant of the ability hypothesis', according to which we should think of experiences, not in terms of what is experienced (where experiences become reified) but in terms of how things are experienced. What makes his account non-reductive is that 'it surrenders all explanatory ambition'.

Although I am very sympathetic to much of what Hutto says here, I have three worries about his account. My first worry concerns just what kind of account it is. It certainly is not the 'how it works' kind of account, for that has been rejected; it is precisely in respect of this that 'explanatory ambition' has been surrendered. But, although non-reductive, it is not obviously, or at least not only, an account that sets out to be descriptive of the phenomena, in spite of his saying at one point that "in order to understand experience we must give attention to what is involved in the exercise of certain abilities *descriptively*" (Hutto, Sec. 2, my emphasis). I think the idea, rather, is to provide a kind of historical account of our abilities, which appeals to both phylogenetic and ontogenetic principles. My worry here is partly that what Hutto provides is simply too programmatic. But perhaps this is his intention at this stage; more will follow in other work. However, as far as it goes at this stage, his account still seems to be entirely consistent with the kinds of 'how it works' account that he is at pains to reject. (Compare here the consistency of a historical account of the development of the heart with a 'how it works' account.) What one is looking for from Hutto, perhaps, is a positive account that entails the impossibility of the kind of account that he does reject; and this seems to be missing. To be clear, we do not want a positive account that entails the rejection of an object-based schema; we want a positive account that entails the rejection of any kind of how-it-works account, including those that, in being thoroughly impersonal in their perspective, have no mention of experiences in their explanation – only in their explananda. So it would be interesting to see – even in a programmatic way – how such an account might work; after all, it amounts to nothing more than the abandonment of cognitive science.

My second worry is that Hutto, in his entirely admirable rejection of what he calls strong individualism, goes too far in his historical account in emphasising the communicative function of our emotions. For example, he says, "we react and feel as we do because it is natural for us to see and be moved by specific expressions of emotion in others". Why do we feel disgust and fear? Surely an essential part of the answer is to do with the advantage that we gain, as individuals or as a species, in being able to recognize the disgusting or dangerous properties of non-human things in the world, such as berries and volcanoes, and our being able to respond effectively to those things through involuntary physiological changes and through voluntary action. Of course, recognizing others' facial expressions can also lead us to respond by being 'moved' emotionally ourselves. But, as Hutto remarks, we often respond with entirely different emotions to those emotions that we recognize –with fear to an angry expression, with anger to a contemptuous expression, and so on. (I will return to this point in a moment.) And, as in my example of the berry, we often respond without any emotion at all. The mistake of the individualist, as Hutto rightly urges on us, is to make our responses to inanimate things central and primary, leaving our inter-human recognitions and responses as peripheral and secondary. But Hutto perhaps goes too far in the other direction. There need be no priority in Hutto's non-reductive historical account between our ability to recognize and respond appropriately to emotions in other humans on the one hand, and, on the other hand, to recognize and respond to other things in the world such as berries and volcanoes.

However, and this is my third worry, in spite of this lack of priority there is something radically distinct about our capacity for what Hutto says we shouldn't call mind-reading: our capacity to recognize and respond to others' thoughts and feelings. We no longer animate all things (if we ever did), and volcanoes are no longer 'read' as being angry. But we do 'animate' each other, and angry gestures are read as being expressive of an angry mind. Hutto rightly insists that this is not an inference from people's facial expressions and behaviour; we do not "ascribe mental states [to others] by means of the cold inferential processing of such 'exterior' signs" (Hutto, Sec. 1). "Crucially," he says, "the 'perception of emotion' can be accounted for without introducing anything like the idea that the creature doing the signalling is doing so knowingly or that in responding appropriately the consuming creature is making any inferences" (Hutto, Sec. 4). We should all agree with this, although my berry example does show that emotional expression can be both genuinely expressive of emotion and knowingly deployed to communicate. Although such cases are not typical, it is well worth remembering that we give much more outward expression to our emotions when in the company of others than we do when alone.

However, Hutto seems to couple together rejection of the thoroughly implausible account of cold inference with having "strong grounds for doubting that appeals to tacit knowledge are necessary in order to explain how, in our normal environments, we reliably respond to the actions and expressions of others to whom we are calibrated and vice versa" (Section 4). So, as an alternative to tacit knowledge, he is led to appeal to Robert Gordon's idea of simulation as 'transformation' rather than 'transportation'. This, however, as has been shown elsewhere, fails to explain anything about how we grasp others' thoughts, let alone solving the conceptual problem of other minds. Rather, it presupposes what is to be explained[2]. As Heidegger pointed out, to appeal to empathy 'to provide the first ontological bridge' to the other subject is to get things entirely the wrong way round[3].

I know this is something that Hutto has dealt with at length elsewhere, but it would be helpful to hear what he has to say about another, more sensible, kinds of account of the epistemology of others' emotions that appeals neither to cold inference nor to Gordon's notion of simulation. One such account could argue that we grasp another person's emotion non-inferentially, in a way which is phenomenologically immediate, but which is nevertheless based on what we perceive – on the other's facial expressions and behaviour. Thus we could say that we can gain non-inferential perceptual knowledge that someone is, say, sad; we know that they are sad from the way they look (or sound), and yet we have not inferred that they are sad from the way they look. This kind of account has been well argued for elsewhere.[4] It does, of course, imply an epistemic asymmetry between our grasp of our own emotional states as compared with those of other people, but, first, this asymmetry is independently plausible and, secondly, it in no way implies any equivocation between first- and third-personal use of emotion terms –an equivocation which Hutto is surely right to resist. But perhaps Hutto's worry about this kind of account of non-inferential perceptual knowledge of others' emotions is that its plausibility does rely on the possibility that there is a story to be told, in terms of information processing at what is sometimes called the 'sub-personal' level, about how we are able to tell that someone is sad from the way they look. However, I would have thought that it is here that Hutto can bring to bear his historical stories, of training of the individual, and of development in the species, and thus can avoid any appeal to the obscure notion of 'transformation'.

Notes

1. See, for example, Nagel 1974; Levine 1983; Levine 1993, and Papineau 2004.
2. See, for example, Heal 2000.
3. In Heidegger 1962: 124.
4. See, for example, Millar 2000.

References

Heal, J. 2000. "Other minds, rationality and analogy." *Proceedings of the Aristotelian Society* 74 (1): 1–19.
Levine, J. 1983. "Materialism and qualia: The explanatory gap." *Pacific Philosophical Quarterly* 64: 354–61.
Levine, J. 1993. "On leaving out what it's like." In *Consciousness*, M. Davies and G. W. Humphreys (eds), 121–136. Oxford: Blackwell.
Heidegger, M. 1962. *Being and Time*. Tr. J. Macquarrie and E. Robinson. New York: Harper and Rowe.
Millar, A. 2000. "The Scope of Perceptual Knowledge." *Philosophy* 75: 73–88.
Nagel, T. 1974. "What is it like to be a Bat?" *Philosophical Review* 83: 435–450.
Papineau, D. 2004. *Thinking about Consciousness*. Oxford: Clarendon Press.

Embodied expectations and extended possibilities

Reply to Goldie

Daniel D. Hutto

1. What do I think I am doing?

Although he is generally sympathetic to my larger programme, Goldie – like Myin, De Nul and Crane – holds that my attempt to expose the philosophical damage caused by a misguided commitment to the object-based schema fails to get to the root of problem: i.e. the real impediment to our understanding of the emotions. He says what we want is “a positive account that entails the rejection of any kind of how-it-works account” (Goldie: this volume). It is not enough simply to have a “positive account that entails the rejection of an object-based schema” (Goldie: this volume). This is because, as he sees it, the desire to provide how-it-works accounts – and not merely those of the kind that model experience on ‘objects’ *per se* – is the true source of our tendency to misunderstand emotional experience.[1]

On this, I *think* we disagree. I say this in a tentative voice because Goldie does not offer a substantive critique of my diagnosis of the role I see the object-based schema playing in supporting certain kinds of ‘how-it-works’ accounts. For, by my lights, it is only *certain* kinds of ‘how-it-works’ accounts that should be rejected – i.e. those that seek to ‘make experiences intelligible in other terms’, for it is only those accounts that foster the insuperable metaphysical problem of consciousness. My claim is that the object-based schema plays a pivotal role in engendering the idea that *that* problem can be solved. For that reason, if it can be shown that it is a mistake to try to model phenomenal experiences on objects we would have the basis for an in-principle objection to explanatory physicalist approaches – at least those that are, in one way or another, committed to the object-based schema. In particular, any attempt to give a straight answer to the *how*-variant of the hard problem – any attempt to close the explanatory gap by supplying a satisfying explanation – is doomed to fail. Goldie is entirely right about which *general* considerations engender and promote interest in the metaphysical problem, but my aim in exposing the role the object-based schema plays in certain explanatory projects is to trace its *specific* and non-obvious source of the temptation to take the problem seriously. My aim is to show why we cannot – not ever – answer the question: "*How* could such phenomenology arise from, or be correlated with, or be identical to, these physical causes and effects?" (Goldie: this volume, emphasis added). Despite this – despite the fact that we will never know *how* – I maintain that we have good independent reasons to believe *that* the mental and physical *are* identical (Hutto 2000: ch. 5).

My philosophical approach is unusual in that I do not offer an all-embracing account or theory. Certainly, I would not dream of trying to provide a positive metaphysical account that *entails* the falsity of physicalism (see my reply to Rudd). For this reason, I cannot supply what Goldie asks for in the passage below:

> What one is looking for from Hutto, perhaps, is a positive account that entails the impossibility of the kind of account that he does reject; and this seems to be missing… it would be interesting to see – even in a programmatic way – how such an account might work; after all, it amounts to nothing more than the abandonment of cognitive science (Goldie: this volume).

Even so, we do not require a single replacement account in order to force a rethink of the standard assumptions of cognitive science (and most, if not all, of the traditional assumptions need re-thinking). I have however attempted to expose all *explanatory* forms of physicalism as hopeless by exposing their misguided commitments; that was my intention in *Beyond Physicalism*.

That my general approach is unorthodox may explain why Goldie isn't quite sure what it is that I propose to put in place of the standard offerings. He lists some of the usual options and wonders whether mine is a/an:

1. 'how it works' account;
2. 'description of the phenomena' account;
3. 'history of our abilities' account;
4. 'application of emotional concepts to ourselves and to others' account.

In my view, all of these accounts must be given if we are to understand emotional experience, expression and response; which one we start with will depend on the nature of the particular inquiry. We should not privilege one sort of account above all others nor should we attempt to reduce them all to one. The trouble with much current philosophical thinking, particularly attempts to supply theories of consciousness, is that this simple truth is not always appreciated – nor, indeed, are the consequences of failing to acknowledge it. Explanatory physicalism is a manifestation of this. All of the accounts above are relevant for understanding different aspects of experience – and moreover what we say about any one of these may potentially influence what we think about the others; sometimes what we learn about one domain may set new criteria of adequacy for our thinking in another. For example, recent discoveries such as inattentional and change-blindness have both challenged standard 'descriptions of the phenomena' in that they suggest that our experience of the world may not be as seamless and as all encompassing as many have supposed, and – on the back of this, new ways of understanding the mechanisms that underlie such responding have been proposed (see O'Regan and Noë 2001). This is but one example, but a quite powerful one, in which there is interesting cross-fertilization between 'description of the phenomena' and 'how it works accounts' but it serves to establish that such interplay is not only possible but valuable.

In encouraging a healthier metaphysical attitude, one inspired by Bradley, I hold that it is possible to address questions about the mechanics, intentionality, phenomenology, origins, development and epistemology of experience – each in their appropriate context. This does not involve providing a single overarching account or theory (programmatic or otherwise). Hence, the aim of the target paper and much of my previous work has been to (1) explore *what* it makes sense to ask in each of these domains and (2) to provide suggestions, sketches and proposals about *how* we might practically and legitimately prosecute such inquiries. In surveying the possibilities, and making them explicit, I hope to have been doing some clarifying philosophical work; staking out clear boundaries and exposing misguided ambitions and assumptions along the way (see Hutto 2003/2006: ch. 6). In particular, I hold that a strong case can be made for a developmental claim (both phylogenetic and ontogenetic) about the primacy of our unprincipled engagements with the world and others. But more than this, I also hold that these basic modes of 'feeling towards' remain in play even in sophisticated cases of emotional interactions between adult humans. Unlike certain evolutionary psychologists (those who promote the view that the mind is massively modular) I do not hold that we are *simply* ancient beings living in a modern environment. But in large part that is true – we are complex mosaics having inherited many of our abilities from a variety of ancestors, the last combination of *mechanisms* that support emotional expression and response having been passed on to us directly from our hominid forerunners. Modern humans are not hominids, but we owe the latter a lot. It helps therefore in understanding the full range of our emotional responsiveness to consider which are the more ancient and which the more recent, distinctively human, aspects of our ways of interacting with the world and others. This is true even in those cases in which it is *not* possible to disentangle or cleanly separate the basic from the cultural elements, as in those cases in which our emotions become re-formed through cultural training and education (here it is worthy of note that even our ancient ancestors had 'cultural' practices of a sort that are highly relevant to the ways emotional interactions are shaped, see Hutto 2007b). So, the reason I place such a great emphasis on historical accounts – even starting with the birds and the bees – is that I believe these can offer important insights into the *basis* of our existing interactions (Gallagher & Hutto 2007). And this exercise can also help us to re-think and perhaps see the nature and character of these interactions in a new and revealing light.

2. Embodied expectations and transformations

Goldie suspects that my construal of emotional engagements as 'unprincipled' may leave me unable to provide an adequate account of shared knowledge of the world – shared knowledge of the sort that is derived from perceiving the responses of others. As he sees it, I mistakenly "couple together rejection of the thoroughly implausible account of cold inference with having 'strong grounds for doubting that appeals to tacit knowledge are necessary'" (Goldie: this volume).[2] Connectedly, he thinks my preferred method of escape from the standard 'theory of mind' accounts drives me –unnecessarily – into the arms of Gordon's radical simulationist account and its ill-explicated 'transformation' metaphor. And since he is not at all impressed by what is on offer on this front, he wonders what I would have to say "about another, more sensible, kind of account of the epistemology of others' emotions… [that] we grasp another person's emotion non-inferentially based on what we perceive – we can gain non-inferential perceptual knowledge that someone is, say, sad" (Goldie: this volume).

Before examining this proposal in more detail, let me say a quick word about the use I wanted to make of the transformational metaphor in saying that we ought to 'follow Gordon'. I had not thereby intended that we should adopt his variant of the simulation theory when it comes to understanding basic emotional engagements. Rather my thought was that the transformation metaphor can and should be given a non-simulative grounding (this is a clearer and more direct way of putting what I have tried to say in my earlier work, see for comparison Hutto 2000, 2002). Nevertheless, I hold the transformation metaphor has real purchase. It is especially apt when it comes to understanding embodied responding and expectations of the sort involved in subliminal emotional contagion, motor mimicry and goal emulation. In such cases onlookers are *literally* transformed. And noting this gets the direction of affection the right way around – as I have long argued – unlike projective varieties of simulation. For in responding to others emotionally, typically it is what they do that affects and moves us (and *vice versa*). We do not first project ourselves onto them (or even into their circumstances). This is true not only in cases in which we mirror the other but also in cases in which we deploy more varied script-like modes of responding, of the sort that constitute the majority of intersubjective interactions.

What Gordon is surely right about is that our basic modes of emotional engagement operate "primarily at the sub-verbal level" (Gordon 1986: 170). Moreover, they are 'hot'; they directly exploit "one's own motivational and emotional resources" (Gordon 1996: 11). In saying that we should follow his lead my aim was to stress that any good account of emotional engagements must acknowledge the importance of these phenomenological and embodied features. I like Gordon's general approach for these reasons and also because it, like mine, is fundamentally opposed to the offerings of theory-theorists and certain other simulationists who insist that even basic acts of seeing another's intention or emotion are inferentially mediated.

But what about the idea that basic emotional responding yields knowledge that is based on a kind of non-inferential perception? As it happens, I think there is some truth to this, but great care must be exercised when unpacking what is meant both by 'perception' and 'knowledge' if we are not to go wrong. Thus while I am prepared to agree with Goldie's line, it is important to say a bit more about how I understand the nature of perceptual acts in cases of basic end-directed responding. To do so I will first amplify what I said in the target paper about basic worldly engagements. These are best understood in terms of Action Coordination Routines (ACRs) – routines that are indexically-inspired by organisms' informational sensitivity to natural signs; that sensitivity drives cooperating mechanisms in a way that sponsors characteristic patterns of response. Such selective responsiveness to specific cues (single or multiple) give rise to patterns of action that can be either simple or complex; but the point is that for most animal species – even the social ones – the general format of such responding will be *pre-scripted*. This is because ACRs are well worn hand-me-downs: working alone or in conjunction, the patterns of response of any existing organisms will have been good enough to meet the fundamental needs of their forbearers in their everyday dealings (however informationally hostile their home environments will have been). This is just another way of saying that standard response routines have been 'selected for' in historically normal contexts. As such, creatures who rely heavily or solely on inherited ACRs – of whatever sophistication – will run up against natural limitations; for example they can be expected to do poorly when they 'play away from home' – e.g. in those cases when they attempt to apply their stereotypical patterns of response in the face of novel challenges or challengers. This happens, for example, when they are placed in ecologically unusual situations. Of equal importance is the fact that even though ACRs might be extremely subtle and complex, for the great bulk of creatures, these routines are purely indexically driven.

ACRs that are highly fixed – and even adult humans have inherited some of these – have features that might be thought to be best explained by appeal to 'perceptual modules'. For the fact is that many ACRs are only sensitive to select stimuli and they sponsor reactions that are quick and characteristic enough to be counted as 'unthinking'. These are mandatory, involuntary and operate below the level of access consciousness. And, as Fodor would have it, they may be sub-served by mechanisms that have a relatively fixed neural architecture – one prone to specific forms of malfunction. Yet if I am right there are no subpersonal, subdoxastic representations – no mental states with informational content (see my reply to Crane). Therefore, even if we imagine that task-specific devices do in fact subserve at least some ACRs these cannot be identified with 'modules' of the sort postulated by Fodor and Carruthers. For the way such devices (should any exist) are responsive to worldly offerings does not involve representing these.

I reject Fodor's model of the mind based on a 'trichotomous functional taxonomy' of transducers, input systems/analyzers (i.e. modules) and central cognitive mechanisms (see Fodor 1983: 41–42). Perceptual signals do not have any informational content 'contained in' them to be acquired and then manipulated in the way that his theory supposes. Indeed, because there is no contentful 'input', it is – strictly speaking – a mistake to speak of 'input' devices, even purely perceptual ones. Of course, this is not to deny that organisms are complex mechanisms that respond selectively and sensitively to certain natural signs (signs which covary reliably enough with certain worldly items); many organisms robustly track particulars and kinds (sometimes using multiple sensory channels – and sometimes even using multiple channels within a single sensory modality – see Sterelny 2003: ch. 2). Nevertheless, if we think of these tracking and guidance abilities in terms of informational sensitivity instead of in terms of the acquisition of informational content, then the standard implications of talk of 'information processing' must be re-interpreted. Crucially, according to my deflationary proposal, 'informational content' is not first received *via* the senses and then further manipulated and formatted by specialised mechanisms (a process by which it is thought that much content is lost but only some retained). I do not deny that something like this process occurs, but I do deny that it should be understood in terms of the processing of acquired contents. Nor, for this reason, is the product of the process the creation of representations – representations which preserve the same basic content acquired via the senses, only re-casting it in a form that is "accessible to thought" (see Fodor 1983: 40). This is simply not possible if there is no 'received' content to be processed in the first place.

Those who endorse the 'modular' approach make the traditional mistake – the very one I complained about in the closing section of my reply to Crane – of confusing legitimate talk of 'carrying information', which can be explicated in terms of covariance, with talk of 'carrying information' in which contents are imagined to be somehow 'contained in' a signal. We can see the two ideas at work in Fodor's thought when he first introduces his construct of a module: "*Any* mechanism whose states covary with environmental ones can be thought of as *registering information about the world*; and given the satisfaction of certain further conditions, the *output* of such systems can be reasonably thought of as *representations* of the environmental states with which they covary" (Fodor 1983: 39, second emphasis added).

According to Fodor, there are two intervening steps that take place when informational content is reformatted so as to be used in inferential forms of cognition. The first step involves the transduction of low-level proximal stimulations (presumably, as Dretske would have it, this involves a reformatting of information from analogue to digital form). The second step involves transformations of the content that are post-transductive and inference-like but which are, despite this, not conducted by central cognitive mechanisms. Making transformations of the second kind is the dedicated work of modules. Thus: "the inferences at issue have as their 'premises' transduced representations of proximal stimulus configurations, and as their 'conclusions' representations of the character and distribution of distal objects" (Fodor 1983: 42). Hence, modules are 'interface' devices that take relatively shallow inputs, those having low-level informational content, and yield full-fledged representations as output.[3]

In contrast, by my lights, if there are any dedicated mechanisms that support specialised responding then these are best understood as devices that are driven by on-line indexically-based informational sensitivities. Each one would have its own designated task to perform and set routines for performing it but they would operate by the manipulation of 'informational contents' or 'representations'. In all, like Hurley, I take it to be a mistake to think of basic *perceptual acts* in traditional input and output terms (Hurley 1998). We must retire the thought that perception and action are in the first instance disintegrated, at least in basic cases of non-verbal responding.

Hardwired mechanisms driving fixed ACRs would be like Fodorian modules in that they operate entirely independently of central cognition: in pre-dating language-mediated forms of thinking and believing, they would have to be. Such mechanisms will have been fashioned to respond to specific environmental prompts, initially guiding organisms that had no beliefs – and *a fortiori* no background beliefs. In other words, the mechanisms that drive such responding will have been fashioned to function in creatures, our immediate ancestors included, that lacked higher-order cognitive processes of the sort that could have penetrated them in any case. This follows automatically if the creatures that relied on them were simply incapable of harbouring propositional attitudes (see my reply to Hobson). I take it, therefore, that indexically-inspired response routines are *naturally* cognitively impenetrable: they are in essence non-representational, lacking the kinds of forms and contents that would allow them to enter into *bone fide* inferential liaisons, full stop.

ACRs kick in without any background thought. And, surely, this is a good thing. If creatures had to wait for the top-down verdicts of central cognition before responding in the simplest cases they would be effectively crippled. Karmiloff-Smith's assessment of Fodorian modules therefore also applies perfectly well to basic ACRs: "They are the stupidity in the machine – but they are just what a young organism might need to get initial cognition off the ground speedily and efficiently" (Karmiloff-Smith 1995: 3). Indeed, without some such bottom-up responding to get a grip on worldly offerings there would be no way for 'central cognition' to judge, on reflection, *which* considerations are relevant to particular cases.

This does not mean that ACRs are impervious to influence by higher-level judgements – for it is at least possible that, in some cases, the patterns of response initiated can be controlled, overridden or overcome, albeit indirectly. In a significant number of cases, despite being directly unresponsive to reason, many of our unprincipled modes of response are open to education and training, learning and enculturation. This is true in the human case and seems equally true to some extent of other species as well: with effort at least some perception-response links of some ACRs might be re-tied.

What is true of *basic* worldly perception and action looks to be true of the social variety too. Many social engagements bear the hallmarks of being driven by modules. Consequently, unless we rein ourselves in, we 'see' and are irresistibly moved to 'react to' agency, animacy and emotional expression – *even* in cases where we know there is nonesuch. For example, seeing a series of illuminated dots that move in the particular manner or suitably animated geometric figures provokes characteristic responses from us – responses of the same sort that are evoked in encounters with genuine agents (Baron-Cohen 1995: 34, Nichols and Stich 2003: 95, McGeer 2007). The way we respond in such cases is on a par with responses to the infamous Müller-Lyer illusion: we cannot help but *see* two lines being of different lengths, even when we *know* that they are of equal length (see my reply to Rudd). In cases of this kind our routine patterns of response are not quelled even if we are in possession of the relevant background knowledge that no agency is present.[4]

This has led some to posit the existence of Social Intelligence Modules (or SIMs) (Currie and Sterelny 2000). These are imagined to be second-order modules which take in representational inputs from more basic perceptual modules – those designed to target social scenes – and which yield 'intentional markers', representations of specific social kind, as output. Examples of such markers are: 'means me harm', 'is friendly' or 'is angry'. In the place of SIMs it may be that there are hard-wired mechanisms that perform the very same social functions; that of driving certain fixed other-directed responses, but in a non-modular way – i.e. without trading in informational contents or subdoxastic representations. Rather, if any such mechanisms exist, they would sponsor Interaction Coordination Routines (or ICRs) – these can be thought of as sub-species of ACRs that have the proper functions of exploiting social affordances. In the simplest cases scripted patterns of response would be indexically prompted, inspiring the sorts of responses to another that *would be* appropriate *if* that other 'means me harm', 'is friendly' or 'is angry' (and, for most creatures, these reactions would be inspired because doing so was selected for in the historically Normal environments of the organisms in question).

Crucially, in acting on such perceptions, neither the organisms nor their internal devices are engaging in subpersonal operations of a kind that can be rightly understood as involving 'acts of interpretation'. They are not processing informational inputs that are inferentially transformed to yield intentions, predictions, explanations or any other contentful representations as output. Basic social responding is bound up with the characteristic perception of expressions which in turn foster what I call 'embodied expectations'. The visceral patterns of response these exemplify are best understood in terms of affect programmes which follow basic scripts, as I argued in the target paper (as inspired by both Griffiths and Goldie). I see no obstacle to including mention of the *character* of such reactions – understood in terms of sensations and feelings of the sort that are part and parcel of the ensuing actions or states of readiness to act. Only, on my account, these phenomenal 'aspects' are neither additionally generated phenomenal properties nor intentional contents; rather they should be understood in an actional way. I supply more details of this approach in my reply to Myin and De Nul.

In all, I propose that our basic unprincipled engagements – which are based on a sensitivity to signs that drive our acting on worldly offerings and interacting with others – are best understood as promoting a kind of responsiveness that can be explicated by appeal to biosemiotic proper functions. In the service of particular organismic needs, embodied responding and perceiving are thus, at least in basic cases, tightly bound together.

The crux is that our primary modes of worldly and social responding do not involve the manipulation of representations or any inferential thought. Primitive interactions – those of social animals (including human beings) – are not accomplished by bringing any psychological or behavioural theories (or principles) to bear. No comparisons are made with others by means of analogy. Rather it is sensitivity to the expressions of others – here understood widely to include gestures, stances, movements, etc. – that act as the relevant spurs. And the intervening cognition (or cognitive processing) is not fuelled by representational proxies that serve to indicate the 'internal' states of others. On the contrary, we are intentionally directed at the intentional and affective attitudes of others (that is what we are meant to target) by means of natural signs – the expressions of others. These expressions are reliable enough guides to 'other minds', at least in historically normal conditions. But it is not just the world-directedness of such informational sensitivity that matters; we must also always consider the way in which such signs are consumed by organisms. We must give appropriate attention to the imperative response patterns that they drive. It is thus more correct to say that we are *directly moved* by another's psychological situation rather than that we *directly perceive* it (or at least where the latter is heard in the way supporters of a model of passive perception hear it). Or, put otherwise, if we heed Hurley's corrective about the ties between perception and action and explicate these in biosemitotic terms, then I agree with Goldie that such responding can be understood as a kind of 'direct perception' (cf. Millikan 2004: 104, Bermúdez 2003: 37). Of course, saying this does not rule out that social animals can learn to control their emotional expressions or even to send false signals. It is just that these are secondary developments. As Wittgenstein observes "One can say 'He is hiding his feelings'. But that means that it is not *a priori* they are always hidden" (Wittgenstein 1992: 35e).

Having stressed my views about the non-representational nature of the prompts and internal processes involved in embodied responding, let me say more about what I take to be wrong with the received view of the 'outputs' of emotional engagements. It should be clear by now that, as I understand them, unprincipled engagements do not yield *propositional* or *factual* knowledge. Indexically-based responding serves to coordinate social interactions, but not by intellectual means. Thus to the extent that knowledge of the other or of the world is made available to the participants in such interactions, it will not be of the propositional (or of a sub-propositional, referential variety) – it will not be knowledge *that*. However complex, ACRs (and by implication ICRs) do not involve the manipulation of informational contents *via* inferential mediation, hence they will generate no more propositional knowledge than do the on-line responses that coordinate the interactions of ants or honeybees.

This principle holds despite the fact that many ICRs are more interesting and variegated than the interactions of such creatures. It is useful to get a sense of the range of possibilities. Some ICRs are fairly universal; others are peculiar to certain taxonomic families – even to particular species within these. The capacity to recognise and respond to animacy, for example, has very ancient history and is widespread throughout much of the animal kingdom (Baron-Cohen 1995: 33–43). And well it might be, given that being able to distinguish self-propelled agents from that which is externally moved would be important for the vast majority of creatures, even if they have no other social graces. Mammals, for example, are typically highly sensitive to the visual attention of others, and to binocular visual attention in particular (Sheldrake 1999, 2005: 11). This is a good thing. As nature is red in tooth and claw, it is particular important to know when one is being regarded or, worse, stared at by a 'pair of eyes' – and it is better still if one can discern whether the other doing the staring is friendly or malign. This latter requires more than being able to monitor another's gaze: it demands an ability to 'perceive' the intention or emotion behind such acts of attention – such as hunger, anger or sexual interest. These are expressed in the other's gaze, stance, movement or posture.

The capacity to detect and respond to these sorts of signals and signs is commonplace amongst social animals, but certain of the higher primates have abilities that go beyond this. They are adept at keeping track of complex third-party relations and, some of the great apes have shown some ability with gaze monitoring and eye-tracking and a limited sensitivity to perceptual access of certain others, such as competing conspecifics when faced with certain kinds of task (see Call and Tomasello 2005). There is even some evidence that some great apes can distinguish between intentional as opposed to accidental actions on the part of others, at least to some extent.

How should we understand such abilities? The most modest 'theory of mind' account on the market holds that *very* simple mindreading abilities might do the trick. Thus Nichols and Stich have postulated the existence of an Early Mindreading System which is driven by the direct manipulation of mental state representations and powered centrally by a practical reasoning mechanism – with the support of various mechanisms of other kinds (see Nichols & Stich 2003). Although 'unprincipled' in the sense that such systems do not entail the having or using of a 'theory of mind', this proposal nevertheless rests on acceptance of the Basic Architectural Assumption, according to which "the mind contains two quite different kinds of representational states, beliefs and desires" (Nichols & Stich 2003: 15). But ascribing such states to non-verbals, although a common enough everyday practice with instrumental value, is a mistake when it comes to providing a serious psychotechtonics. For example, despite strong evidence that apes are and hominids would have been capable of a kind of proto-logical instrumental thinking, there also are good reasons to suppose that this is driven by recreative imaginative abilities as opposed to the manipulation of propositional attitudes in acts of *bona fide* practical reasoning (Bermúdez 2003, Hutto 2007b).

Perceptually-based images and not propositional attitudes are the likely basis of such non-verbal acts of extended cognition. Such imagery can be understood as the result of the relevant perceptual mechanisms operating in an off-line mode (Currie 1995).[5] In such instances, non-standard triggers might result in non-standard responses; images rather than actions. For example, visually remembering something – as opposed to currently seeing it – may be brought on by seeing, hearing or smelling something quite different – something that evokes associations that literally *re-mind* us of the original. Animals capable of recreative imagination of this kind would be able to respond both to worldly offerings and the attitudes of others in flexible ways that go beyond being locked into reactions to what is immediately perceptually present. Cognition of this kind should be distinguished from purely indexically-based responding. The cognitive steps are off-line and iconically-based.

Nevertheless, imaginative thinking retains many of the features of indexically based responding of the more immediate perceptual variety. This is because, being derived from perceptions, the images that fuel acts of recreative imagining *resemble* their founders – indeed, it has been argued that they are in a very literal sense 'copies' or 'reproductions' of perceptual images.[6] Understood as having been created by off-line perceivings, there can be as many types of images as there are perceptions, including those associated with the perception of motor actions.

Being replicas of perceptions, images are restrictively bound up with certain types of activities, specifically those of the sort that their counterpart perceptual acts would have been operative. Hence unless extended by analogy, iconically guided actions are naturally domain specific. All the same, creatures capable of recreative imaginative abilities have additional abilities, such as the capacity to delay action – and more importantly to rehearse, plan and initiate new kinds of responses in outcome-sensitive ways. Such thinkers would not be chained to purely reactive, on-line responding that would tie them to signs immediately present in their here-and-now environments. In this way, they would be able to 'break free' (at least to some extent) from the sort of scripted ACRs that mark the behaviours of most animals.

Despite conferring this degree of freedom, iconic guides must not be confused with structured representations that have determinate propositional content: they do not have proper parts that denote worldly items nor, taken as wholes, do they say anything (they neither speak truths or falsehoods). Unlike purely indexical guides, however, it might be appropriate to think of them as 'presentations' of a sort because they can be objects of attention in their own right (indeed much of what we think of as consciously aware 'seeing' may in fact be perceptual re-enactments with particular attentional foci). Images, despite having some combinatorial properties, are not composed of discrete parts that connect in the way that logical symbols do (see Prinz 2002). Lacking appropriate internal structures, they are at best *only* capable of sponsoring associative and analogical modes of thought.[7] But even though they are not – strictly speaking – logical, images can surely act as the pivotal instrumental components in quite sophisticated off-line thinking and planning.

The point is that even if we suppose that such imaginative abilities are implicated in unprincipled forms of social engagement they should be understood as fuelled by the manipulation of non-propositional components – perceptions, images, motor schema, etc. For this reason interactions based on acts of recreative imagining cannot be construed in the way Nichols and Stich propose. This is because the boxes of their Early Mindreading System are filled with the wrong sort of contents. At best non-verbal animals might be capable of imagining *non-propositional* goals. But clearly their imaginative abilities would be limited. And, most importantly, as relates to the BAA, it is simply not possible for a creature to have a belief imagistically: it makes no sense to talk of believing an image, only believing propositions will do. This is reason enough to think that even sophisticated non-verbal intersubjective engagements only ever involve intentional but not propositional attitudes.

If we assume that chimpanzees had such extended imaginative capacities this may explain why their social dynamics are much more interesting than those of other primates – for while both involve multiple ICRs and require strong general intelligence to remember and re-identify patterns and particulars – chimp interactions have a noticeably more political dimension than that of other primates (Byrne 1999: 79). Still, the crucial point holds: in responding to others the reactions of these animals can themselves serve as *guides*, setting up a complex interplay. But however complex these interactions become, the creatures that rely on such prompts are steered and directed based on what is perceived in the expressions and responses of their fellows.

This brings us to the heart of the matter. For such creatures are also able to use the responses of others as guides, not just to the emotional states of others, but to how things stand with the state of the world. This is the point of Goldie's example in which one person learns something from seeing how another reacts to the taste of sour berries. At least some non-verbals, upon witnessing the reactions of their compatriots in such a case might 'get the message' – i.e. that such berries should be avoided. But it is easy enough to understand this in terms of their using the other's expression as yet another kind of indexical guide, one that moves them to respond to worldly features without thereby representing them. They may learn something important from such encounters but, for the reasons given above, we should tread cautiously in how we characterise what is learnt. Certainly, it is not 'knowledge' of the propositional kind.

Some non-verbal creatures can attend to and re-identify particulars (not just worldly features or kinds). This is, for example, true of rats: they have sophisticated recognitional abilities. Other creatures – possibly certain of the great apes and certainly human infants of a certain age – are not only capable of attending to and re-identifying objects, they can also attend to them jointly. This seems to involve, *inter alia*, mutual recognition of one another's attentional focus. Yet, I would argue that none of these abilities presuppose a capacity to represent the objects in question either referentially or propositionally (for further details see my reply to Hobson).

Recognising berries in the sense of being able to re-identify them is one thing, recognising them *as* berries – i.e. conceptually identifying them and categorising them 'as such' is quite another; it is something that must wait on the development of linguistic abilities. So, again, as long as we are careful in saying what *kind* of knowledge basic social interactions yield, I am quite happy to agree that we can "learn about the properties of the non-human world from the reactions and responses of others" (Goldie: this volume). To keep things straight it is better to say that, at the basic level, social creatures – including humans – can attend to the responses of others and to worldly features and to use those responses as a guide to their own.

A similar moral applies to those non-verbal expressions that are purpose-driven, deliberate and seemingly knowing. Such acts can be interpreted in richer or leaner terms. Richly construed, we might think that they imply an understanding of propositional attitudes – on the presumption that the communicator has an understanding of other's state of mind in such terms (indeed, this may require several orders of intentionality). It was once hotly debated whether chimpanzees had this sort of capacity for metarepresentational intentional attribution. In one famous case it was claimed that at least one chimpanzee, Rock – a dominant male, certainly did and that his understanding took a quite complex form. Thus Byrne and Whiten attributed to him the following thought: "Rock *believes* that Belle will *think* that he no longer *wants* to discover what she *knows* about hidden food" (Byrne and Whiten 1991: 131). But we have good reason to resist this characterisation given the now well-established consensus that chimpanzees are incapable of understanding the concept of belief (Papineau 2003, Povinelli & Vonk 2003, Tomasello, Hare and Call 2003a, Sterelny 2003). If chimpanzees have any understanding of another's seeing or knowing they do not understand these states in propositional attitude terms. Nevertheless, their interactions are complex enough to tempt us to think that they would be capable of this – and this, in and of itself, is important.

On the leaner reading which I promote, the expressive animal need only harbour non-propositional intentional attitudes towards another's attitudes. Its 'knowing' acts of communication – perhaps fuelled by memories of past encounters in situations with similar features, or even memories of past encounters with specific individuals who are counted as 'friends' or 'enemies' – need not be based on beliefs *per se* nor need they constitute an attempt to convey *propositional* knowledge, as opposed to complex attempts to control or direct the other's behaviour. Given that chimpanzees can interact in these complex ways without possessing the concept of belief, it should be clear that it is not necessary to represent the other's propositional attitudes in order to gauge the likely reception or value of such communiqués. Much more would need to be said to make this proposal fully convincing. I have elsewhere tried to say more, explicating in more detail what I call intentional attitudes (for more details see my reply to Hobson). However, for the purposes of this reply, it suffices that we are motivated to try to give such an account, spurred on by what we know both about the sophistication of chimpanzee social responding as well as its natural limitations.

It will be correctly observed that we are not chimpanzees. Nevertheless it is plausible that humans will have inherited at least *some* basic modes of social responding (likely with important modifications) from our simian ancestors (just as they will have inherited more basic ways of detecting agency from yet more venerable ancestors, systems that may also have been passed on to us). My supposition is that we come equipped, as standard, with a battery of low-level, specialised devices and set routines for conducting many basic, unprincipled social engagements. That said, while some ancient adaptations may be common to both humans and some of our non-human brethren, others – specifically those that rely on our powerful imitative abilities – may be unique to our branch of the primate line. In promoting the idea that a hominid capacity for imaginative rehearsal served as the font for powerful mimetic skills, Donald has convincingly argued that "By 'parachuting' a domain-general device of this power on top of the primate motor hierarchy, previously stereotyped emotional expressions would have become rehearsable, refinable, and employable in intentional communication" (Donald 1999: 147). This would have yielded more flexible and malleable modes of social interaction than seen in any other species – indeed looks like the best explanation of the wide range of refined and modifiable responding we find in modern humans. Such abilities would have opened up an enormous number of possibilities for expression and response, complicating social dynamics to no end. But the general principle holds: basic social interactions, even of this sort, would be unprincipled and embodied (even though they would be iconically supported).

All of this is in keeping with the idea that those capable of taking on a 'second' nature – those capable of benefiting from cultural training as well as forming and reflecting on explicit judgements about social matters – might modify and rescript their ICRs (or at least *some* of them) in important new ways (see my reply to Rudd). It is of no small importance that for linguistically competent animals – human beings – basic perception-response patterns *as a whole* can be objects of attention and reflection. The development of reflective abilities of this power would have provided the basis for vastly transforming the possibilities for and modes of our emotional engagements.

I take it that no inferential reasoning processes are involved and no propositional knowledge is acquired (not of the world or of others) in non-verbal acts of emotional responding. But, given that humans are language using creatures, it is surely the case that *we* can gain propositional knowledge on the basis of perceiving another's emotion. For us, I think uniquely, both possibilities exist. Thus deciding how best to characterise the 'knowledge' gained in any particular case may be tricky. Therefore, despite agreeing with Goldie that emotional encounters can yield a kind of 'perceptual knowledge', I want to stress again that the products of *basic* emotional engagements (even in the human case) are not propositionally-based judgements; they are not instances of knowledge *that*. My worry is that, without qualification, unguarded talk of 'perceptual knowledge' is apt to mislead on this score. And the same applies, *mutatis mutandis*, to talk of others *knowingly* communicating in *basic* expressive acts.

3. Extended possibilities and neutral responses

In closing, I want to say something about how we have come by the capacity for more neutral, emotionless responding since Goldie raises a question about this too. Humans have powerful recreative imaginations, likely inherited from our hominid forerunners. But decoupled iconic thinking is still embodied and visceral because of its re-enactive character, it is therefore quite unlike the kind of reflective or neutral responding afforded by the manipulation of truly abstract symbols. This latter capacity is something humans have to a degree that, indisputably, no other species does: it is the capacity to represent objects and situations using complex linguistic signs. A *kind* of reflective thinking is surely possible without language, but augmenting our cognitive toolkit with abstract symbols our ancestors would have been able to make new and better use of those pre-existing tendencies and thus would have had truly transforming effects. Used to enable certain forms of reasoning, linguistic symbols would have brought about a major *extension* of pre-existing practices, radically altering the space of cognitive possibilities. I follow Clark supposing that the acquisition of language was the 'ultimate upgrade' (Clark 1998:177, 179, 180).

I take it that it is the ability to engage in such abstract thinking that explains why we, but not every kind of social creature are able to "often respond without any emotion at all." (Goldie: this volume). Consider, by way of comparison, the plight of Sheba, a chimpanzee, who after years of intensive training eventually learned to use some basic symbols to represent different quantities of food. A series of experiments revealed that by deploying these symbols as intermediaries she was able to override her otherwise irresistible natural pre-disposition, shared with others of her kind, to reach for larger amounts of food whenever these were on offer. This proved important since in the test conditions her doing so consistently resulted in her getting a lesser amount. Much to her manifest frustration, Sheba could not overcome this tendency even after she apparently cottoned on to the experimenter's rule (indeed, the experiments were designed to see if she could master it). Yet after she was trained in the use of simple conventional symbols a new possibility in her behavioural repertoire emerged: she became able to curb her base tendencies. Representing the object of her desire in a more abstract way gave her a new means of achieving an old end. She was able to use the symbol as a go-between – as a kind of detached representation of the food quantity – and this freed her from her 'more natural', non-symbolic embodied mode of responding.

It is important not to overstate Sheba's abilities. To count as a truly autonomous act of symbolic thinking, one that meets the generality constraint, she would have had to be capable of using the symbol in question freely in a wider system of signs and across multiple contexts. Learning a handful of individual symbols falls a long way short of having mastery of a stable system of complex signs, ones with recurring sub-units: i.e. natural language sentences. This is what is required for a more sophisticated representation and properly logical reasoning about 'ends' and 'means' of the sort that permits reflective evaluation and freedom of choice of the highest order. This looks to be beyond the cognitive reserve of wild chimpanzees; for only those that have been enculturated exhibit any capacity for only very limited symbol use; this is brought home by tracing the painstaking and roundabout route through which Sheba came to be in a position to solve her problem. Her training required an extremely long regime in order to establish the relatively simple associative link between different quantities of food and symbols for these.[8] Nor did she reach a new decision about how to act based on a series of inferential steps calling on her pre-existing instrumental beliefs. Yet it is easy to imagine the greater kind of freedom and flexibility of response she would have had if she could have engaged in linguistically-mediated practical reasoning. Her mastery of even this basic symbol, although of limited use, was a hard-won but important achievement for this chimpanzee.[9] For truly emotionless responding it seems symbol use is necessary: we humans, of course, have the capacity in spades. Hence we are capable of blowing both hot and cold when faced with emotionally-charged situations because we are uniquely capable of responding on a variety of levels. In understanding our true range for emotional expression and response it is vital to distinguish these possiblities, looking carefully at the particularities of each case.

In all, I want to thank Goldie. His comments proved valuable for they have required me to state, for the record, in precisely what sense I think that the embodied expectations that feature in basic emotional engagements are transformative and why they should neither be understood as generated *from* propositional knowledge nor as *generating* such knowledge.

Notes

1. Goldie is very clear on this point: "I myself do not think that the difficulties arise only if we are in the grip of this object-based model of experience; I think they arise naturally as part of the contrast between the impersonal explanatory perspective of the sciences and the personal perspective involved in capturing what is to be explained" (Goldie: this volume, emphasis added). Yet he does not further support his claim that "The force of the question does not depend on one's being persuaded to adopt the object-based schema, whatever its particular merits or demerits" (Goldie: this volume). I have given details of the key role of the object-based schema in fuelling explanatory physicalist accounts in my previous work; I regret not having said more about this in the target paper. Not doing so has generated misunderstanding about the scope of my claims and the focus of my concerns and this has emerged, not only in Goldie's commentary, but also in those of Myin and De Nul and Crane. However, it would be interesting to see if Goldie's assessment would remain the same once my diagnosis involving that schema has been clarified, as I have attempted to do in reply to those others.

2. This is Goldie's 'third' worry. He also expresses a second: that my account may over-emphasise "the communicative function of our emotions" (Goldie: this volume). Thus while he endorses my rejection of individualism he thinks that I risk going "too far in the other direction" (Goldie: this volume). He urges that between the individual and communal functions of the emotions "there need be no priority" (Goldie: this volume). I thoroughly agree. I take this to be an open question and I had hoped that this was clear in the target paper. For I only ever claimed that once freed of individualist prejudices "there is no reason to deny that the function of at least some of our capacities for emotional recognition and response are primarily social" (Hutto this volume, emphasis added).

3. Despite the fact that modules manipulate representations of the right form and content to participate in inferential operations they are supposed to be shut off from the operations of central cognition. In a word, they are 'encapsulated'. A virtue of the no-content account is that it relieves the need to explain how or why the domain-specific 'representations' of the various modules are 'corralled' from the rest of cognition. For that view raises a number of important questions. Are representations somehow farmed out to a domain-general inferential mechanism (and then returned) every time a bit of intramodular thinking goes on or does each module have its own internal inferential mechanism? Perhaps questions like these can be answered, but we can avoid them altogether if we deny the existence of modules and the representational entities that fuel them. On the account I am propounding there simply are no logically structured representational contents of the sort that classical cognitivists postulate and so no need to concern ourselves with worries of this sort.

4. These basic response tendencies are in place very early on. "Psychologists have studied people's responses to filmed displays of points of light, produced by having people in a darkened setting wear reflective patches on their joints and at other places on their bodies. Normal adults can recognise the resulting display as indicative of a human figure, even with very brief display times, and infants of only three months old respond selectively to them" (Currie and Sterelny 2000: 158–159). Moreover, most adult humans have notable tendencies to focus strongly on social aspects of scenes and events, without being aware of this. This has been revealed by comparing the results of eye-tracking experiments conducted with both normal and autistic subjects.

5. If this thesis is true it would explain why images are similar in key respects to perceptual experiences since they are both produced by substantially the same mechanisms. That images are similar to perceptions in certain respects might be explained by the fact that there is only a *partial* overlap in the relevant processing paths (Rollins 1994: 355, see also Podgorny & Shepard 1978, Segal & Fusella 1970, Farah 1985).

6. Currie and Ravenscroft call images 'counterparts' of perceptions (Currie & Ravenscroft 2003).

7. It is easy to find those happy to catalogue, in great detail, reasons why "the imagist theory of thought is hopelessly inadequate as an account of all forms of thinking – or, indeed, as an account of any of our propositional thoughts" (Carruthers & Boucher 1998: 7, emphasis added, see Fodor 2003). This is perfectly true. But it does not follow that images do not underwrite non-logical forms of thinking and that these were used by our ancient ancestors.

8. There remains a tremendous gulf between ape and human capacities for learning symbols. Enculturated apes struggle to learn even a small number of basic symbols and the process is very slow (Li & Hombert 2002: 190).

9. Unlike in cases of purely indexically or iconically-based responding, this is a situation in which a simple public sign is being used to 'stand for' something, denotationally and referentially. Here we might *begin* to legitimately talk of informational content.

References

Baron-Cohen, S. 1995. *Mindblindness: An Essay on Autism and Theory of Mind*. Cambridge, MA: MIT Press.

Bermúdez, J. 2003. *Thinking Without Words*. New York: Oxford University Press.

Byrne, R. 1999. "Human Cognitive Evolution." In *The Descent of Mind: Psychological Perspectives on Hominid Evolution*, M.C. Corballis and S.E.G. Lea (eds), 71–85. Oxford: Oxford University Press.

Byrne, R.W. and Whiten, A. 1991. "Computation and Mindreading in Primate Tactical Deception." In *Natural Theories of Mind*, A. Whiten (ed.). 127–141. Oxford: Blackwell.

Call, J. and Tomasello, M. 2005. "What Chimpanzees Know about Seeing, Revisited: An Explanation of the Third Kind." In *Joint Attention: Communication and Other Minds*, N. Eilan, C. Horel, T. McCormack and J. Roessler (eds), 45–64. Oxford: Oxford Univeristy Press.

Carruthers, P. and Boucher, J. 1998. "Introduction: Opening Up Options." In *Language and Thought: Interdisciplinary Themes*, P. Carruthers and J. Boucher (eds), 1–18. Cambridge: Cambridge University Press.

Carruthers, P. 1998. "Thinking in Language? Evolution and a Modularist Possibility." In *Language and Thought: Interdisciplinary Themes*, P. Carruthers and J. Boucher (eds), 94–119. Cambridge: Cambridge University Press.

Carruthers, P. 2003. "Moderately Massive Modularity." In *Minds and Persons*, A. O'Hear (ed.), 67–89. Cambridge: Cambridge University Press.

Clark, A. 1998. "Magic Words: How Language Augments Human Computation." In *Language and Thought: Interdisciplinary Themes*, P. Carruthers and J. Boucher (eds), 162–183. Cambridge: Cambridge University Press.

Currie, G. 1995. "Visual Imagery as the Simulation of Vision." *Mind and Language* 10(1–2): 25–44.

Currie, G. and Ravenscroft, I. 2003. *Recreative Minds: Imagination in Philosophy and Psychology*. Oxford: Oxford University Press.

Currie, G. and Sterelny, K. 2000. "How to Think about the Modularity of Mind-Reading." *The Philosophical Quarterly* 50: 145–60.

Donald, M. 1999. "Preconditions for the Evolution of Protolanguages." In *The Descent of Mind: Psychological Persepctives on Hominid Evolution*, M.C. Corballis and S.E.G. Lea (eds), Oxford: Oxford University Press.

Farah, M.J. 1988. "Is Visual Imagery really Visual?: Overlooked Evidence from Neuropsychology." *Psychological Review* 95: 307–313.

Fodor, J.A. 1983. *The Modularity of Mind*. Cambridge, MA: MIT Press.

Gallagher, S. and Hutto, D.D. 2007. "Primary Interaction and Narrative Practice." In *The Shared Mind: Perspectives on Intersubjectivity*, J. Zlatev, T. Racine, C. Sinha and E. Itkonen (eds). Amsterdam/Philadelphia: John Benjamins.

Goldie, P. 2000. *The Emotions: A Philosophical Exploration*. Oxford: Oxford University Press.

Gordon, R.M. 1986. "Folk Psychology as Simulation." *Mind and Language* 1(2): 158–71.

Gordon, R.M. 1996. "Radical Simulationism." In *Theories of Theories of Mind*, P. Carruthers and P. Smith (eds), 11–21. Cambridge: Cambridge University Press.

Hutto, D.D. 1999. *The Presence of Mind*. Amsterdam: John Benjamins.

Hutto, D.D. 2000. *Beyond Physicalism*. Amsterdam: John Benjamins.

Hutto, D.D. 2002. "The World is not Enough: Shared Emotions and Other Minds." In *Understanding Emotions*, P. Goldie and F. Spicer (eds), 37–53. Aldershot: Ashgate.

Hutto, D.D. 2003/2006. *Wittgenstein and the End of Philosophy: Neither Theory nor Therapy*. Basingstoke: Palgrave Macmillan.

Hutto, D.D. 2006. "Unprincipled Engagements: Emotional Experience, Expression and Response." *Consciousness and Emotion* 7.

Hutto, D.D. 2007a. "First Communions: Mimetic Sharing without Theory of Mind." In *The Shared Mind: Perspectives on Intersubjectivity*, J. Zlatev, T. Racine, C. Sinha and E. Itkonen (eds). Amsterdam/Philadelphia: John Benjamins.

Hutto, D.D. 2007b. *Folk Psychological Narratives: The Socio-Cultural Basis of Understanding Reasons*. Cambridge, MA: MIT Press.

Hurley, S. 1998. *Consciousness in Action*. Cambridge, MA: Harvard University Press.

Karmiloff-Smith, A. 1995. *Beyond Modularity: A Developomental Perspective on Cognitive Science*. Cambridge, MA: MIT Press.

Li, C.N. and Hombert, J. 2002. "On the Evolutionary Origin of Language." In *Mirror Neurons and the Evolution of Brain and Language*, M. Stamenov and V. Gallese (eds), 175–205. Amsterdam/Philadelphia.

Nichols, S. and Stich, S. 2003. *Mindreading: An Integrated Account of Pretence, Self-Awareness and Understanding of Other Minds*. Oxford: Oxford University Press.

McGeer, V. 2007. "The Regulative Dimension of Folk Psychology." In *Folk Psychology Re-Assessed*, edited by D.D. Hutto and M. Ratcliffe. Dordrecht: Springer.

Millikan, R.G. 2004. *Varieties of Meaning: The 2002 Jean Nicod Lectures*. Cambridge, MA: MIT Press.

O'Regan, J.K. and Noë, A. 2001. "A Sensorimotor Account of Vision and Visual Consciousness." *Behavioural and Brain Sciences* 24: 939–1031.

Papineau, D. 2003. *The Roots of Reason: Philosophical Essays on Rationality, Evolution and Probability*. Oxford: Oxford University Press.
Podgorny, P. and Shepard, R.N. 1978. "Functional Representations Common to Visual Perception and Imagination." *Journal of Experimental Psychology* 4: 21–35.
Povinelli, D.J. and Vonk, J. 2003. "Chimpanzee Minds: Suspiciously Human?" *Trends in Cognitive Sciences* 7: 157–60.
Prinz, J. 2002. *Furnishing the Mind: Concepts and Their Perceptual Basis*. Cambridge, MA: MIT Press.
Rollins, M. 1994. "Re: Reinterpreting Images." *Philosophical Psychology* 7: 345–58.
Segal, S.J. and Fusella, V. 1970. "Influences of Imaged Pictures and Sounds on Detection of Visual and Auditory Signals." *Journal of Experimental Psychology* 83: 458–64.
Sheldrake, R. 1999. "'The Sense of Being Stared At' Confirmed by Simple Experiments." *Biology Forum* 93: 209–24.
Sheldrake, R. 2005. "The Sense of Being Stared At: Part 1: Is it Real or Illusory?" *Journal of Consciousness Studies* 12: 10–31.
Sterelny, K. 2003. *Thought in a Hostile World*. Oxford: Blackwell.
Tomasello, M., Call, J. and Hare, B. 2003a. "Chimpanzees Understand Psychological States – The Question is Which Ones and to What Extent." *Trends in Cognitive Sciences* 7: 153–6.
Wittgenstein, L. 1992. *Last Writings on the Philosophy of Psychology Volume 2: The Inner and the Outer*. Oxford: Blackwell.

From feeling to thinking

(through others)

Peter Hobson

1. Introduction

It is true: although many psychologists would make a (seemingly) respectful nod towards the idea that emotions have a place in explaining the workings of the mind, or that emotions might be relevant for how the mind develops in early childhood, there are also many who would cast a disapproving frown at the suggestion that emotional experience is pivotal for such accounts. In the current vogue for cognitive neuroscience, even emotional goings-on are subsumed under the term 'cognitive', and little wonder if they slip out of view altogether. Personally, I have had the experience of being treated with kindly indulgence as the 'affect man' in the world of autism research, notwithstanding my struggles to convey that my approach is as intimately connected with thinking as most other work in the field.

So Hutto is not tilting at windmills. Nor is his characterization of attitudes towards emotional experience unfamiliar. There is, as he states, a widespread tendency to treat experience as an object. Many do suppose that what we need to explain is how, from the stance of a spectator observing behaviour (or worse, behaviours), it is possible for one person to understand another as having a mind. The idea that our experience of other people *as* people with their own subjectivity is mediated by some form of inference is pervasive and pernicious. It perplexes me how innocently psychologists and even philosophers trot out the argument that understanding minds operates by drawing analogy from one's own case to that of others. But since I am a developmental psychologist and not a professionally trained philosopher, it would be unbecoming of me to comment upon the philosophical/conceptual aspects of Hutto's approach, even if I felt able to do so. On the other hand, inspired by Piaget, I do have a longstanding interest in genetic epistemology, that is, the conditions that make the acquisition of knowledge possible. So perhaps it may be worthwhile if I pinpoint where Hutto's account works for me, and where I think something more is needed.

2. Emotion and thought in developmental perspective

If there are indeed people who wish to analyze emotions entirely in terms of propositional attitudes, then more's the pity. The reason I say this, is because there is much about emotional experience and emotional relations that occurs *both* before a human being has the ability to think propositionally, even implicitly, *and* that operates at a psychological level that is more basic than articulated thought. In addition, the developmental route through which an infant and then a very young child needs to pass in order to arrive at the ability to think propositionally, is one that commences with feelings and the interpersonal co-ordination of emotional attitudes. According to this perspective, it is not merely that culture shapes our emotional responses like a sculptor shapes clay. Rather, some elements of culture are woven into the very fabric of our thinking, including our propositionally styled thinking, through the emotional engagements we have with other people.

Before I am carried away with the interpersonal aspects of all this, I should express my agreement with Hutto's approval of Goldie's notion of 'feeling towards'. The critical thing is that emotional life is relational, just as perception is relational. Relational towards the world-as-experienced, that is, and certainly not relational towards 'propositions' that merely articulate the aspect or description under which the world might be subsumed for a person. I am more or less happy with Hutto's line of thinking about feeling being a way of experiencing, if by this he means a quality of experiencing rather than a particular form of experiencing. I add this qualification because I think feelings are part and parcel of what makes experiences, any experiences, what they are. Indeed I would argue that similar issues arise in relation to attention: we always attend to something in such a way as to have a quality of relatedness to that something (or imagined something), and we would do better to consider how a person relates to something attentively, and not be misled into talking as if attention were somehow something added on to our psychological orientation.

I imagine that for people who think about babies, few are likely to disagree with Hutto that there are nonconceptual capacities for experience. That is not to claim that infants' experiences are in the same class as many of our adult experiences – they have what William James (1890) called sciousness, rather than the kind of self-reflective consciousness in which we are aware of being aware. And again, it makes a lot of sense to think of levels of consciousness as how things are experienced. Surely it is also appropriate for Hutto to highlight what are surprisingly common among cognitive psychologists (and perhaps, though I had assumed not, among philosophers): those lapses into anthropomorphism where the brain is said to judge, or assume, or conclude things. The excerpts from Millikan's work bring out how *our* seeing things as symbolic does not entail that the creatures or mechanisms that respond to those icons recognize them to be symbolic. Yet this also reminds us that we need to provide a conceptual as well as developmental map of how children do come to see things as symbolic, and knowingly so.

Somewhere in the heart of his discussion, Hutto considers 'the kind of ends that emotional experiences and their expressions are likely meant to serve'. I can appreciate the phylogenetic (and from a different point of view, the polemical) significance of such considerations. Personally, although I find just-so stories interesting, I also find them less than persuasive. It is something else that convinces me that we need to place the interpersonal aspect of emotions centre-stage in our account of human mental life and thought.

In fact, it is a set of something elses that convinces me. Firstly, it does not make sense to me that one can understand what a smile or an anguished grimace means – to take but the facial aspects of what are prototypically whole-body and whole-person expressions – unless one has what one might call 'feeling perception'. As Wittgenstein (1980) noted, it is *in* another person's expression that we apprehend joy or sadness, but we could not apprehend those states if we were not able to feel things ourselves.

Secondly, and connected with this, we are *involved with* other people from very early in life, as is well illustrated by a two-month-old's emotional reactions to a caregiver who adopts an unresponsive, still-face posture. If self-in-relation-to-other is a starting-point for social development, then as Hutto states, 'strong individualism does not make sense at this fundamental level'. The quality and power of our engagement with others throughout life is quite different from that which might be suggested by more intellectual accounts of social relations. Just as, for that matter, the kind of commitment we have to many of our thoughts and beliefs betrays how much more than computations are involved in thinking.

Thirdly, and critically, I believe that our account of the emergence of concepts of self and other *requires* non-conceptual, non-inferential forms of emotional connectedness and differentiation in the early months of an infant's life. More than this, I strongly suspect that the ability not only to recognize/conceptualise, but even to have, propositionally styled thoughts, is dependent upon interpersonal engagement and the forms of non-verbal communication that such engagement makes possible.

From a developmental perspective, then, I would resist the temptation to give primacy to the proposition component of propositional attitudes, and instead dwell on the attitude component. If a person's emotional attitudes and the behaviour they encompass establish the relation between that person and the world, then one can begin to envisage how personally-anchored perspectival takes on the world, and the descriptions-for-persons or propositions in terms of which those takes can be characterized, are constructed as distillations of what those attitudes entail. Elsewhere (e.g. Hobson 1993) I have offered an account of symbolic functioning, itself grounded in social-communicative transactions, as anchoring such distilled attitudes. If all this sounds like little more than a promissory note, I would add that if the starting point is for infants to register and respond *to* bodily expressions of attitude in others, in such a way that it is possible both to assume and assimilate something of those attitudes alongside one's own starting-state – and if, moreover, the other person's attitudes are perceived to have directedness towards the same objects and events that one relates to oneself, as is the case for typically developing infants at the end of the first year of life – then the scene is set for developing insight into person-anchored perspectives on the world. It is a matter of great import that, as Vygotsky (1962: 8) expressed it: '…every idea contains a transmuted affective attitude toward the bit of reality to which it refers'.

Let me express the matter differently. There are grounds for believing that a child's increasingly sophisticated concept of persons-with-minds is founded upon the twin foundations of a) emotionally configured experiences of people (whose bodies are experienced as expressive), and b) the ability to recognize and *identify with* the attitudes of other people, as these are directed to a shared, visually-specified world. The reason that these two aspects of early psychological development are so critical, is that they provide pre-conceptual bases for the one-and-a-half-year-old's newfound conceptual understanding that each person has a self with a particular perspective on the world. Along with this, the child also acquires understanding, prototypically expressed in symbolic play, that he or she can bring new meanings to apply to objects and events.

The upshot is that, in my view, epistemological considerations point to human social life, and the sharing and/or co-ordination of experiences, as the starting-point of growth in interpersonal understanding. For an infant or young child or adult to share and/or co-ordinate subjective attitudes with someone else, there needs to be some self/other structuring to experience, for otherwise the sharing (for example) would not amount to sharing. This is why colleagues and myself have been giving so much emphasis to the process of 'identifying with' another person as critical for early psychological development – and critical, incidentally, for the developmental psychopathology of autism.

3. Final reflections

And yet… I am not so sanguine as Hutto, that in the face of this kind of account of natural person-to-person emotional reactions, 'the conceptual problem of other minds evaporates' (Hutto, this volume). True, the problem is re-framed in a much more appropriate way, so we do not have to be preoccupied with the gulf between bodily appearances and what those appearances express, nor daunted by the gap between self and other. Nevertheless, the task of detailing just how interpersonal relations yield concepts in general, and more specifically, concepts of mind that are applicable both to self and other, over the early years of life, still presents a challenge. As does the task of understanding a condition such as autism, where such relations and such understanding are compromised. To take just one example connected with Hutto's discussion of selective attention: I think that the (often non-inferential, often non-intended) 'pull' towards assuming the psychological orientation of others is interiorised, in the manner Vygotsky (1978) described, and becomes a means to flexible, context-sensitive thinking within the individual's own mind. I also believe the relative lack of such interpersonal pushes and pulls accounts for a substantial part of the cognitive inflexibility and lack of creativity among individuals with autism. Yet there is much to do by way of conceptual analysis, as well as empirical study, before such an idea can be justified or refuted.

And then there is the question of self and other, and how, even beyond the rather constricted domain of mental state concepts, we come to experience and think of ourselves according to these categories. For example, as clinical accounts suggest and as we are currently investigating, children with autism appear to have very partial experiences and concepts of themselves and others as, for example, in competition for things or possessors of things. Yet there are other kinds of emotional engagement with others, such as relations of attachment or jealousy, that appear to be relatively intact among these children. So we still have much to learn about the kinds of emotional engagement, as well as the degrees of emotional engagement, that do the job of… well, making human understanding of thoughts and things, self and other, and the personal and not-so-personal world, quite what it is.

References

Hobson, R.P. 1993. *Autism and the development of mind.* Sussex: Erlbaum.

James, W. 1890. *The principles of psychology* (Vol. 1). New York: Dover.

Vygotsky, L.S. 1962. *Thought and Language.* Translated by E. Hanfmann and G. Vakar. Cambridge, MA: MIT Press.

Vygotsky, L.S. 1978. Internalization of higher psychological functions. In *Mind in Society: The development of higher psychological processes*, M. Cole, V. John-Steiner, S. Scribner and E. Souberman (eds), 52–57. Cambridge, MA: Harvard University Press.

Wittgenstein, L. 1980. *Remarks on the philosophy of psychology* (Vol. 2). G. H. Von Wright and H. Nyman (eds). Translated by C. G. Luckhardt and M.A.E. Aue. Oxford: Blackwell.

Four Herculean labours

Reply to Hobson

Daniel D. Hutto

1. Points of agreement

There is much about which Hobson and I concur – for example, he claims to be 'more or less happy' with my "line of thinking about feeling being a way of experiencing, if by this [Hutto] means a quality of experiencing rather than a particular form of experiencing. I add this qualification because I think feelings are part and parcel of what makes experiences, any experiences, what they are" (Hobson: this volume). This has long been my view, but I hope to have made my commitment to it clearer in that I endorse an ineliminable place for feelings in our understanding of experiencings in the target paper (see also my replies to Myin and De Nul and Crane). Nevertheless, as I stressed there, we must be very careful about what we imagine 'feelings' to be and we must also realise the practical limits – those set by our own perceptual and imaginative capacities – on how we can study and understand such feelings.

Most substantively, Hobson agrees with me in denying "that infants' experiences are in the same class as many of our adult experiences" (Hobson, this volume). This is of interest given the challenges raised by other commentators in this volume (see especially Rudd's commentary). Thus Hobson and I stand together in thinking that an "account of the emergence of concepts of self and other requires non-conceptual, non-inferential forms of emotional connectedness and differentiation in the early months of an infant's life" (Hobson: this volume). More than this, we agree that the development of second nature is a complex and transformative business for, "it is not merely that culture shapes our emotional responses like a sculptor shapes clay. Rather, some elements of culture are woven into the very fabric of our thinking" (Hobson: this volume).

Although Hobson recognises the polemical significance of my emphasis on the natural history of our recognition-response systems, he remarks that despite finding "just-so stories interesting" he also finds them "less than persuasive" (Hobson, this volume). For the record, my interest in propounding 'just-so' biological stories is not merely to persuade us to take interpersonal engagements seriously (though it is true that they aid that cause). They also play a vital role in helping us to understand: (1) the nature of basic intentional directedness and (2) the origins of experience (see my replies to Rudd and Crane). This is true even if we are less than confident that we can fill in the precise details. That said, I accept that focusing on the phylogenetic to the exclusion of other factors would be a grave mistake. For this reason the role I earmark for such considerations remains only a *limited* one (see my replies to Rudd and Goldie).

In all, Hobson and I agree about quite a lot. It may be for this reason that he raises a number of challenges for me rather than a series of objections. On a critical note, however, he questions my optimism about having dealt decisively with the conceptual problem of other minds. As he sees it I have not so much shown how it evaporates but merely re-framed it (albeit in a more amenable fashion). Technically, I disagree. Even so, I think – here again – we are united in spirit. The conceptual problem of other minds is an intractable philosophical puzzle about how it is *so much as possible* for us to have developed psychological concepts that apply equally to both ourselves and others (Avramides 1999, 2001). It arises inevitably if we assume an individualistic model of basic interpersonal interaction – one that presupposes that a strong first/third person divide is in place from the start. For, on this assumption, it appears that we have just two unpalatable choices. We either learn our basic psychological concepts by making essential reference to our own experiences or we do so by observing the outward behaviour of others. If they are learned in either of these opposing ways our mentalistic concepts will lack the requisite asymmetry that they appear to have – an asymmetry that allows us to apply them equally to both ourselves and others without special qualification (for full details see Hutto 2002). I claim that in rethinking the nature of our primary engagements we can crack this logical nut – and I see such nut-cracking as my main job as a philosopher.

The essence of my proposal is that this impasse can be avoided if we abandon the assumption that we come equipped with a mature conception of the self/other contrast from the start – and, in particular, one that is in place *prior* to the child's learning of his or her most basic psychological concepts. In contrast, I claim that our mature understanding of the self/other contrast unfolds in stages. As I see it, it is minimally based upon *at least* three kinds of distinguishing contrasts, including the capacities to distinguish: (1) oneself as a perceiver within a contrast space of perceivers, (2) an agent within a contrast space of agents, and (3) a bearer of reactive attitudes within a contrast space of other bearers of reactive attitudes (Bermúdez 1998: 248). I would add two others to this list: (4) a believer in a contrast space of believers and (5) a person who acts for reasons in a contrast space of others who do likewise.

Each of these self/other contrasts requires detailed attention (and we should also say how they interrelate). But if strong individualism is incoherent in the context of basic social engagements, then there is no hard choice to make when it comes to understanding the acquisition of mentalistic concepts. Neither first nor third personal perspectives could have been privileged in the beginning, for these would have only come into view at a much later stage of development. To accept this is to surrender to the idea that infants *could* be in a position to make 'self-other ascriptions' in their first interactive engagements with others.[1] The result: there is no conceptual problem of other minds – the very idea that there could be such a problem is only sponsored by commitment to a misleading picture of the character of our *basic* relations with others.

Very well: but Hobson is absolutely right to think that we still have *many* miles to go before we sleep. In clearing up the philosophical confusion we have at once opened a path for hard and interesting work. It is a long road that stretches ahead, and Hobson correctly identifies its important milestones. We need detailed accounts of how interpersonal relations:

1. yield concepts in general;
2. yield concepts of mind that are applicable both to self and other, over the early years of life;
3. yield concepts of the attitudes in particular;
4. are impaired with respect to certain conditions, such as autism;

I will say a bit about each of these topics, with the aim of sketching how I would take up the challenge and adventure of tackling the Herculean tasks that Hobson sets.

2. The emergence of symbolic thinking

Hobson is absolutely right to "resist the temptation to give primacy to the proposition component of propositional attitudes, and instead dwell on the attitude component" (Hobson: this volume). I would add that in order to understand the attitudes we must also get to grips with what it is to be directed at worldly offerings in non-content involving ways. I attempted this some time ago by introducing the notion of intentional attitudes (see Hutto 1999: ch. 4).

There can be no doubt that to successfully execute actions animals must be informationally sensitive to select features of their environments – typically in indexical ways. This sensitivity should be understood as having been selectively forged by end-directed needs to respond appropriately to particular kinds of things and states of affairs. This fact explains why many of the outward behaviours of non-verbal animals are sophisticated enough to warrant interpretation using folk psychological apparatus. Watching cat and mouse antics, for example, offers a spectacle of high-level anticipatory predator/prey interactions in which the participants exhibit knowledge of their legendary opponents (i.e. knowledge of the sorts of things that cats and mice are, in general, likely to do). Moreover, such interplay involves more than general understanding; each animal must also form expectations about what their current adversary, as a token of a more general type, is doing or is about to do in light of the particular circumstances (i.e. 'Jerry is about to scurry behind that obstacle'; 'Tom is giving me space to run', etc.).

It is quite compelling – almost irresistible – for us to want to say that such creatures are acting out of beliefs and desires – even if we stop short of supposing that they can ascribe such states of mind to one another. We see them as weighing up possible courses of action, comparing them against others and assessing these in light of their strongest desires (presumably, they do all this at an unreflective sub-organismic level). Minimally, it seems that they reason practically about what to do next. The product of such reasoning is the formation of 'intentions-to-act', where these are understood as some kind of motivating imperative (e.g. 'Leap to the right', 'Make a run for it').

In standard parlance, such processes of reasoning are described in fully fledged mentalistic terms – Tom *wants* to catch Jerry and he *thinks* that Jerry will appear from his hiding spot just here and right about now. And if Jerry fails to do so, it is Tom's false belief that putatively explains his ineffective mouse-catching behaviour on this occasion. It is not uncommon to hear claims such as the following:

> A cat is conscious, I assume, and it *has the sort of consciousness whose content can be put into words* only with the help of the first person pronoun. A cat *could never* catch a mouse if it couldn't have thoughts representing the world from its own egocentric perspective, thoughts with the English-language equivalents such as 'I'm gaining on it' or 'I've got it' (Velleman 2004: 2, emphases added).

However tempting they may be, it is just these sorts of content ascriptions that must be avoided. The waters here are muddied because our command of the folk psychological schema enables us to make crude generalisations, which work in predicting the behaviour of many, many things – even those to which we clearly would *not* want to seriously ascribe beliefs and desires. For this reason there is an uninteresting sense in which folk psychological predicates can be *applied to* non-verbal responding. But this neither commits one to the supposition that such responding *in fact* (or really) involves the harbour of propositional attitudes nor that the organisms in question are genuinely capable of reasoning about means to end in 'deciding' on a course of action by manipulating such attitudes.[2]

And no creature can engage in *bona fide* practical reasoning unless it manipulates internally-structured propositional representations. It is not enough for such representations to be intentionally directed at a particular states of affairs, they must be compositionally structured. Consider our cat again. Tom can only form an intention-to-act in the way described above if we assume that he apprehends the state of affairs concerning Jerry's location under a given mode of presentation. Moreover, this mode of presentation must have a structured format of the right kind if it is to be tied at significant points with the mode of presentation under which Tom apprehends the relevant desired state of affairs (i.e. his apprehension of Jerry). Crudely, his beliefs and desires must have the right forms and contents if they are to interrelate logically, so as to join forces in the formation of intentions. Only if they have such features is it possible that they can serve as motivating reasons.[3]

Against the dominant trend of thought, I hold that non verbals are not practical reasoners in this sense. The world-directed actions of Tom and Jerry are best explained in terms of *intentional* rather than propositional attitudes; or, if you like, in terms of propositional attitudes *extensionally* rather than *intensionally* construed.[4] In saying this I am not motivated by the epistemological worry that we cannot specify precisely under which mode of presentation Tom represents the state of affairs 'Jerry will emerge here and now' (compare by way of contrast the fact that we can know roughly what it is that the cat is directed at – what its putative 'belief' is about, in extension). My complaint is more fundamental. It is rather that in order to explain the way in which nonverbals are 'normally' attuned to certain worldly offerings (and why, on some occasions they are not) we should not (and need not) invoke the idea that they are directed at structured representations of the intensional variety. That sort of contentful attribution is neither needed nor warranted. The non-verbal intentional attitudes of animals, infants and even those of adult humans are not to be understood in contentful terms, *full stop* (see my replies to Crane and Goldie). Non-verbal responding is not content-involving. And animals and infants are only capable of harbouring intentional attitudes, not propositional ones.

For a creature to have an attitude directed at a proposition – for it to apprehend a state of affairs intensionally so to speak – it must have the capacity to direct its attention at that state of affairs *via* structured vehicles of some appropriate sort (the public sentences of natural language are the paradigm). Since I reject the Language of Thought hypothesis, for me, the only vehicles that permit this are uniquely those of natural languages – their complex public symbols alone allow us to conduct the kind of logical operations that depend on having a compositional semantics. For members of the species *Homo sapiens sapiens*, the sentences of such languages are mediums that enable us to focus on new objects of attention, the propositions expressed by such sentences. It is competence with language that enables humans to have *propositional* attitudes and to conduct acts of practical reasoning based on these.

The story of exactly how this happened in our pre-history is extremely complex and not something I could provide in complete detail (nor, being a philosopher by trade, do I see this as my job). It is possible, however, to say something about the logic of such developments – i.e. to identify which capacities would have had to come first in the order of things. Indeed, in seeking an intellectually satisfying account it should be possible to go further and say a bit about the mechanisms and practices that provided the platforms for the various stages of this development.
It is generally supposed that there must have been a major cognitive upgrade (more likely a series of upgrades) in the hominid line that explains the special set of cognitive abilities associated with the emergence of the first humans. Some think this took the form, *inter alia*, of the introduction of a series of special-purpose modules; task-specific mechanisms which contain specialised knowledge in representational form. Substantially reconstructed, along the line of mechanisms that support non-representational action coordination routines, this may be part of the story. However, I hold that, overshadowing this was the development of a capacity for recreative imagination of the sort detailed in my reply to Goldie. A new brand form of domain-general intelligence was added to the basic cognitive equipment during this period (or a vastly improved version, on the assumption that apes already had some abilities in this regard).[5]

The big features of my proposal can be best illustrated if we make some important modifications to Mithen's cathedral model of psychotechtonic architecture (see Figure 12.1, modified from Mithen 1996: ch. 4).[6] Like Mithen, I take it that the most ancestral modes of cognition are bound up with capacities for associative, trial-and-error learning – which for him fall under the heading of 'general intelligence'. Hence, the earliest and most fundamental structure of the mind, like that of the simplest churches, is represented by a nave, standing on its own.

This nave is eventually encompassed by four self-contained, radiating chapels, each devoted to one of distinct domain-specific competencies, which he identifies as: technical, social, natural history and linguistic intelligences.[7] While some others would seek to characterise 'intelligences' in terms of 'modules' or 'folk theories' relating to physics, psychology, biology and grammar, I object to such characterisations. In my view, there are no non-linguistic representational contents to fuel the putative inferential acts in which such mechanisms are supposed to engage. Softer talk of competencies, in line with my proposals about action coordination routines, is therefore to be preferred.[8] Thus, to take one prominent example, human children inherit a language-ready brain which prepares them for the rapid acquisition of language but this does not imply the existence of a special kind of psychological mechanism that incorporates 'a theory of grammar'; if I am right there is no sub-personal device decked out with the appropriate concepts and principles concerning the behaviour of linguistic universals.[9]

In any case, for us the main point of interest is that Mithen only postulates three major moments in the construction of the cathedral of the mind. I add a fourth, proposing that a transept of recreative imagination must have been added in the third phase – probably at an early point during the hominid evolution – during the reign of *H. erectus*. This will have made for cruciform layout, offering additional domain-general central support to all of the pre-existing chapels. It would have provided iconic resources enabling off-line responding and instrumental planning within specified domains. Moreover, it would have permitted some cross-domain commerce by means of analogy and metaphor (of the non-linguistic variety). These imaginative abilities would have provided a basis for interpersonal and mimetic abilities that pre-dated full linguistic competence (see Hutto 2007 for full details).

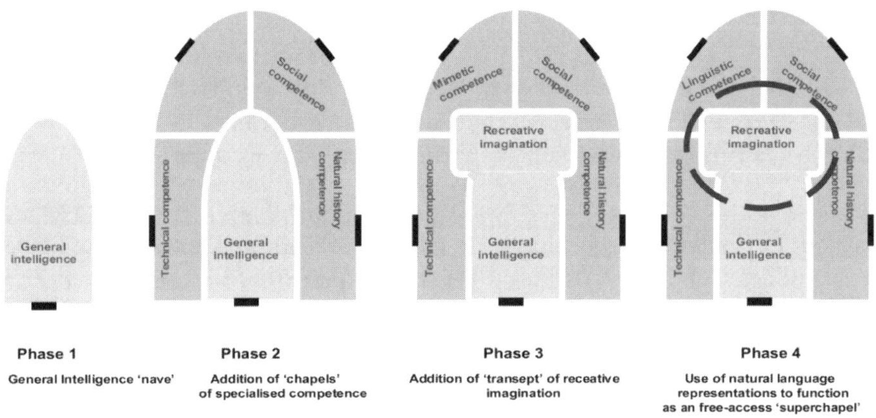

Figure 12.1 Mithen's Cathedral – with modifications

As impressive as this development would have been, it would not have permitted the kind of free flow of movement between domains afforded by the inferential manipulation of abstract symbols (of which more in a moment). Yet it would have made space for sophisticated non-verbal intersubjective engagements, such as joint attention involving intentional attitudes – engagements that may otherwise be hard to account for without invoking full-fledged 'theory of mind' abilities.

The phenomenon of joint attention deserves special comment since it is a sophisticated kind of triangulation – one of a quite different order from other kinds of more basic interactive responding, such as declarative pointing, gaze following and social referencing. For an account of joint attention requires explicating how object-focused triangles are formed. And more – it requires an explanation of how, "two or more subjects [can] focus their perception simultaneously, as a consequence of attending to each other, on a shared object of attention" (Brinck 2004: 194–195).

It can look as if such triangulation is in debt to the services of some kind of inference-based theory of mind abilities. For awareness of another's visual take on a situation can certainly seem to require a capacity to make 'inferences from me to you' based on assumptions of similarity (i.e. the assumption that you and I are alike in relevant psychological respects – at least at some level). Thus, while it may be conceded that Interaction Coordination Routines (ICRs), as described in my reply to Goldie, and mimetic abilities might underwrite social interaction in a wide range of basic cases, to some it seems that genuine joint attention entails the application of full fledged mindreading abilities involving propositional attitudes. But it ain't necessarily so. There are richer and leaner ways of understanding even this more sophisticated form of intersubjectivity (Carpendale & Lewis 2004: 85).

It helps to break the phenomenon up a bit before trying to understand it. Those engaged in non-verbal acts of joint attention must be capable of:

1. Harbouring intentional attitudes – not propositional ones (Hutto 1999: ch. 3, 4);
2. Relating to objects experientially (Hutto 2000: ch. 1, § 3);[10]
3. Recognising that one's response and that of the other are co-directed.

The final condition is the killer. It requires attending, not just to the other's behaviour but to "the intention behind the behaviour (yet without entertaining higher order thoughts about it)" (Brinck 2004: 196). Apart from a capacity to identify with the other, what is also required, it seems, is a complex ability to shift one's attention across two axes – focusing both perceptually on some worldly focal point (objects, events, etc.) and intersubjectively on attention of the other to the same. It is often assumed that as the latter is not just a mechanical tracking of gaze: it requires a kind of simulative leap.[11] Simulation is often presented as being a kind of imaginative attempt to adopt another's perspective on events, a coming to see how the world looks from the other's perspective. It is as if I had climbed in behind your eyes, while at the same time recognising that I am not you.

Something like this may be needed to account for the understanding of distinct perceptual takes that occurs in nonlinguistic forms of joint attention. But in explaining the basis of this ability, there is no reason to suppose that rudimentary forms of nonlinguistic shared attention involves making full fledged propositional attitude ascriptions. Seeing another's seeing does not involve representing the other's *cognitive* take, it only requires recreatively imagining the other's *perceptual* one.[12]

Apart from enabling this kind of perspective shifting (and visual perspective shifting in particular), the development of the recreative imagination would have laid the ground for sophisticated imitative abilities and thus the unique kind of mimetic competence we can suppose our ancestors enjoyed. This would have vastly altered the possibilities for expressing and responding to emotions; making possible flexible new forms of intersubjective engagement. I claim that the Mimetic Ability Hypothesis (or MAH) is abductively superior in accounting for the key stages of hominid development as compared with rival proposals that make appeal to theory of mind mechanisms (see Hutto 2007a, 2007b. 2007c). Indeed, it is very plausible that a capacity for mime was the bridge from perceptually-based forms of joint attention to triadic referential acts involving the use of symbols.

The idea is that iconically-based thinking of sort sponsored by the recreative imagination would have made cross-domain analogies possible (see my reply to Goldie). Miming may have been the ultimate – if unstable – basis for directing another's attention to some distal, absent something (a happening, an action or an object). This may have been achieved by drawing on bonds of association holding between certain features the thing designated and certain features of a particular mimetic act.[13] For example, highly stylised gestures, such as wriggling one's arm in slithering fashion may remind another of snakes might have been used (rather like what goes on in the game of charades). This kind of act would have been used in a quasi-symbolic way, without thereby signalling the actual presence of snakes (or inspiring any of the other characteristic responses that encounters with real snakes normally call forth). To wriggle one's arm in such a way so as to trigger thoughts of snakes is not an imperative act. It does not prompt the other to run, nor is it a signal to get the other to use their arms in similar ways. Rather it is an attempt, albeit a crude one, at symbolism.

Even a rudimentary capacity to use and appreciate mime would have brought unheralded degrees of freedom and new possibilities for communication.[14] In key respects, its advent would have made the character of our ancestors' first communicative efforts, quite literally, 'dramatically' different from the sorts of signals used for coordination by other animals. Still, lacking a conventional basis, early mimetic acts would have traded only on 'resemblances', thus they will have depended upon the existence or forging of powerful associations for their success. It is not easy to communicate by means of pantomime, for it requires that others make the appropriate connections: one's partner must recognise the *significance* of the communicative act. And to be sure this is a hit and miss affair: definitely more miss than hit, unless the miming is supplemented in important ways. For example, such acts can be made more reliable through the use of conventionalised gestures: these help with disambiguating the 'meaning'.

There are serious proposals afoot about how simple mimicry and basic pantomime might have eventually given way to the first, if still very basic detached symbols. The idea is that mimetically-based modes of co-referring prepared the ground for the fashioning of a more abstract symbol system – one eventually cut free from, although initially rooted in, strong associations. We can see the kind of process that was likely involved in the generation of a basic public symbol system in the context of Chinese calligraphy. Arbib provides an example of how the pictograph for 'mountain' started life in this form:  – having some prominent features resembling, in outline, that of which it is an icon. But we can imagine how it slowly took on its decidedly more abstract current form of ; this being a modification of the intermediate symbol  (Vaccari and Vaccari 1961).

Using manual iconic gestures rather than written signs, early mimetic acts may have followed similar conventional paths towards abstraction. This, it is speculated, may have resulted in a kind of proto-sign. Its forging would have been an important move away from the kinds of potentially unreliable mimetic acts described above and a step toward publicly established systems of conventional symbols.[15] Arbib provides a handy and very plausible outline of a likely seven stage development of linguistic competence, reproduced below.

1. Grasping;
2. A mirror system for grasping (i.e. a system that matches observation and execution);
3. A simple imitation system for grasping;
4. A simple imitation system for grasping (underpinning pantomime – permitting the miming of actions outside the panto-mimic's own behavioural repertoire (e.g., flapping the arms to mime a flying bird);
5. 'Protosign' comprising conventionalized manual (and related oro-facial) communicative gestures. Conventional gestures are used to formalize and disambiguate pantomime (e.g., to distinguish 'bird' from 'flying');
6. 'Protospeech': a vocal-based communication systems which breaks through the closed nature of primate vocalizations as a result of the 'invasion' of the vocal apparatus by collaterals form the communication system based on F5/Broca's area;
7. Language: the change from the action-object frames to the verb-argument structures to syntax and semantics: co-evolution of cognitive and linguistic complexity (from Arbib 2003: 192 and 2005).

Special care must be exercised when it comes to understanding the role and nature of the conventions that act as a putative foundation for basic linguistic practice in stage five. Drawing an important conclusion from his radical interpretation thought experiment, Davidson notoriously claimed that when it comes to understanding others, at root "the notion of a language, or of two people speaking the same language does not seem to be needed" (Davidson 1984: 157). This is often read as a claim that in radical interpretation we must develop speaker-relative theories of meaning. Speaker meaning, as understood by Davidson, is not determined by appeal to the practices of linguistic communities but by unearthing the best possible T-theory for a particular individual's utterance, a T-theory that will be different at different times (see Hutto 1999b, ch. 5).

For this reason, Davidson bade us to recognise that the very notions of 'languages' and 'language communities' are terms of practical convenience – they are idealisations, useful because in daily life they allow us to make some standard, quick and dirty, assumptions about the way speakers are using their words. It is only with the advent of stable conventional uses that, "language devices have an independent source of function. They are selected for outcomes satisfactory at once to both partners in communication. They have their own natural purposes, often coincident with, but derived separately from, the purposes of individual speakers and individual hearers who use them" (Millikan 2001: 400). Echoing Davidson's conclusion, yet reaching it from a different direction, Millkan remarks that "strictly speaking, on this view there is no such thing 'as language'. There are only large raggedy collections of reproducing patterns" (Millikan 2001: 404). Talk of an utterance belonging to this or that natural language is of practical value, reflecting the fact that we do not have the time or energy to engage in the serious interpretation of individual speakers each and every time one opens his or her mouth.

Despite this, it is clear that *ultimately* in interpreting the communicative acts of others, even of those who speak our home 'language', we do not *have to* depend on fixed practices or conventions about the use of words. Inverting received thinking on this topic Davidson insists that, "convention is not a condition of language. I suggest, then, that philosophers who make convention a necessary element of language have the matter backwards. The truth is rather that language is a condition for having conventions" (Davidson 1984: 280).

Stated in this bald form, I take issue with this last claim for two reasons. Firstly, establishing conventions about the use of linguistic labels is *necessary* for and *prior to* the development of compositional syntax and semantics. Secondly, it is pretty clear that not all conventions are linguistically-based. There is no bar to thinking that conventions hammered out through associations forged in mimetically-based practice could not have provided an essential basis for fully symbolic language. The second-order miming of one another's mimetic acts – which Donald calls 'reciprocal mimesis' – is a plausible explanation of how non-linguistic conventions might have been first established (Donald 1991: ch. 6).

We must be especially careful in explicating this idea. Basic co-referential acts of miming are intentional acts in some sense. Yet in avoiding commitment to theory of mind mechanisms (or ToMMs), we must beware of falling into the trap of assuming that these communications would have been underwritten by a mutual capacity on the part of speakers and hearers to understand and decode the full-blown *propositional* attitudes that lay behind them. By appeal to the apparatus of intentional attitudes and embodied expectations, we can get by without this version of the Gricean assumption.

If this is right, mimetic practices can be called on to do some philosophical heavy lifting; potentially, even offering a solution to the rule-following paradox (see Hutto 2003/2006: ch. 4). I leave it for the reader to think about how this might be possible, by considering two pregnant passages from Wittgenstein.

> If one of a pair of chimpanzees once scratched the figure | – - | in the earth and thereupon the other series | – - | | – - | etc., the first would not have given a rule nor would the other be following it, whatever else went on at the same time in the mind of the two of them.
>
> If however there were observed, e.g, the phenomenon of a kind of instruction, of *shewing how* and of *imitation*, of lucky and misfiring attempts, of reward and punishment and the like; if at length the one who had been so trained put figures which he had never seen before one after another in sequence as in the first example, then we should probably say that the one chimpanzee was writing rules down, and the other following them (Wittgenstein 1983: VI § 42, emphases added).
>
> This was our paradox: no course of action could be determined by a rule, because every course of action can be made out to accord with a rule... What this shows is that *there is a way of grasping a rule which is not an interpretation but which is exhibited* in what we call 'obeying the rule' and 'going against it' in actual cases (Wittgenstein 1953: § 201, emphasis added).

Whereas Davidson is certainly right in thinking that a capacity for rudimentary co-referential interaction and not linguistically-based convention makes language possible, mimetic abilities of a certain kind, those which sponsor *non-linguistic* conventions, may have been at least one necessary foundation for the development of linguistic and other symbolically-based conventions. When it comes to 'understanding others' returning to a more rudimentary base is always possible, however inconvenient. Doing so is absolutely necessary when normal communication *breaks down* or in cases where the supporting conventions do not exist. This would have been the situation of our forebearers in the distant past. Co-attentive, imaginative, associative and mimetic abilities lie at *the true core* of human communication.[16]

These do not require or add up to a facility with propositional attitudes. As I noted earlier, genuine propositional thinking (and hence attitudes) requires the manipulation of complex public symbols – i.e. those with appropriate internal structures. The appearance of these would have had to wait on other developments, in particular: (1) a sensitivity to basic syntax (at least) and (2) the fashioning of complex public symbols with recombinant elements. Capacities for proto-declarative pointing, joint attention and the practice of ostensive naming would surely have been a necessary pre-condition for formation of such symbols. Although I object to talk of modules, I agree with the core idea behind Gómez's suggestion that a "SAM [Shared Attention Module] could easily have been evolutionarily modified into a first kind of LAD – a lexical LAD" (Gómez 1998: 88, Clark 1998: 175, Tomasello 2003).

It is quite plausible that our most immediate ancestors, archaic humans, developed a basic grammatical LAD as well sometime prior to 1000,000 years ago. Working in combination with its lexical cousin, these two LADS might possibly explain the basic linguistic pre-dispositions of modern humans. But note: as I see it, the grammatical LAD need only have performed a very limited function. Its job would have been to act as, "a filter controlling the aspects of the language a child hears that it will reproduce, or, in practice, the same thing, determining what aspects will be perceived as functionally significant aspects" (Millikan 2001: 399, emphasis added). This being so there is no reason to think it must have incorporated some kind of 'grammatical theory' – and there is good reason to think otherwise. Even Gopnik, and arch-theory theorist, rejects the representionalist construal of grammatical knowledge, arguing that, "There is nothing out there that the syntactic representations are representations of. Knowing a syntactic structure and having a syntactic structure are just the same thing … the same arguments that say syntactic knowledge is not a kind of theory call into question whether it is really a kind of knowledge either" (Gopnik 2003: 251).

According to my 'just so' story, despite being forged at different stages in the homo line, by learning to play well together these two LADS may have been the main foundations of human competence with complex languages. Both lexical and grammatical abilities would have had to have been developed in order to deal with combinatorial semantics. Coupling an ability to use and forge lexical symbols, already evolving in the hominid line, with an independent sensitivity to and facility with recursive, core syntactical structures would have provided the ultimate basis for a symbolic explosion, allowing for the generation of countless new symbols. On the one hand, this is consistent with the continuist view that sees human language as having evolved from primate call systems. On the other hand, it is equally at home with the claim that the emergence of mimetic capacity originally fostered a gesture-based mode of communication in hominids.

Accordingly, the path of the development of linguistic competence in hominids and early humans would have been elliptical – having gone through a period in which manual gestures dominated and only later shifted back to speech-centred modes of communication and expression. Posting this circuitous route of the evolution of language-related abilities, in which the lowering of the larynx looks to have been the crucial turning point for the onset of syntactical abilities, is at least one credible selectionist explanation of how humans may have come by brains and bodies that are so apt to receive language. This was surely not achieved by the forging of a single mechanism. Rather it involved the multi-stage, gradual evolutionary development of several.[17] It follows that certain high-profile features of chapel of linguistic competence, those to do with the production and comprehension of syntax, were only completed late in the day – likely along with or *just before* the arrival of *Homo sapiens sapiens*.

It is crucial that the evolution of such linguistic capacities should not be confused with the origin of languages. Complex languages are intricate cultural mosaics. In contrast, the ability to acquire them is built on several biologically-driven anatomical foundations, all of which look likely to have been uniquely constructed in the homo line. Whatever the exact timing of the appearance of these foundations in our pre-history, the emergence of language would have still had to wait on the development of certain socio-cultural *practices*, such as naming, classifying and reporting. It would have had to wait on the arrival of certain socio-cultural practices – the fashioning and use of public symbols – that would have made completely unrestricted access between the various domains of competence possible.

Significantly, this would not have required any further changes to the fundamental psychotechtonic architecture.[18] The space of central cognition – Mithen's superchapel – can be thought of as a *virtual* space: its creation would not have required adding further structures to the brain (or indeed modifying existing ones in a hardwired way).[19] New possibilities for thought were instead afforded by external forms that public language (and their inner proxies) make available. Public language symbols allowed for higher-order abstract reflection upon (and logical integration of) domain specific activities for the first time. This is because it provided a vantage point from which to survey all; a point from which to connect one's thinking in these domains in genuinely inferential and not merely analogical ways.[20]

I propose that it was through the use of new cognitive tools, those provided by public language symbols that our embodied practices became (and still become) extended. And with complex language comes new objects of attention (propositions). In short sketch, this is my understanding of *how* propositions and symbols (linguistic concepts) emerged and emerge.

3. Acquiring concepts of the attitudes

Hobson wonders not only how concepts in general might be forged from interpersonal interactions; he also asks how we come by mental concepts during our early years. In particular, he is interested in those that are applicable to both self and other.

It is worth saying at the outset what I take it that mental concepts are *not*. They are not "having something in one's head that serves to represent the objects of one's thoughts" (Fodor 2003: 21). That is to say, they are not, as denotational atomists would have it, acquired (as opposed by being learnt) by a proprietary 'triggering' process (Leslie et al. 2004). This is the favourite story of proponents of a certain kind of theory of mind mechanism account. Nor are they scientific constructs; fashioned through dynamic – but rationally constrained – theory development.[21] Nor are they objects of introspective attention; distinguished by their distinctive qualitative features. I offer detailed arguments against each of these conjectures (see Hutto 2007b).

In their place, I do not offer an alternative theory but a general recommendation. To understand what it is to 'have' a concept one must ask what kind of abilities one would have to have in order to satisfy the criteria for practical possession of that concept. Answering that question therefore yields a detailed understanding of what command of any particular concept comes to. Following through on this idea, I propose that in order to understand how children acquire mentalistic concepts we must focus on their practical (not their imagined theoretical) abilities. Accordingly, we can expect (at least sometimes) that new concepts will be gained only as new abilities are – and also that a firmer command of concepts comes with greater mastery of a certain abilities.

Making this our focus, we can interrogate the basis of such abilities: i.e. what underwrites and engenders them. This type of investigation will yield a unique ability profile for each 'concept' – detailing the necessary pre-requisites for its acquisition, in terms of:

1. More basic abilities/capacities (whether these are nonconceptual or themselves conceptual);
2. Special supports that extend the practical possibilities (e.g. material or linguistic constructions that act as cognitive tools);
3. Engendering or enabling socio-cultural practices and institutions.

With respect to the acquisition of the standard folk psychological concepts – desire and belief – children gain a practical grasp of these in piecemeal fashion. In what follows, I illustrate the process.

Very early on young children can attend to the intentional attitudes of others (preferences, goals or intentions-in-action). These are expressed and responded to in embodied ways. What changes in the course of childhood development is that as children learn how to use linguistic signs they gain an understanding that such attitudes can be directed at different kinds of objects, or more precisely that others can be directed at the world in linguistically mediated ways. Words – and eventually whole sentences – serve as replacement descriptions of desired items; they allow children to represent what it is that someone wants in ways that are simply beyond the scope of creatures that are restricted to embodied modes of responding. Using their linguistic abilities, human children are able to make ascriptions about what another wants that go beyond what can be perceived by attending to the intentional attitudes that others adopt towards aspects of their immediate environment. So it is that children come to recognise that others may want things that are currently out of sight or temporally beyond their reach (Wellman 1991). Mastery of language reveals the existence of, what we might for convenience call, linguistic objects of attention and co-attention. Children powerfully augment and extend their possibilities for engaging with others when they learn how linguistic signs can serve both to designate other objects and states of affairs *as well as* being the focus of another's desires or attention. This, in turn, engenders new kinds of expectations: those of a properly inferential and of the less visceral sort (see my reply to Goldie). Young children, in command of this ability, can thus make desire-based predictions, albeit of a low-level sort. For example, they are able to *say* what others will likely do if their desires are fulfilled, frustrated or merely satisficed (as opposed to properly satisfied).[22]

As one might expect, the nature of these ascriptions develops in tandem with their growing command of linguistic constructions.[23] Typically, two-year olds begin by ascribing desires for objects. Then they begin to see that others can want that certain actions should take place and, eventually, that certain state of affairs should obtain. Children progress from making attributions such as "Mummy wants ice cream" to those incorporating infinite complements, such as that "Mummy wants to go upstairs", and eventually to those using finite complement clauses, such as "Mummy wants that Emerson should go to school". Typically, the last of these – attributions of the full-blown propositional or situational variety – comes late in the two-year old's repertoire (but this is not always so).[24]

All of these linguistic constructions can serve as new focal points for co-attention; becoming the key points of interest in early dialogues, which are typically carer-led. They provide a necessary medium for children to *say* what they want and equally or discussing what parents, siblings and others want (or for parent's to say what children want – see McGeer 2007). These linguistically scaffolded abilities set the stage for social dramas of an entirely different order than those that typify purely embodied contexts of interaction.[25] All the same, this new way of representing and understanding the foci of intentional attitudes is – in an important and clear sense – a natural outgrowth of more rudimentary embodied activity. For, as Hobson would have it, the *attitude* of 'wanting' is already familiar.

Some have claimed this sort of understanding of desires implies having a metarepresentational ability – not just an ability to represent a new kind of focus for intentional attitudes, but also a capacity to represent other perspectives on these as well (Goldman 2001, Leslie et al. 2004, Nichols & Stich 2003). But this overlooks the fact that there are important conceptual differences in our understanding of desires and beliefs. While the desire attributions of two-year olds are impressive, they fall short of the kind of understanding of perspectives that one needs in order to recognise that another has a false belief (i.e. that some part of the world is not in fact as the other takes it to be). It is clearly easier to grasp that the other wants something (or wants that something be the case) in the absence of the relevant object or state of affairs than it is to imagine that the other thinks that a particular state of affairs obtains when it quite clearly does not (from the child's point of view). Put otherwise, psychological dramas concerning what others want typically unfold *within* a single epistemic frame, but understanding full fledged metarepresentational attitudes, i.e. beliefs, requires a leap of the imagination of a quite different sort. Thus, as Harris proposes, even when it comes to understanding advanced desires it is sufficient to regard others as 'goal-directed agents', but to understand others as believers requires being able to see them as 'epistemic subjects'.

Confusion on this score can be alleviated if it is acknowledged that facility with complementation as a linguistic device is necessary, *inter alia*, for making propositional attitude ascriptions, but it is insufficient for making those of the metarepresentational variety. *That*-clauses operate in quite distinctive ways when they relate different types of psychological attitudes in content-involving ways to propositions. For example, this is why philosophers explicate the concept of desire in terms of 'satisfaction' and that of belief in terms of 'truth' (or aiming at truth): the former exhibits a mind-world direction of fit, the latter exhibits a world-mind direction of fit.

It is certainly true that understanding desires as propositional attitudes entails an ability to understand truth-conditional propositional contents. But having a capacity to understand the truth-conditional content of utterances does not automatically imply an *epistemic* understanding of truth. Indeed, in the run up to their third year of life, children show signs of understanding propositions without attributing knowledge and thought to others in a properly 'epistemic' way. This is evidenced by their predominate tendency to refer mainly to their own states of knowledge (Bartsch & Wellman 1995: 62). Although others are typically treated as indicators (reliable or otherwise) about the state of worldly affairs, they are not initially understood to be believers. For example, a child may note that 'Mummy knows/thinks that Alex is hiding'. This is sometimes described as their having a grasp of the knowledge/ignorance contrast. Yet even though epistemic verbs are used in the making of such attributions, it does not follow that young children possess a full-fledged understanding of knowledge – at least not one of the sort in which having a contingently true (i.e. possibly false) belief features as a condition for having it. Children of below the age of three apparently cannot make sense of the possibility that the other might be wrong; they are unable to imagine the other as having a divergent cognitive take on the situation in question. This does not prevent them from noting, say, that a state of affairs does not obtain when another *says* it does – as in the case in which Mummy says 'Alex is hiding' and he manifestly is not. This is likely to provoke such responses as 'No, Alex not hiding', 'Not hiding', or 'There he is' and so on. But these responses are not equivalent to first ascribing and then trying to correct mother's false belief.

Mummy's words are not yet interpreted in the context of her having made a *claim* about the world despite the fact that the child understands what it is that she says. In effect, mother's words are treated as mere factual broadcasts – announcements about how things stand, which the child simply endorses or rejects. For younger children all there is are falsehoods, there is as yet no false thinking – no false believing. To regard others as the sources of factive statements does not require even a weak ability to understand them as adopting attitudes of belief towards worldly affairs. It requires an understanding of propositional representations and their specific content (in a sense closer to that of indication). More than this is needed to understand metarepresentation which admits of the possibility that the other is making an error of judgement. In engaging in their first dialogical interchanges, children have yet to step out of what is, in effect, a solipsistic point of view – for each child, the world is *their* world and any knowledge others may have of it is firmly evaluated against how they (the child) takes things to be (which, for them, is the same as how things are). This is the easiest way of explaining why younger children appear to make no distinction between 'what they take to be the case' and 'what is the case'.[26]

Being able to understand the factual content of propositions, however impressive, does not add up to an understanding of beliefs. By the same token having the ability to ascribe propositionally focused desires does not imply a capacity for metarepresentation either. Mastering the idea that the other might have a cognitive take on a situation that might diverge from one's own is tantamount to gaining an understanding of false beliefs, and thus beliefs *per se*. This is definitional. Until children can make such distinctions they are not in a position to question or reflect on the 'correctness' of their own epistemic takes on the world in the way adults can. In their younger years, children do not understand that they or others adopt 'cognitive takes' on the world at all.[27]

This neatly explains the well-documented gap not only in children's talk about desires and beliefs but also their early facility with desire attributions and their delayed passing of false-belief tasks. These differences show up clearly in the developmental profile. Desires come first in our mentalistic understanding of things: children are capable of attributing and understanding them long before they can make comprehending belief ascriptions.[28] They not only mention desires before beliefs, but they show comprehension of advanced desires, involving contrastives, roughly six months before they can do the same with respect to beliefs. If there are, in fact, significant differences in what is required for an understanding of the attitudes it is hardly surprising that the concepts of desire and belief are mastered at such a temporal distance.

To think of oneself as having *a* possibly *fallible* view of things entails being able to think of oneself as having one view amongst possible others: that is what is required to have a concept of belief. What changes in the interactive careers of children such that they come to grasp the concept of it between the ages of 3 and 4? It is extremely plausible that "a critical pre-condition for understanding beliefs but not desires – participation in the exchange of information through conversation – is not obtained by most children until the third year" (Harris 1996: 208). Accordingly, it is "the child's growing experience, not as an agent, but as a conversationalist [that] plays a critical role" (Harris 1996: 209–210). On this account, an understanding of belief – one requiring acknowledgement of divergent *cognitive* perspectives – is forged and fostered by encounters with and having to confront and accommodate different cognitive takes on worldly states of affairs: this experience is part and parcel of what goes on in conversations.[29] Metarepresentational understanding is thus forged by the relevant exercise of the imagination in repeatedly experiencing the clash of different points of view and dealing with the cognitive friction this generates.

But children must be prepared in quite particular ways for this. As with desires, they are familiar with an analogue activity in the landscape of action: i.e. they are accustomed to using their non-propositional recreative imagination in a somewhat similar way. Prior to this point, they will have exercised it mainly in the form of visual perspective shifting during acts of non-verbal joint attention. Discursive conversations, like embodied forms of joint attentional engagements, are dynamic affairs; participants are constantly forced to establish and re-establish a common focus while keeping track of another's attitudes on it as well. The difference is that in the linguistically-mediated context children are dealing with new and more complex objects of interest and trade: content-involving propositions. Thus the perspective-taking in question is discursively mediated and thoroughly cognitive – it requires a prior capacity to talk about the state of the world in contentful terms and to imagine how others might see things differently. Because of their peculiarly discursive nature conversations require children to operate on a new playing field, bringing what are in essence old skills to bear in relation to new objects of attention.

More than this, engaging in full-blown conversations requires more than just trading remarks about how things stand in the world – typically one's take on things is up for debate, discussion and challenge. Mature conversations involve a bit of give and take. Perhaps the most prominent feature of good conversations is that participants are unavoidably forced to monitor one another's understanding of things and how these evolve over time (or indeed to separately monitor those of several others). In this way "Conversation constantly underlines the centrality of point-of-view" (Harris 1996: 218, see also Bohman 2000: 227). If one already understands what is said, and the relevant imaginative capacities are in tact, then repeatedly engaging in this sort of activity would foster recognition of the fact that one's own take on things is just one amongst many possible such takes.

What this tells us is that long before acquiring a practical grasp of mentalistic concepts normally developing children must be able to navigate the social matrix using embodied skills, interacting with others in ways which require no understanding whatsoever of propositional attitudes or reasons for action. With a growing command of language they are able to make use of syntactical constructions, with embedded complement clauses. These eventually become new linguistic objects of attention and co-attention. At first this enables them to extend their understanding both about what they and others might desire. But focusing on these 'linguistic objects' with others by exercising the same kind of recreative imaginative ability needed for engaging in joint attention tasks, children are able to participate in conversations. And it is by engaging in such conversations that they come by understanding the propositional attitude belief.

3. Accounting for autistic impairments in understanding the concept of belief

The task of explaining what underlies autism is a mammoth one. Those suffering from this syndrome have a range of impairments that can be classed under the broad headings of: interpretation, social interaction, communication, and creative imagination (see Baron-Cohen 2000). Autism is characterised, indicatively not comprehensively, by specific problems relating to:

a) Joint or shared attention;
b) Reciprocal relating and empathy;
c) Perceiving complex emotions;
d) Understanding false beliefs and understanding beliefs about beliefs;
e) Distinguishing appearance from reality;
f) Executive control and forward planning tasks;
g) Paucity of 'pretend' play, inability to role-play;
h) Understanding and correctly using pronouns;
i) Conversational pragmatics;
j) Prosody, metaphor and irony;
k) Understanding stories involving reasons for action;
l) Recognising what is significant or relevant;
m) Rigidity and repetitiveness of behaviour.

It is widely recognised that the full range of symptoms associated with autism are unlikely to have a single cause. It has been proposed that we will make better progress by abandoning the attempt to treat autism as a unitary syndrome and instead to characterise it as a multidimensional one – one with a great many satellite symptoms and associated disorders.[30] This being the case it is simply not credible that all of its related disorders could be explained in terms of 'mindblindness'.

Even so, those with autism have profound and well-documented difficulties both interacting with and understanding others.[31] One of the best known is the fact that such individuals have difficulties passing 'false belief' tasks of both the first and second order varieties, despite the fact that they demonstrate strong levels of general intelligence. It is evident that, "autistic children have severe and specific difficulty with understanding mental states. Even with a mental age of 7 years, these children mostly fail in tasks which are normally passed around ages 3 and 4" (Leslie & Frith 1988: 315).

Without supposing that its root cause can be identified, it has been claimed – all the same – that 'mindblindness' is the "core and possibly universal abnormality of autistic individuals" (Baron-Cohen 2000: 3). Supporters of this view claim that malfunctioning 'theory of mind' mechanisms (or ToMMs) are responsible for the poor performances of autistic persons in a range of interpersonal interactions – at least, for obvious reasons, when it comes to explain failures to perform on false belief tasks.[32] Typical malfunctions to sub-components of ToMMs, such as the Shared Attention Modules (or SAMs), are thought to explain why autistic individuals are unable to jointly attend and, possibly, why they do not engage in pretend play. With suitable adjustments, something like this account may be right. But I hold that it is false to think that those with autism fail on metarepresentational false belief tasks because they lack properly functioning ToMMs of the mature variety. According to the received view, such mechanisms are what enable unimpaired children, or at least those of the appropriate age, to perform such tasks successfully. The natural corollary of supposing this is to hold that those who systematically fail in such tasks must have 'damaged' or 'malfunctioning' ToMMs. It is against this background that debates have ensued for many years over which *type* of subpersonal ToMM – those of the truly theory-based or simulative variety – might be best suited to explain these selective disabilities exhibited by autistic individuals (see Hutto 2003).

Despite the popularity of this idea, it should be noted straightaway that the available evidence from autism only securely establishes that folk psychological understanding is highly domain specific. And this fact in no way lends conclusive support to claim that an inability to successfully execute 'mentalistic' tasks is best explained by damaged or imperfect ToMMs. As a general rule, we should be immediately suspicious of any explanation that is as convenient as this; it is rare in science that the *explanans* should so neatly fit the *explanadum*.

But there are other reasons to be suspicious of what I call the 'restricted mindblindness hypothesis'. Before turning to these, it is worth getting clear about the scope of its claim. To simply call autistic persons 'mindblind' without further clarification is misleading. The fact is that they are only 'blind' to *some* but not all aspects of the psychological life of others. They are not wholly oblivious to 'agency' or 'intentions' as such: they are able to see that others seek and desire things and to note the kinds of things to which they react. But seeing and responding to basic intentions, desires and goals can be achieved without requiring any understanding of other content-involving points of view. Importantly, responding to others while navigating the landscape of action in these limited ways does not require stepping outside of one's own perspective.

There is evidence that autistic individuals are capable of understanding at least *certain* psychological concepts – at least to some extent. For example, Goldman cites the case of:

> an able autistic young man who despite suffering from autism is very helpful with household chores and errands. One day, as his mother was mixing a fruit cake, she said to him "I haven't got any cloves. Would you please go out and get me some." The son came back a while later with a carrier bag full of girlish clothes, including underwear, from a High Street boutique. Clearly, the boy had misperceived the word 'cloves' as 'clothes'. But what normal young man would assume his mother asked him to casually buy her clothes, just like that? (Goldman 1992: 112)

Goldman plausibly concludes that the boy's mistake derives from his inability to read the situation – a failure to grasp what it is *normal* for someone to ask for in these circumstances. This explains why he doesn't question what otherwise *ought* to be regarded as a very strange request from his mother. But what stands out from this example is that he has a practical understanding of what it is for someone to *want* something. His actions show that he grasps this notion perfectly well.[33] It follows therefore that those with autism cannot be *completely* mindblind; they are capable of understanding and using at least some propositional attitude terms. Indeed, it is also worth bearing in mind that not all of those who suffer from autism fail false belief tasks, only some do.[34]

Interestingly most autistic individuals do suffer from profound difficulties with joint attention.[35] They even typically fail to meet the eyes of others, let alone make attempts to attract or attend to another's attention.[36] This important mode of social interaction is poignantly, "missing in the development of even quite able autistic children" (Kennett 2002: 347, Andrews 2002).[37] I think this may, in part, stem from a more fundamental impairment in their recreative imaginative abilities. And imaginative impairment of this kind could explain why autistic children tend not to engage in even the most basic forms of pretend play.

It has been claimed that the mechanisms of pretence may be the true source of our metarepresentational abilities – that even the simplest acts of pretence involve "an early manifestation of the ability to understand mental states [and hence represent] the specific innate basis of our commonsense theory of mind" (Leslie 1987: 412). But this conjecture has not held up well under scrutiny. The fact is that early forms of pretend play have no direct connection to imagining mental states; instead they mostly involve imagining that certain objects are of a different kind than they in fact are. While it is hard to deny that *this kind* of imaginative capacity might fuel metaphoric thinking it surely does not entail an ability to think of 'others' having possibly divergent *cognitive takes* on situations – i.e. it is hardly constituted or need be based upon a metarepresentational ability. The very fact that children who do not suffer from autism engage in pretend play as early as age two is enough to suggest that these imaginative feats are *at best* a platform for a metarepresentational activity that develops later on, rather than the other way around. Therefore a basic capacity for pretence is not identical to a capacity for metarepresentation (nor does it developmentally presuppose the latter).

Recent evaluations of experiments using picture choice tasks support this conclusion – for children systematically pass these tests early on when the relevant requests are framed using the language of pretending, but not that of thinking (Astington and Jenkins 1999: 1318). And it has been demonstrated, in a way that is even more directly pertinent, that in a number of trials, "3-year olds understand pretence in terms of observable action, whereas 4-year olds are capable of attributing relevant states about a pretend sequence to an absent actor" (Berguno and Bowler 2004: 541). Thus with direct reference to Leslie's earlier work, the authors of this study argue that a failure to make this kind of distinction has resulted in the data from previous experiments on pretence being interpreted ambiguously. In all, it seems safe to conclude that the pretend play of young children, even those involving the rehearsal and miming of the observed actions of others, does not entail having mature ToM abilities.

But what is well established is that those with autism demonstrate great difficulty in *simultaneously* entertaining or imagining more than one perspective on events and/or situations. This shows up not just in their basic interpersonal interactions but also in more advanced forms of pretend play. For this reason, although autistic individuals are sometimes characterised as having an impoverished perspective on others, it is in fact closer to the truth to say that they are unable to recognise that others (or indeed that they, themselves) have 'perspectives' on situations at all.[38]

In line with the claim that we only acquire a practical understanding of 'belief' by engaging in conversations, it looks likely that an inability to imagine alternative perspectives would make it difficult, if not impossible, to achieve an understanding of such a concept. For if an embodied capacity such as imagination – likely one taking the form of visual perspective shifting – is a non-negotiable pre-requisite for engaging in the relevant kinds of conversation then we should expect that those that are imaginatively impaired would have problems even entering into such exchanges. And if those problems were severe enough, we can predict that they would be unable to acquire an understanding of the concept of belief.[39] Assuming, of course, that I am correct to think that engaging in conversations is a non-negotiable pre-requisite for distinguishing oneself as a believer within a contrast space of other believers.

Put simply, the characteristic problems autistic individuals have when it comes to engaging in conversations can be put down to impaired imaginative capacities. This is what thwarts them from developing an understanding of most important folk psychological attitudes.[40] This explanation has the virtue of being parsimonious. A basic ability to engage in imaginative acts of visual perspective shifting sort is required both for non-verbal joint attention and for developing a *bona fide* metarepresentational understanding. If this proposal is right then the proponents of ToMMs have things exactly backward; it is not that autistic individuals lack the concept of belief because they lack a working mentalistic ToMM! Rather, they have trouble in getting to grips with the concept of belief, and this is what prevents them from properly mastering folk psychology. This is because mastering an understanding of *belief* is necessary for understanding *reasons* – and an understanding of reasons, of the complex interplay between beliefs and desires, is needed for folk psychological understanding. Without an understanding of the concept of belief one could not understand intentions performed *for reasons*. I claim that children only come by the latter ability by being exposed to and engaging in a distinctive kind of narrative practice (I briefly explain how I think this works in my reply to Gallagher).

An inability to engage in conversation would sponsor other serious problems too. For as Bohman notes "we establish and maintain relationships to others in dialogue and conversation" (Bohman 2000: 224). Conversations provide one of the main routes into the norm-ridden social world, thus an inability to cope with them may explain why autistic sufferers are so socially awkward; showing such a limited capacity to understand such things as jokes or displaying insensitivity to the ethical dimensions of most situations (see McGeer 2001: 113).[41] On the supposition that dialogue is an important means of instilling norms – i.e. to teach us what is appropriate and what is not. For an understanding of such boundaries emerges through recognising and sometimes confronting the views of others. Imaginative flexibility therefore looks to be a requirement for the development not only of alternative sets of values, but also our own first set. Hence, the fact that autistic individuals are unable to engage in such conversations properly might explain other limitations in their behaviour. Lack of this important source of training might explain not only why autistics are somewhat ethically oblivious, but also why they have such trouble seeing what is "important, meaningful or relevant" (Frith 1989: 109, cf. also 5–6, 12, 108, 120, 134).[42] Both capacities require being attuned to social norms.

Still, it may seem less than obvious how an inability to understand the concept of belief relates, if it does at all, to the fact that, "children with autism appear to have very partial experiences and concepts of themselves and others" (Hobson: this volume). My guess is that the links are complex: if a practical grasp of the concept of belief is a requirement for acquiring full-fledged folk psychological abilities, it may be that the latter is in turn required for certain kinds of self understanding. If so, this could potentially explain why autistic individuals have a limited understanding of what it is to be a 'person'. For example, it is plausible that whatever sense we have of our existence across time as people who lead, not just live, lives may depend on our being able to understand what it is to act for a reason and being able to understand such intentional actions within larger narratives (at least to some extent). If so, a fundamental inability to understand and produce folk psychological narratives would restrict one to a very limited, attenuated sense of self (see Hobson 1993: 236–7).

To sum up: Why do autistics have such difficulty in understanding narratives involving people *who act for reasons*? My claim is that it is not because of a malfunctioning metarepresentational mechanism – rather it is to do with imaginative difficulties related to perspective shifting – difficulties that make it hard, if not impossible, for sufferers of autism to carry off the leaps of imagination required for gaining an understanding of belief. This inability has exponentially bad downstream effects. Accordingly, the typical pattern of symptoms that is associated with the autistic disorder does not flow from a single source, like arms radiating from a central hub. Many characteristic problems stem from a basic impairment, one that initiates a kind of domino effect. As the severity of the disorder and its particular manifestation varies from case to case, this may well explain why there is no common profile to the impairments suffered by autistic individuals.

I realise that this reply hasn't dealt fully, but only suggestively – at best, with Hobson's fourth challenge – his question about the source of our understanding of selves. I will not be able to do justice to it here, but I say more in response to in my reply to Gallagher (see also Hutto 1997, Hutto 2007d, Gallagher & Hutto 2007).

Notes

1. Lest I be accused of setting up a strawman, I state for the record that there are those who believe that this is possible. For example, Gopnik, tells us that "infants seem to be born believing that people are special and that there are links between their own internal feelings and the internal feelings of others" (Gopnik 2004: 22).

2. Belief/desire psychology used in this way could be thought of as a type of calculus for predicting behaviour of many, many complex systems. But when folk psychology is used in this way it has only such instrumental value – as such its predicates need be treated like calculation-bound' entities generally. Their 'real' existence is no more entailed than that of centres of gravity, as Dennett has long argued. Accordingly, he invited us to think of the 'posits' of intentional psychology as species of *abstracta* and not as serious theoretical posits (i.e. *illata*). An example of *abstracta* would be Dennett's lost sock centre, defined as "the center of the smallest sphere that can be inscribed around all the socks I have ever lost in my life" (Dennett 1991: 28).

3. This is why, for example, mental images and pictures are incapable of doing the work of propositions, since they lack appropriately analysable contents and internally structured logical forms. In essence, Fregean thoughts or 'senses' are required. For Frege these were objective entities that had to be intellectually 'grasped' in acts of reasoning – otherwise they were causally inert. Indeed a numerically identical thought would have to be grasped more than once by the same individual during acts of inferential reasoning. Although few today would endorse the above claims without serious qualification, these core insights remain deeply influential. Despite the fact that treating thoughts as graspable abstract objects did not survive the naturalistic turn, the Fregean picture of propositional thought has been retained: Fodor's theory of mind, re-jigs Frege's basic idea. Fodor embraces an industrial strength intentional realism that is staunchly committed to 'the philosopher's notion of the proposition'. The main difference is that Frege's 'thoughts' or 'senses' are not re-construed as inner mental representations nor as abstract objects; they become internal-to-the-cranium representations in the Language of Thought (or LOT) (see Fodor 2003: 143–144). Thus, representationalists of the Fodorian ilk convert Fregean talk of 'grasping one and the same 'thought' more than once when reasoning' into talk of 'harbouring numerically distinct token representations of the same type in one's head'. For contemporary representationalists, the 'mode of presentation' metaphor is naturalistically unpacked by identifying such things with the internal structure of the representational tokens themselves. Accordingly, "modes of presentation are sentences (of Mentalese), and sentences are individuated not just by their propositional content but also by their syntax" (Fodor 1994: 97). And it is the syntactical properties of Mentalese sentences that, on this account, matter to computational operations and transformations. Reasoning is conducted only in virtue of the formal properties of representations.

4. Thus in making quotidian, off-the-cuff belief or desire ascriptions for the purposes of predicting (i.e. not genuinely explaining) the behaviour of complex systems, it does not matter which of the great range of possible belief/desire pairings is ascribed. This is revealed by the fact that typically saying exactly which belief or desire contents non-verbals harbour does not matter (for examples see Hutto 1999: 90–91).

5. To a limited extent apes can make tools and jointly attend to objects and actions. This suggests that they have *some* of the relevant imaginative abilities. But the differences with human

capacities are enormous, suggesting we have "an evolutionarily different version" (Gómez 2005: 80, see also Leekam 2005: 225).

6. The cathedral analogy was inspired by his experience of church excavations and his detailed knowledge of the developmental psychology literature. It has the nice feature of preserving the notion of a layered mind, diachronically constructed. And this allows us to give the idea of synchronous interacting levels a long deserved rest. This, of course, doesn't preclude our being interested in taking a look in the crypt. Importantly, just as with the more familiar boxological approaches, we must observe the standard health warning that this imagery only has schematic value. It should not be confused with proposals about the anatomy of the brain. This allows us to leave questions about which exact mechanisms are involved in supporting cognition and the nature of their precise modes of operation for future empirical investigation. For example, face recognition looks to be sub-served by a specialised device and is not just fallout from more general recognitional abilities. And we know this because we have discovered that the systems which subserve it can be neurally isolated – i.e. it is possible to damage them while sparing other recognitional abilities (Currie & Sterelny 2000: 148).

7. Mithen borrows this terminology from Gardner (1983, 1993).

8. Since tasks decompose endlessly, it makes sense to talk in terms of higher level competencies, grouping the subservient action coordination routines together under broader intuitive headings; this can be done in just the way Karmiloff-Smith distinguishes 'domains' and 'micro-domains' (Karmiloff-Smith 1995: 6).

9. On certain readings Chomsky's famous proposal that an innate Universal Grammar (or UG), which provides knowledge of linguistic universals, is thought to take the form of a device containing grammatical principles (but principles open to parameterisation). It is this knowledge that pre-disposes language learners to hit on the right local grammars with minimal effort or to develop full blown ones, even when confronted by degenerate inputs (Chomsky 1986, Bloom 1998: 206). Hence, such principles putatively explain the grammatical expectations of very young children, which are thought to be in place from birth. Chomsky has notably vacillated in his views about the character of this linguistic 'knowledge'. Yet according to Fodor's Neo-Cartesian interpretation, to have a Chomksyian language acquisition device (or LAD) entails having some kind of 'language of thought'. There is considerable exegetical disagreement about Chomsky's actual commitments on this front. Jackendoff, for example, has challenged Fodor's reading, calling it a "serious misconstrual" (Jackendoff 1999: 311). And this is because Jackendoff maintains that the generalisations of generative grammar are formal computations devoid of propositional content.

10. Indeed the perceptual modality in question must allow for the possibility of sharing responses, as the visual medium does (Hutto 2000: 34–35, 2002: 45–6).

11. As Brinck notes non-verbal joint attenders must also (i) make attention contact, and (ii) alternate gaze between each other and the object. The first capacity might be explained by appealing to fairly basic SCRs. But meeting the second condition requires at least one participant in the referential triangle to ensure that the other focuses on the object (event or action) that is to be the common focal point of co-attention (assuming – as will often be the case – that the participants are not already separately attending to this thing). This can be achieved through a combination of pointing, physical manipulation, gaze alteration and monitoring, etc. Although this may all sound relatively mechanical, in fact, none of this could be accomplished without a capacity for perspective shifting.

12. What I am proposing here can be best understood if we make significant modifications to Nichols' and Stich's Early Mindreading System (which they call the Desire and Plan system). It is thought to be triggered by low-level feature detection mechanisms for the targeting of suitable subjects, on my account these will be SCRs. Ultimately, for Nichols and Stich, this device explains why, but not how, "infants tend to attribute goals to people but not to mechanical objects" (Nichols and Stich 2003: 95). For the basic detector does not make any attributions itself. That is achieved by other components of the system working in conjunction with the Planner. The result is that a simple heuristic is employed for making propositional attitude predictions – effectively supposing that others desire or seek whatever it is that the attributor would desire or seek in the same circumstances. We can retain much of the guts of this model, while replacing a few key mechanisms, and re-thinking its representationalist commitments (for full details see Hutto 2007b).

13. Evidence that this kind of use of associated meanings lies at the root of communication is reflected in feature of our mature linguistic behaviour. The ancient mimetic mind and the deep associations on which it thrives, still apparently governs the 'metaphors by which we live' and a continued reliance on gesture looks to have stayed with us as something more than an inert cognitive vestige (Lakoff & Johnson 1980, Corballis 2003). For some, the many aspects of the responses of modern humans have changed little or not at all since the time of early human societies.

14. It is known that apes do not display a capacity for sign use in the wild or even with conspecifics in captivity, but some pick this up after enculturation with human trainers. Thus Call and Tomasello note that "Apes with human contact are also the only apes to produce imperative pointing... The use of declarative gestures is much less frequent in apes, and may be confined to apes with extensive human contact" (Call & Tomasello 1996: 382). In order to explain these limitations they suggest that "although apes can master the 'referential triangle' in their interactions with humans for instrumental purposes when they are raised in humanlike cultural environments, they still do not attain humanlike social motivations for sharing experience with other intentional beings" (Tomasello & Call 1997: 393).

15. There would have been both costs and benefits in moving to such a symbol system. Learning abstract symbols is harder and takes longer, but once learned they make for less ambiguous, speedier and more reliable communication. This obviates the need for protracted, on-line and possibly noisy processes of clarification (see Corballis 2003: 211–2). In thinking about this, it is useful to contrast the ease with which human children pick up the syntax of local grammars with their difficulty in learning to read written forms.

16. There can be no doubt, nor does Davidson deny, that we are conditioned to follow and obey the norms of our community in the initial stages of learning a local public language. It is because of this that he tells us "It is easy to misconceive the role of society in language. Language, to be sure, is a social art. But it is an error to suppose we have seen deeply into the heart of linguistic communication when we have noticed how society bends linguistic habits to a public norm" (Davidson 1984: 278, emphasis added).

17. Given this there is no need to postulate a theoretically-based understanding of language, one genetically hard-wired or coded within us, in order to explain our language acquisition abilities. Nevertheless, we come equipped with built-in mechanisms and abilities that pre-dispose unimpaired members of our species, in each generation, to rapidly pick up a first language with relative ease, even when faced with minimal or degraded input. Consequently, the mere fact that we are geared up to acquire language – being especially receptive to basic grammars – lends no special support to the claim that we have a built-in theory of grammar.

18. Mithen proposed that the final development of the cathedral of the mind was that free access was established between all of the individual chapels. From a design point of view he considered two possibilities for how this might have been achieved, either through (1) the erection of a superchapel, permitting access to all points from the centre or by means of (2) the introduction of a series of doors, windows and internal arches allowing for circumambulatory flow from each chapel to all of the others. The superchapel model has been the clear favourite, but it is usually understood to have involved some structural alteration – in effect the introduction of the machinery that enabled central cognition or mimicking its effects. It is generally thought that some explanation needs to be given as to how the domain-specific representations of the chapels are themselves represented or re-described in the making of unrestricted inferences (Sperber 1994, Karmiloff-Smith 1995). Some have suggested this may have been made possible by fashioning a common cognitive coin – inner speech – initially using the vehicles provided by natural language (Carruthers 1998). Mithen speculates that this would have been a prolonged and noisy business, involving the knocking in of existing walls or building substantial new structure. Others, he claims, have mistaken this activity for the sound of a single cultural explosion. In his view the Middle/Upper Paleolithic was the scene of extensive building works (Mithen 1996: 152). I favour a much quieter account of the superchapel construction.

19. Human infants are born with a biological inheritance that sets each of them up for the construction of their own superchapels anew in every new generation. This provides a basis for new and more efficient forms of reasoning and reflection that would have been unavailable to purely associative and mimetic minds. Although this is always an individual achievement, development of a capacity for propositional thought only occurs if the right socio-cultural supports are in place. Language is not something innately embedded in the architecture of the human mind, although we are pre-disposed for language and propositional thinking.

20. As anyone familiar with the modification of an existing building will know, none of these changes should be construed as simple additions to existing structures – in each case the final product will have been wrought through a mix of preserving the old and substantial re-modelling. Much of the old would remain in tact, and indeed in service. Still, the introduction of new features will have transformed the space in quite dramatic ways.

21. According to this theory-theoretic variant of inferential holism a concept's content is constituted by its relations with other concepts or its role in a coherent network of laws or principles.

22. For example, Wellman and Wooley discovered that 2 ½ year olds predicted different responses from story characters when, in seeking a desired object, they were confronted with three different types of outcome: finds-nothing, finds-wanted, finds-substitute (Wellman & Wooley 1990, Wellman & Phillips 2001: 130).

23. On the view I am propounding, it is therefore not at all surprising that we find strong ties between linguistic capacity and theory of mind performance. Based on the results of a detailed longitudinal study, it has been confidently concluded that "theory of mind depends on language" (Astington & Jenkins 1999). Recent findings demonstrate that "by far the most significant variable in predicting success on ToM tasks is the production and comprehension of sentences containing propositional complement clauses… it is precisely familiarity with discourse in which propositions figure as objects ('Sally says/thinks that [proposition]) that enables children to propose mental states in which propositions figure as objects" (Garfield et al. 2001: 520). Indeed, it has been independently argued that mastery of complementation is needed for the metarepesentational embedding of propositional clauses (de Villiers & de Villiers 1999). While

the studies conducted by Astington and Jenkins are consistent with this hypothesis – in that they found syntactical abilities were most strongly correlated with ToM abilities – they acknowledge that there is a softer possibility that the mastery of syntax might not take the form of complementation *per se*.

24. Up until the age of two-years, English-speaking children typically use only simple two-word constructions (Pinker 1994). Yet some children make quite early use of fully tensed that-clauses that can be used to represent the complex objects of desires – apparently this is true of German children. Even so, it has been shown that such children still lack an understanding of false belief (Perner et al. 2003). This gives us reason to reject the strong form of linguistic determinism that de Villiers and de Villiers promote.

25. Eventually, with further adjustments such propositional desires can play their part explicating the processes of practical reasoning –– either by taking the form of imperatives or by modalizing the indicative form (Mahoney 1989: 20–21, Carruthers 2004).

26. One might hold that this is merely a case of appearance not reality; specifically, a case of performance masking true competence. But unless this competence can be unpacked by appeal to some type of subpersonal mechanism (as I argue it cannot) then, we should take this appearance at face value.

27. Prior to this point, "understanding remains on the level of action. During this early developmental period, language is being learned and used but it is not yet a vehicle for conveying the representation of narrative" (Nelson 2003: 27). The actional level is that of intentional attitude psychology involving mimesis, emotional responsiveness, and so on. But what it does not involve is "taking a perspective on events that is not one's own" (Nelson 2003: 27). Thus "at 2 years of age the child has only a few of the rudiments that enter into narrative, mainly the landscape of action, the child's own perspective on canonical events" (Nelson 2003: 27).

28. Evidence gleaned from the conversations of young children reveals that they "do not use such terms as intend to, on purpose, or mean to until about 3, 4, or 5 years, but as early as 1 ½ years they talk about persons' goals and desires, primarily with the term want" (Wellman & Phillips 2001: 130).

29. It is clear that young children do not begin life with this capacity. Initially when one asks a child "for the contents of a[nother] person's belief, they consistently, resistantly cite the facts" (Gopnik & Wellman 1992: 152). The development of the concept of belief is fashioned as we gain an "understanding of different perspectives on the world of experience, perspectives that are revealed especially in narrative discourse and that are not discernable in actions alone" (Nelson 2003: 29).

30. As Boucher noted some time ago "there is a range of different symptoms associated with different disabilities such as Kanner's and Asperger's Syndromes that are both regarded as forms of autism. This makes it unclear whether in speaking of autism we are talking about a syndrome, with a single common cause, a set of related but different subtypes or something better understood as a continuum" (Boucher 1996: 225–6). In adopting the latter view, I reject the following "two assumptions: that a single cognitive abnormality exists in all austistic individuals, and that all symptoms that characterise autism stem from that single abnormality" (Coltheart & Langdon 1998: 139).

31. Autistic individuals display a profile of disorder that is the reverse of that of sufferers from Williams' Syndrome. The latter normally suffer from moderate mental retardation and have severe difficulties with spatial cognition but they exhibit extreme, sometimes over-exuberant,

hypersociability and affective responding. Those with William's syndrome regularly seek to engage others emotionally and have a tendency to focus closely on facial expressions. Garfield et al. observe "Williams' syndrome children have fewer problems with ToM tasks than do autistic individuals, despite often comparable or lower levels of nonverbal intelligence. This disability, apparently representing the other half of the double dissociation between general intelligence and ToM, has been taken by proponents of a strongly modular account of ToM to demonstrate domain specificity in both the ToM capacity and its impairment in the case of autism" (Garfield et al. 2001: 522).

32. Thus it has been proposed that what autistics lack is "the relevant normally developing mechanism… for creating and handling meta-representations" (Leslie and Frith 1988: 315, emphasis original). But if offered as complete explanation of the disorder it is hard to square with the fact that "There are symptoms of autism, some of them apparently rather significant, which fall outside of the classic triad. There is a pattern of disabilities which seem to reflect deficits of what is called executive function" (Currie 1996: 253). Executive function is required for flexible planning and control and its impairment is likely related to characteristic autistic symptoms such as the lack of pretend play. Currie proposes that this may go some way to explain why "People with autism are upset by trivial changes in their surroundings, wish to adhere rigidly to the details of familiar routines, have narrowly focused, fact-based interests, and engage in stereotyped behaviour. Also, their behaviour does not seem to be future oriented; they don't anticipate the consequences of behaviour, are unself-reflective, impulsive and appear to delay or inhibit responses" (Currie 1996: 253). In defence of ToMM theories Carruthers has replied, saying that recorded lack of engagement in pretend play on the part of autistics might be accounted for on other grounds, such as motivational disinterest rather than cognitive disability or lack of competence (Carruthers 1996a). But this is already to concede the point that their having a malfunctioning ToM is not a viable candidate for explaining all of the symptoms associated with the disorder.

33. Stich and Nichols have objected to Goldman's reading on the grounds "Neither the term 'want' nor any other mentalistic language occurs in the anecdote, and there is no indication that the young man 'has a perfectly good grasp of the mentalistic notion of wanting'" (Stich and Nichols 1995: 104). Actions speak louder than words, and it is clear from what the boy does that he understands what 'want' means in this context.

34. Thus it is often observed that "although most autistic children fail tests which assess their mentalising ability, there is a substantial minority of such children who regularly succeed" (Coltheart and Langdon 1998: 143). Ozonoff and colleagues have conducted experiments which reveal that, unlike High Functioning Autistics, Asperger's Syndrome sufferers are able to pass first-order false belief tasks. However they write "We also found that severe executive function impairments were present in both AS and HFA subjects, suggesting that this may be one deficit primary to the disorders of the autistic spectrum. The lack of theory of mind deficit may not be primary to all of the autistic continuum, but may be a correlated deficit, present in more severely affected autistic individuals" (Ozonoff et al. 1991: 1118). Yet it is also worth noting that "AS subjects were able to pass the theory of mind tasks used in the present study, yet had great difficulty applying a theory of mind when chatting to the examiner between tests (instead of discoursing at length on weather patterns or vacuum cleaners, despite obvious signs from the examiner of boredom)" (Ozonoff et al. 1991: 1118).

35. Indeed, it has been said "Ask any clinician to describe the earliest and most significant impairments in autism, and the chances are that they will put joint attention at the top of the list" (Leekam 2005: 205). Still, as with 'theory of mind' abilities one must be cautious here. It would

be unwise to postulate a singular, 'monolithic' joint attentional ability that one simply has or has not got (Gómez 2005: 79). There are complexities at this level too. What can be safely said is that the autistics' trouble in this regard cannot be put down to mere attentional defects: they tend to be exceptionally good at attending to things for long periods.

36. For example, they are quite unlike normal children, who by the end of their first year, engage in social referencing and respond, even in experimental conditions when confronted by such things as visual cliffs, only after taking cues from their mothers' emotional orientations. Thus a mother's expressions of happiness or anxiety systematically affect infant reactions. Describing this perhaps too richly Hobson remarks that what such interactions involve is something like the recognition that, 'I am seeing this as a frightening situation, she sees it as OK' (Hobson 1993: 235).

37. Thus "Although autistic children may make requests for objects and actions and may understand other people's pointing gestures that convey instructions, they rarely make gestures such as showing, giving or pointing in order to share awareness of an object's existence or properties or comprehend such gestures when they are made by others" (Hobson 1993: 242, see also Baron-Cohen 1995: 66).

38. Thus autistic individuals have metarepresentational problems even with respect to their ability to understand complex emotions. Baron-Cohen reports that in viewing photographs of people expressing emotions "most children with autism were able to match happy and sad, but significantly more children with autism made errors in matching pictures of surprised expressions. They mistook these for non-cognitive states such as yawning or being hungry, focusing on the open mouth" (Baron-Cohen 1995: 79). He opines that this is because surprise is a 'belief-based' emotion, one that is likely to require recognition of the other's cognitive take on things. It also fits with their kind of 'phenomenalist' errors to which they are prone in appearance-reality tests (Baron-Cohen 1995: 82).

39. Hence their "difficulty in disembedding from a particular point of view and acquiring the capacity to adopt a variety of 'co-orientations' to given objects or events, for example to pretend a matchbox 'is' a car" (Hobson 1993: 243). This is consistent with the fact that this facet of autism be understood as an "innately determined biological disorder" (Gopnik et al. 2000: 51).

40. Indeed a basic impairment to both the recreative imagination and a secondary impairment to metarepresentational ability would make problematic the entertaining of counterfactual possibilities and complex future planning, which could explain some of their difficulties associated with executive control (see Currie 1996: 253). It might also be the source of ultra-literal tendencies and difficulties with metaphor and analogy displayed by autistic individuals, since these require capacities for a kind of aspect-switching. An imaginative inability of this kind would also make it difficult, if not impossible, to negotiate conversational pragmatics. Such a deficit may also shed light on why autistic individuals have particular problems in the use and understanding of pronouns, since "Pronouns and deictic terms must be produced and understood with respect to a given point-of-view" (Harris 1996: 218, see Frith 1989: ch. 8, 11).

41. For example, autistic sufferers "show little interest in how their actions affect others and how other's actions are meant to affect them. They may often be confused about what other people do, but show little capacity to be hurt by intentionally malicious behaviour, or touched by intentionally kind behaviour whether or not the behaviour is experienced as beneficial. They may be amused by other people's physical 'antics', even when those antics betray extreme distress or pain. They understand sabotage, but are blind to deceit and other forms of slyness. Jokes, as opposed to pratfalls, are impossible to 'get'" (McGeer 2001: 113).

42. Returning to the case of the boy who mistakenly fetches his mother some clothes instead of cloves, it appears that despite understanding the relevant psychological attitude, he has little or no understanding of what people normally desire in such and such circumstances. He seems to have little truck with cultural norms.

References

Arbib, M. 2003. "The Evolving Mirror System." In *Language Evolution*, M. Christiansen and S. Kirby (eds), 158–181. Oxford: Oxford University Press.

Arbib, M. 2005. "From monkey-like action recognition to human language: An evolutionary framework for neurolinguistics." *Behavioral and Brain Sciences* 28(2): 105–24.

Andrews, K. 2002. "Interpreting Autism: A Critique of Davidson on Thought and Language." *Philosophical Psychology* 15: 317–32.

Astington, J.W. and Jenkins, J.M. 1999. "A Longitudinal Study of Relation Between Language and Theory of Mind Development." *Developmental Psychology* 35: 1311–20.

Avramides, A. 1999. "Davidson and the New Sceptical Problem." In *Donald Davidson: Truth, Meaning and Knowledge*, U. Zeglen (ed), London: Routledge.

Avramides, A. 2001. *Other Minds*. London: Routledge.

Baron-Cohen, S. 1995. *Mindblindness: An Essay on Autism and Theory of Mind*. Cambridge, MA: MIT Press.

Baron-Cohen, S. 2000. "Theory of Mind and Autism: A Fifteen Year Review." In *Understanding Other Minds: Perspectives from Developmental Cognitive Neuroscience*, S. Baron-Cohen, H. Tager-Flusberg and D. Cohen (eds), 3–20. Oxford: Oxford University Press.

Bartsch, K. and Wellman, H. 1995. *Children Talk About the Mind*. New York: Oxford University Press.

Berguno, G. and Bowler, D. 2004. "Understanding Pretence and Understanding Action." *British Journal of Developmental Psychology* 22: 531–44.

Bermúdez, J. 1998. *The Paradox of Self-Consciousness*. Cambridge, MA: MIT Press.

Bloom, P. 1998. "Some Issues in the Evolution of Language and Thought." In *The Evolution of Mind*, D.D. Cummins and C. Allen (eds), 204–223. Oxford: Oxford University Press.

Bohman, J. 2000. "The Importance of the Second Person: Interpretation, Practical Knowledge, and Normative Attitudes." In *Empathy and Agency*, H.H. Kogler and K.R. Stueber (eds), 222–42. Boulder: Westview Press.

Boucher, J. 1996. "What Could Possibly Explain Autism?" In *Theories of Theories of Mind*, P. Carruthers and P. Smith (eds), 223–41. Cambridge: Cambridge University Press.

Brinck, I. 2004. "Joint Attention, Triangulation and Radical Interpretation." *Dialectica* 58: 179–205.

Call, J. and Tomasello, M. 1996. "The Effect of Humans on the Cognitive Development of Apes." In *Reading into Thought*, A.E. Russon, K.A. Bard and S.T. Parker (eds), 371–403. New York: Cambridge University Press.

Carpendale, J.L.M. and Lewis, C. 2004. "Constructing an Understanding of the Mind: The Development of Children's Social Understanding within Social Interaction." *Behavioural and Brain Sciences*: 79–151.

Carruthers, P. 1996a. "Simulation and Self-Knowledge: A Defence of Theory-Theory." In *Theories of Theories of Mind*, P. Carruthers and P. Smith (eds), 22–38. Cambridge: Cambridge University Press.

Carruthers, P. 1998. "Thinking in Language? Evolution and a Modularist Possibility." In *Language and Thought: Interdisciplinary Themes*, P. Carruthers and J. Boucher (eds), 94–119. Cambridge: Cambridge University Press.

Carruthers, P. 2004. "Practical Reasoning in a Modular Mind." *Mind and Language* 19: 259–78.

Chomsky, N. 1986. *Knowledge of Language: Its Nature, Origin and Use*. New York: Praeger.

Clark, A. 1998. "Magic Words: How Language Augments Human Computation." In *Language and Thought: Interdisciplinary Themes*, P. Carruthers and J. Boucher. Cambridge: Cambridge University Press.

Coltheart, M. and Langdon, R. 1998. "Autism, Modularity and Levels of Explanation in Cognitive Science." *Mind and Language* 13: 138–52.

Corballis, M.C. 2003. "Gestural Origins of Language." In *Language Evolution*, M. Christiansen and S. Kirby (eds), 201–218. Oxford: Oxford University Press.

Currie, G. 1996. "Simulation-Theory, Theory-Theory and the Evidence from Autism." In *Theories of Theories of Mind*, P. Carruthers and P. Smith (eds), 242–256. Cambridge: Cambridge University Press.

Currie, G. and Sterelny, K. 2000. "How to Think about the Modularity of Mind-Reading." *The Philosophical Quarterly* 50: 145–60.

Davidson, D. 1984. *Inquiries into Truth and Interpretation*. Oxford: Clarendon Press.

Dennett, D.C. 1991. "Real Patterns." *Journal of Philosophy*: 27–51.

De Villiers, J.G. and De Villiers, P. 1999. "Linguistic Determinism and the Understanding of False Beliefs." In *Children's Reasoning and the Mind*, P. Mitchell and K. Riggs (eds), 189–226. New York: Psychology Press.

Donald, M. 1991. *Origins of the Modern Mind: Three Stages in the Evolution of Culture and Cognition*. Cambridge, MA: Harvard University Press.

Fodor, J.A. 1994. *The Elm and the Expert: Mentalese and Its Semantics*. Cambridge, MA: MIT Press.

Fodor, J.A. 2003. *Hume Variations*. Oxford: Oxford University Press.

Frith, U. 1989. *Autism: Explaining the Enigma*. Oxford: Blackwell.

Gallagher, S. and Hutto, D.D. 2007. "Primary Interaction and Narrative Practice: From Empathic Resonance to Folk Psychology." In *The Shared Mind: Perspectives on Intersubjectivity*, J. Zlatev, T. Racine, C. Sinha and E. Itkonen (eds). Amsterdam/Philadelphia: John Benjamins.

Gardner, H. 1983. *Frames of Mind: The Theory of Multiple Intelligences*. New York: Basic Books.

Gardner, H. 1993. *Mutliple Intelligences: The Theory in Practice*. New York: Basic Books.

Garfield, J.L., Peterson, C.C. and Perry, T. 2001. "Social Cognition, Language Acquisition and the Development of the Theory of Mind." *Mind and Language* 16: 494–541.

Goldman, A.I. 1992. "In Defense of the Simulation Theory." *Mind and Language* 7: 104–19.

Goldman, A.I. 2001. "Desire, Intention, and the Simulation Theory." In *Intentions and Intentionality*, B.F. Malle, L.J. Moses and D.A. Baldwin (eds), 207–225. Cambridge, MA: MIT Press.

Gómez, J.C. 1998. "Thoughts about the Evolution of LADs." In *Language and Thought: Interdisciplinary Themes*, P. Carruthers and J. Boucher (eds), 76–93. Cambridge: Cambridge University Press.

Gómez, J.C. 2005. "Joint Attention and the Notion of Subject: Insights from Apes, Normal Children and Children with Autism." In *Joint Attention: Communication and Other Minds*, N.

Eilan, C. Horel, T. McCormack and J. Roessler (eds), 65–84. Oxford: Oxford University Press.
Gopnik, A. 2003. "The Theory Theory as an Alternative to the Innateness Hypothesis." In *Chomsky and His Critics*, L.M. Antony and N. Hornstein (eds), 238–54.
Gopnik, A. 2004. "Finding Our Inner Scientist." *Daedalus* 133: 21–8.
Gopnik, A., Capps, L. and Meltzoff A. 2000. "Early Theories of Mind: What the Theory Theory can tell us about Autism." In *Understanding Other Minds: Perspectives from Developmental Cognitive Neuroscience*, S. Baron-Cohen, H. Tager-Flusberg and D. Cohen (eds), 50–72. Oxford: Oxford University Press.
Gopnik, A. and Wellman, H.M. 1992. "Why the Child's Theory of Mind Really 'Is' a Theory." *Mind and Language* 7: 145–71.
Harris, P. 1996. "Desires, Beliefs and Language." In *Theories of Theories of Mind*, P. Carruthers and P. Smith (eds), 200–20. Cambridge: Cambridge University Press.
Hobson, P. 1993. "The Emotional Origins of Social Understanding." *Philosophical Psychology* 6: 227–49.
Hutto, D.D. 1997. "The Story of the Self: The Narrative Basis of Self-Development." In *Critical Studies: Ethics and the Subject*, K. Simms (ed.), 61–75. Amsterdam: Rodopi.
Hutto, D.D. 1999A. *The Presence of Mind*. Amsterdam: John Benjamins.
Hutto, D. D. 1999b. "A Cause for Concern: Reasons, Causes and Explanations." *Philosophy and Phenomenological Research* 59(2): 381–401.
Hutto, D.D. 2000. *Beyond Physicalism*. Amsterdam: John Benjamins.
Hutto, D.D. 2002. "The World is Not Enough: Shared Emotions and Other Minds." In *Understanding Emotions*, P. Goldie (ed.), 27–54. Aldershot: Ashgate.
Hutto, D.D. 2003/2006. *Wittgenstein and the End of Philosophy: Neither Theory nor Therapy*. Basingstoke: Palgrave Macmillan.
Hutto, D.D. 2003. "Folk Psychological Explanations: Narratives and the Case of Autism." *Philosophical Papers* 32: 345–61.
Hutto, D.D. 2004. "The Limits of Spectatorial Folk Psychology." *Mind and Language* 19: 548–73.
Hutto, D.D. 2005. "Starting Without Theory: Confronting the Paradox of Conceptual Development." In *Other Minds: How Humans Bridge the Divide Between Self and Others*, B. Malle and S. Hodges (eds), 56–72. New York: The Guilford Press.
Hutto, D.D. 2006. "Unprincipled Engagements: Emotional Experience, Expression and Response." In *Consciousness and Emotion: Special Issue on Radical Enactivism*. R. Menary (ed).
Hutto, D.D. 2007a. "First Communion: The Mimetic Ability Hypothesis." In *The Shared Mind: Perspectives on Intersubjectivity*, J. Zlatev, T. Racine, C. Sinha and E. Itkonen (eds). Amsterdam/Philadelphia: John Benjamins.
Hutto, D.D. 2007b. *Folk Psychological Narratives: The Socio-Cultural Basis of Understanding Reasons*. Cambridge, MA: MIT Press.
Hutto, D.D. 2007c. "Folk Psychology without Theory or Simulation." In *Folk Psychology Reassessed*, D.D. Hutto and M. Ratcliffe (eds). Dordrecht: Springer.
Hutto, D.D. 2007d. "The Narrative Practice Hypothesis." In *Narrative and Understanding Persons*, D.D. Hutto (ed). Cambridge: Cambridge University Press.
Jackendoff, R. 1999. "What is a Concept, That a Person May Grasp It?" In *Concepts: Core Readings*, E. Margolis and S. Laurence (eds), 305–33. Cambridge, MA: MIT Press.
Karmiloff-Smith, A. 1995. *Beyond Modularity: A Developmental Perspective on Cognitive Science*. Cambridge, MA: MIT Press.
Kennett, J. 2002. "Autism, Empathy and Moral Agency." *The Philosophical Quarterly* 52: 340–57.

Lakoff, G. and Johnson, M. 1980. *Metaphors We Live By*. Chicago: Chicago University Press.

Leekam, S. 2005. "Why do Children with Autism have a Joint Attention Impairment?" In *Joint Attention: Communication and Other Minds*, N. Eilan, C. Horel, T. McCormack and J. Roessler (eds), 65–84. Oxford: Oxford University Press.

Leslie, A.M. 1987. "Pretense and Representation: The Origins of 'Theory of Mind.'" *Psychological Review* 94: 412–26.

Leslie, A.M., Friedman, O. and German, T.P. 2004. "Core Mechanisms in 'Theory of Mind.'" *Trends in Cognitive Sciences* 8: 528–33.

Leslie, A.M. and Frith, U. 1988. "Autistic Children's Understanding of Seeing, Knowing and Believing." *British Journal of Developmental Psychology* 6: 315–24.

Mahoney, J.C. 1989. *The Mundane Matter of the Mental Language*. Cambridge: Cambridge University Press.

McGeer, V. 2001. "Psycho-Practice, Psycho-Theory and Autism." *Journal of Consciousness Studies* 8: 109–32.

McGeer, V. 2007. "The Regulative Dimension of Folk Psychology." In *Folk Psychology Re-Assessed*, D.D. Hutto and M. Ratcliffe (eds). Dordrecht: Springer.

Millikan, R.G. 2001. "Purposes and Cross-Purposes: On the Evolution of Languages and Language." *The Monist* 84: 392–416.

Mithen, S. 1996. *The Pre-History of the Mind: A Search for the Origins of Art, Religion and Science*. London: Thames and Hudson.

Nelson, K. 2003. "Narrative and the Emergence of a Consciousness of Self." In *Narrative and Consciousness*, G.D. Fireman, T.E.J. McVay and O. Flanagan (eds), 17–36. Oxford: Oxford University Press.

Nichols, S. and Stich, S. 2003. *Mindreading: An Integrated Account of Pretence, Self-Awareness and Understanding of Other Minds*. Oxford: Oxford University Press.

Ozonoff, S., Pennington, B. and Rogers, S. 1991. "Executive Function Deficits in High Functioning Autistic Children. Relationship to Theory of Mind." *Journal of Child Psychology and Psychiatry* 32: 1081–106.

Perner, J., Sprung, M., Zauner, P. and Haider, H. 2003. "Want That is Understood Well before Say That, Think That, and False Belief: A Test of de Villiers's Linguistic Determinism on German-Speaking Children." *Child Development* 74: 179–88.

Pinker, S. 1994. *The Language Instinct*. New York: Morrow.

Sperber, D. 1994. "The Modularity of Thought and the Epistemology of Representations." In *Mapping the Mind: Domain Specificity in Cognition and Culture*, L.A. Hirschfeld and S.A. Gelman (eds), 39–67. Cambridge: Cambridge University Press.

Stich, S. and Nichols, S. 1995. "Second Thoughts on Simulation." In *Mental Simulation*, M. Davies (ed.), 87–108. Oxford: Blackwell.

Tomasello, M. 2003. "On the Different Origins of Symbols and Grammar." In *Language Evolution*, M. Christiansen and S. Kirby (eds), 94–110. Oxford: Oxford University Press.

Tomasello, M. and Call, J. 1997. *Primate Cognition*. New York: Oxford University Press.

Vaccari, O. and Vaccari, E.E. 1961. *Pictorial Chinese-Japanese Characters: A New and Fascinating Method to Learn Ideographs*. Vaccari Language Institute.

Velleman, J.D. 2004. "The Centred Self." *Unpublished manuscript*

Wellman, H.M. and Phillips, A. 2001. "Developing Intentional Understandings." In *Intentions and Intentionality*, B. Malle, L.J. Moses and D.A. Baldwin (eds), 125–148. Cambridge, MA: MIT Press.

Wellman, H.M. 1991. "From Desires to Belief: Acquisition of a Theory of Mind." In *Natural Theories of Mind*, A. Whiten (ed.), 19–38. Oxford: Blackwell.
Wellman, H.M. and Wooley, J.D. 1990. "From Simple Desires to Ordinary Beliefs: The Early Development of Everyday Psychology." *Cognition* 35: 245–75.
Wittgenstein, L. 1983. *Remarks on the Foundations of Mathematics*. Oxford: Blackwell.
Wittgenstein, L. 1953. *Philosophical Investigations*. Oxford: Basil Blackwell.

The narrative alternative to theory of mind

Shaun Gallagher

Daniel Hutto, in his essay on "Unprincipled Engagements", is right to link up perception, action, emotion, and interaction with others, and to see them as fully integrated at the most basic levels of experience. And there is, as we hear every now and then (e.g. Merleau-Ponty 1945, and more recently Noë 2004) a certain truth to behaviourism. But it is also the case that all of this action and behaviour leads us somewhere – namely to meaning – and that this must also count as an important aspect that has a looping effect, in the sense that it gets reincorporated back into our experience. The need to satisfy "our own interpretive needs" seems to be a need that is either built into the basic levels of our life, or is something that is generated in and retrofitted into those basic perceptual, emotional, interactive aspects. If, as philosophers and psychologists, we then look for meaning in these very processes, in our quest to understand ourselves, it seems reasonable (as part of a rationality that grows out of this organization) to ascribe reasons, rules, or laws to our own behaviour. This is what leads us on to the kinds of abstract, overly mentalistic and overly propositional explanations that Hutto is attempting to clear away.

Theory of mind (TOM) approaches to explanations of how we come to understand others are typically abstract (third-person when they need to be second-person), mentalistic (starting with the supposition that there are things like minds, beliefs, desires that we have no access to in others, and even sometimes in ourselves), and biased toward theoretical reason (when practical reason is a better way to go). They tend to forget emotion, and our ability to read emotion, not in the minds of others, but on the faces of others, and in their gestures and expressive movements. I have argued against TOM approaches on these grounds (Gallagher 2001). And yet there is incontrovertible evidence that our human experience includes more than basic perceptions, emotions, and embodied interactions. That is, we (together) go on to invent important institutions and create laws, and even puzzle ourselves about whether laws could be natural. I think that the way this tends to happen – and a good way to think about how we get from perceptual experience to rationality – is through the medium of narrative. I want to pick up this idea at Hutto's suggestion about emotion and narrative.

Hutto quotes Goldie on the connection between emotions and narrative: for Goldie emotions are, "typically complex, episodic, dynamic and structured" (Goldie 2000: 16). Emotion can thus constitute "part of a narrative – roughly, an unfolding sequence of actions and events, thoughts and feelings, in which the emotion is embedded" (Goldie 2000: 13, 102). Hutto prefers to say that "emotions and their consequences have a kind of structure that is ripe for narration".

I think that the idea of narrative competence suggests an alternative to TOM approaches, and a better way to account for the more sophisticated understandings (and mis-understandings) we have of others. Here I won't try to trace the entire story of how we move from neurons to narrative, or ontogenetically from primary intersubjectivity, involving face-to-face interactions in which we see, in the other person's bodily movements, facial gestures, eye direction, etc. what they intend and what they feel (Trevarthen 1979; see Gallagher 2001; 2004), to the more nuanced understanding that comes from mature interactions with others. I do think that there is a good deal of evidence that humans have, from infancy onward, direct perceptual access to the intentions and feelings of others in their embodied and situated comportment. Our primary way of understanding others is worked out not via 3rd-person observation or 1st-person simulation, but via real (2nd person) interaction in pragmatic and social contexts. Recent neuroscience has given us some important and fascinating data on motor resonance processes – how our motor system reverberates in our encounters with others. Thus, for example, Gallese writes:

> when we observe goal-related behaviours … specific sectors of our pre-motor cortex become active. These cortical sectors are those same sectors that are active when we actually perform the same actions. In other words, when we observe actions performed by other individuals our motor system 'resonates' along with that of the observed agent (Gallese 2001, 38).

In contrast to Gallese, who suggests that this kind of sensorymotor capacity is already an empathic understanding of the other, Jean Decety (2002, 2005) suggests that a more developed empathic understanding of others would involve these basic resonance processes plus the mentalistic theory of mind capacities. Empathy, he suggests, does not imply simply an emotional response initiated by the emotional state of the other. It also requires a minimal comprehension of the mental states of this person (see Decety & Jackson 2004; Jackson, Meltzoff & Decety 2005).

In partial agreement with Decety I will argue that the more sophisticated understanding of others is something more complex and less automatic than the automatic processes of the resonance system. In contrast to Decety, however, I want to propose an alternative model to TOM (whether theoretical or simulationist versions) as the basis for understanding, since TOM approaches make understanding too much a cognitive, "in the head" process, and not sufficiently situated. The alternative is to think of how we gain and employ narrative competency as a form of understanding.

Around the age of 1 year, according to Trevarthen, and others, the infant goes beyond person-to-person immediacy and enters contexts of shared attention and shared situations in which they start to learn what things mean and what they are for. Peter Hobson (2002: 62) recently summarized the idea, which Trevarthen calls "secondary intersubjectivity".

> The defining feature of secondary intersubjectivity is that an object or event can become a focus between people. Objects and events can be communicated about… the infant's interactions with another person begin to have reference to the things that surround them.[1]

By the time that infants are two years of age they are well practiced in understanding things as other people understand them, and when this practice is combined with several other newly acquired capacities, young children are ready to understand things and people in an emerging narrative structure. The acquisition of language, plus the capacity to recognize their own image in the mirror, feeds a developing conceptual understanding of themselves that is essential to the onset of autobiographical memory.

> By 18–24 months of age infants have a concept of themselves that is sufficiently viable to serve as a referent around which personally experienced events can be organized in memory … The self at 18–24 months of age achieves whatever 'critical mass' is necessary to serve as an organizer and regulator of experience …. This achievement in self-awareness (recognition) is followed shortly by the onset of autobiographical memory … (Howe 2000: 91–92).

Autobiographical memory is one aspect that shapes narrative competency – an ability to see things in a narrative framework. Along with a growing linguistic competency, a developing conceptual sense of self, and the interactions associated with secondary intersubjectivity, autobiographical memory helps to kick-start narrative abilities during the second year of life. Two-year olds may start this process by working more from a set of short behavioural scripts than from full-fledged narratives; and their autobiographical memories have to be elicited by questions and prompts (Howe 2000). From 2–4 years, children fine-tune their narrative abilities via further development of language ability, autobiographical memory, and a more stable objective sense of self. Importantly, it is just at this time, starting in the second year, that children start to show empathic understanding (Decety & Jackson 2004).

I want to suggest that the abilities for intersubjective interaction and understanding that start with primary and secondary intersubjectivity, develop along a route that in most ordinary cases exploits narrative competency rather than the procedures associated with theory of mind (e.g., appeal to folk psychology or simulation routines). This doesn't mean that our understanding of others requires an occurrent or explicit narrative story telling: but it does require the ability to see/to frame the other person in a detailed pragmatic or social context, to understand that context in a narrative way. As Alasdair McIntyre (1981) suggested, for an observer, or for a participant, an action has intelligibility when it can find a place in a narrative. We make sense out of our own actions and out of the actions of others by placing them in a narrative framework. This is not a new theory of understanding. It has its roots in certain hermeneutical traditions. Thus, for instance, Dilthey recognized that it is not sufficient to focus on grasping the mental states of others in order to understand their actions.

It is necessary to distinguish the state of mind which produced the action by which it is expressed from the circumstances of life by which it is conditioned.

> … [In some cases] action separates itself from the background of the context of life and, unless accompanied by an explanation of how circumstances, purposes, means and context of life are linked together in it, allows no comprehensive account of the inner life from which it arose (Dilthey 1988: 153).

This is still too mentalistic; it is not the inner life or the mental life that we attempt to access, but simply the other's life in its worldly/situational contexts, and that is best captured in a narrative form. I encounter the other person, not abstracted from their circumstances, but in the middle of something that has a beginning and that is going somewhere. I see them in the framework of a story in which either I have a part to play or I don't. The narrative is not just about what is going on inside their heads; it's about what is going on in the world. To understand the story of what this person is doing does not require a mentalistic inference or simulation. Our understanding of others is not based on attempts to get into their heads, to access a 'landscape of consciousness' since we already have access to a 'landscape of action' (Bruner 1986) which is constituted by their embodied actions and the rich worldly contexts within which they act – contexts that operate as scaffolds for the meaning and significance of actions and expressive movements.

Janet Astington (1990) has argued that narrative competency requires the acquisition of a theory of mind. Citing Bruner's concept of the landscape of consciousness ("what those involved in the action know, think, or feel, or do not know, think, or feel" [Bruner 1986: 14]), she suggests that to understand narrative we need access to the characters' minds, and to have the latter requires us to have TOM. But Bruner himself offers good experimental evidence against the importance of the landscape of consciousness (LofC) for understanding narratives. Feldman, Bruner et al. (1990), in a study of narrative comprehension in adults, presented two different versions of the same story to two groups, respectively. The first and original story mentions the mental states of the characters as the story develops, and so was rich in the LofC. The second story is the very same story stripped of mental terms, leaving only the landscape of actions (LofA). The results showed no significant differences (1) in subjects using reader-related mental verbs when they recount the LofC narrative; (2) in recounting the facts of the stories – "the retellings were virtually indistinguishable"; (3) in recounting the order of events; and (4) when providing a meaning summary (gist) for the story: "there is no version difference in the kind of gist given".

What does seem important for understanding narrative is the kind of emotional resonance that one finds already in infancy, in primary intersubjectivity. Decety and Chaminade (2003) have shown this connection as it plays out in the brain. In their fMRI study, subjects were presented with a series of video clips showing actors telling sad and neutral stories, as if they had personally experienced them. The stories were told with either congruent or incongruent motor expression of emotion. Subjects were then asked to rate the mood of the actor and how likable they found that person. Watching sad stories versus neutral stories was associated with increased processing activity in emotion related structures (including the amygdala and parieto-frontal areas, predominantly in the right hemisphere). These areas were not activated when the narrator showed incongruent facial expressions. The reasonable hypothesis is that conflict between what we sense as the emotional state of the other person, simply on the basis of seeing their faces and actions, and the narrative content they present, is disruptive to understanding. Whatever is going on in the brain correlates not simply to features of action and expression (and the subjectivity of the other person) but to the larger story, the scene, the circumstance of the other person, and how features of action and expression match or fail to match those circumstances. If the emotional character of the other person is not in character with the narrative framework – with the story that I could tell about her and her circumstances – it is difficult to understand that person.

An important part of narrative competency involves the capacity for self-narrative: one is tempted to say that only when we are capable of understanding ourselves in a narrative way – once we can formulate a self-narrative – we are then able to understand others in a narrative way. But it is not so simple or straightforward. Since we develop in social contexts and normally acquire the capacity for narrative in those contexts, then the development of self-narrative obviously involves others. Katherine Nelson (2003) points out that narrative competency for the landscape of action emerges in 2-year olds, "with respect to the child's own experience, which is forecast and rehearsed with him or her by parents". Self-narrative requires building on our experiences of others and their narratives, so "children of 2–4 years often 'appropriate' someone else's story as their own" (Nelson 2003). Furthermore, to occupy a position within a self-narrative requires more than a minimal, non-conceptual self-awareness – it requires a conceptual, objective, narrative self that is aware of itself as having a point of view that is different from others.[2]

There is much more to say about narrative competency, how it is normally constituted, and how it may change in certain pathologies (see Gallagher 2003a; 2003b). Here my limited aim, in agreement with Hutto, is to suggest that there is no need to appeal to overly mentalistic theory-of-mind explanations for how we understand others. What begins as perceptual and emotional resonance processes in early infancy, which allow us to pick up the feelings and intentions of others from their movements, gestures, and facial expressions, feeds into the development of a more sophisticated understanding of how and why people act as they do, found in our ability to frame their actions, and our own, in narrative structure.

Notes

1. This view is quite consistent with one expressed by Merleau-Ponty about 30 years before Trevarthen. "No sooner has my gaze fallen upon a living body in the process of acting than the objects surrounding it immediately take on a fresh layer of significance. … [The child can appropriate objects and] learn to use them as others do, because the body schema ensures the immediate correspondence of what he sees done and what he himself does … and the unsophisticated thinking of our earliest years remains as an indispensable acquisition underlying that of maturity (Merleau-Ponty 1945: 353–354).

2. Do children pass false-belief tests at the age of four (but not three) because they suddenly acquire a theory of mind, as is the pervasive claim in the theory of mind literature? Or do they gain the capacity to recognize how the other (whether Maxie, or Sally-Ann, or Snoopy, etc.) will act because their narrative competency has sufficiently developed at that point so that they can see others as occupying different character roles that do not have to be identical with their own. It is notable that many false-belief tests are presented in the form of a narrative and could be interpreted as a test for a certain level of narrative competency.

References

Astington, J. W. 1990. "Narrative and the child's theory of mind." In *Narrative thought and narrative language*, B. K. Britton and A. D. Pellegrini (eds), 151–171. Hillsdale, NJ: Lawrence Erlbaum Associates.

Bruner, J. 1986. *Actual Minds, Possible Worlds*. Cambridge, MA: Harvard University.

Decety, J. 2002. "Naturaliser l'empathie [Empathy naturalized]." *L'Encéphale*, 28 : 9–20.

Decety, J. 2005. "Une anatomie de l'empathie." *Revue de Psychiatrie, Sciences Humaines et Neurosciences*, 3(11): 16–24.

Decety, J., and Chaminade, T. 2003. "Neural correlates of feeling sympathy." *Neuropsychologia* 41: 127–138.

Decety, J. and Jackson, P.L. 2004. "The Functional Architecture of Human Empathy." *Behavioral and Cognitive Neuroscience Reviews* 3 (2): 71–100.

Dilthey, W. 1988. "The understanding of other persons and their life-expressions." Translated by K. Mueller-Vollmer in *The Hermeneutics Reader*, 152–64. New York: Continuum.

Feldman, C.F., Bruner, J., Renderer, B., and Spitzer, S. 1990. "Narrative comprehension." In *Narrative thought and narrative language,* B.K. Britton and A.D. Pellegrini (eds), 1–78. Hillsdale New Jersey: Erlbaum.

Gallagher, S. 2004. "Understanding interpersonal problems in autism: Interaction theory as an alternative to theory of mind." *Philosophy, Psychiatry, and Psychology* 11 (3): 199–217.

Gallagher, S. 2003a. "Self-narrative in schizophrenia." In *The Self in Neuroscience and Psychiatry*, A. S. David and T. Kircher (eds), 336–357. Cambridge: Cambridge University Press.

Gallagher, S. 2003b. "Self-narrative, embodied action, and social context." In *Between Suspicion and Sympathy: Paul Ricoeur's Unstable Equilibrium* (Festschrift for Paul Ricoeur), A. Wiercinski (ed.), 409–423. Toronto: The Hermeneutic Press.

Gallagher, S. 2001. "The practice of mind: Theory, simulation, or interaction?" *Journal of Consciousness Studies* 8 (5–7): 83–107.

Gallese, V. 2001. The "shared manifold" hypothesis: from mirror neurons to empathy. *Journal of Consciousness Studies* 8: 33–50.

Goldie, P. 2000. *The Emotions: A Philosophical Exploration*. Oxford: Oxford University Press.

Hobson, P. 2002. *The Cradle of Thought*. London: Macmillan.

Howe, M. L. 2000. *The fate of early memories: Developmental science and the retention of childhood experiences*. Cambridge, MA: MIT Press.

Jackson, P. L., Meltzoff, A. N. and Decety, J. 2005. "How do we perceive the pain of others? A window into the neural processes involved in empathy." *NeuroImage* 24: 771–779.

McIntyre, A. 1981. *After Virtue: A Study in Moral Theory*. Notre Dame: University of Notre Dame Press.

Merleau-Ponty, M. 1942/1963. *La structure du comportement*. Paris: Gallimard. English translation: *The Structure of Behavior*. Trans. A. L. Fisher. Boston: Beacon Press.

Merleau-Ponty, M. 1945/1962. *Phenomenologie de la perception*. Paris: Gallimard. English translation: *Phenomenology of Perception*. Trans. C. Smith. London: Routledge and Kegan Paul.

Nelson K. 2003. "Narrative and the emergence of a consciousness of self." In *Narrative and Consciousness*, G. D. Fireman, T. E. J. McVay and O. Flanagan (eds), 17–36. Oxford: Oxford University Press.

Noë, A. 2004. *Action in Perception*. Cambridge, MA: MIT Press.

Trevarthen, C.B. 1979. "Communication and cooperation in early infancy: A description of primary intersubjectivity." In *Before Speech*, M. Bullowa (ed.), 321–47. Cambridge: Cambridge University Press.

Trevarthen, C. and Hubley, P. 1978. "Secondary intersubjectivity: Confidence, confiding and acts of meaning in the first year." In *Action, Gesture and Symbol: The Emergence of Language*, A. Lock (ed.), 183–229. London: Academic Press.

Narrative practice and understanding reasons

Reply to Gallagher

Daniel D. Hutto

1. Shared ambitions

Gallagher writes, "My limited aim, in agreement with Hutto, is to suggest that there is no need to appeal to overly mentalistic theory-of-mind explanations for how we understand others" and that "narrative competence suggests an alternative to TOM approaches" (Gallagher: this volume). Indeed, he goes further and adds that "Our primary way of understanding others is worked out not *via* 3rd-person observation or 1st-person simulation, but via real (2nd person) interaction in pragmatic and social contexts" (Gallagher: this volume). Those familiar with my previous writings on narrative and folk psychology will recognise that all of this is music to my ears (Hutto 1997, 2003b, 2004). Indeed, making an extended case for these sorts of claims is the primary focus of several of my new papers, edited volumes and my forthcoming book, *Folk Psychological Narratives*.[1] In this reply I highlight some aspects of the approach that I have been developing in those works.

2. The narrative practice hypothesis in snapshot

Folk psychology is a complex skill; the full mastery of which comes over time, but this only happens if children have all the right inherited capacities in tact and if they are supported by their elders, and given the developmental opportunity to engage in specific kinds of social practices, i.e. narrative ones – specifically those with a distinctive subject matter. The core claim of the Narrative Practice Hypothesis (or NPH) is that direct encounters with stories about reasons for acting, supplied in interactive contexts by responsive caregivers, is the normal route through which children become familiar with both (1) the core structure of folk psychology and

(2) the norm-governed possibilities for wielding it in practice, knowing *how* and knowing *when* to use it.

Stories detailing the reasons for which protagonists act serve as exemplars in this sort of initiation.[2] This requires repeated exposure to folk psychological narratives, with which children engage with imaginatively and emotionally, under the guidance of elders. By being supported in this way they acquire an explicit grasp of the *forms and norms* of folk psychology. When encountered in this fashion, this special class of narratives reveals the kinds of invariant relations that hold between propositional attitudes and acquaint listeners to the normal settings in which these operate; revealing what types of factors must be adjusted and accommodated for when making sense of actions in this way. By laying bare these features, stories of this kind familiarise children with the folk psychological schema and the norms governing its practical application.

There are two senses of 'narrative' to distinguish here – narrative in the sense of the third-personal object of co-attention – the folk psychological narrative itself – and acts of narration, the second-personal interactions that constitute story-tellings through which children are introduced to the stories in questions. Both play distinct roles, according to the NPH.

As an object of co-attention the narrative or story itself might be spontaneous production, an autobiographical account, a bit of gossip, or the re-telling of an established text (perhaps a cultural artefact of which there will typically be multiple versions). Here's one such narrative of the last sort (As yet I have no data on how many of these children encounter in the normal course of their development. I imagine the figure to be very high, but for now I leave it to the reader to speculate on this):

> Little Red Riding Hood *learns* from the woodcutter that her grandmother is sick. She *wants* to make her grandmother feel better [she is a nice, caring child], and she *thinks* that a basket of treats will help, so she brings such a basket through the woods to her grandmother's house [beliefs and desires lead to actions]. When she arrives there, she *sees* the wolf in her grandmother's bed, but she *falsely believes* that the wolf is her grandmother [appearances can be deceiving]. When she *realizes* it is a wolf, she is *frightened* and runs away, because she *knows* wolves can hurt people. The wolf, who indeed *wants* to eat her, leaps out of the bed and runs after her *trying* to catch her (Lillard 1997: 268, emphases mine).

Fairy tales, like this famous one, are perhaps the most reliable means of revealing the core folk psychological framework: they show how the core propositional attitudes work together in leading to intentions and (all being well) to action. Typically, such stories include, *inter alia*, illustrations of the nature of means-end planning, the way that projects relate, stack and develop and how a character's purposes can be at odds with those of others, and so on. Crucially, they have *precisely the right form* and content to show how the core propositional attitudes interact in reasoning, exposing their designated inferential roles and relations.[3] Understanding this framework is necessary for reflectively applying mentalistic concepts when understanding the novel actions of others (and reflectively understanding one's own) in terms of explanations that, at root, involve belief/desire pairings.

The countless folk psychological narratives children encounter provide exemplars of the structure of practical reasoning in action. Ideally, they are presented in a very rich interactive setting, with engaged participants on both sides, both storytellers and children. It is helpful to remind ourselves of this, lest we are swayed by misguided poverty of the stimulus arguments into thinking that children are disembodied *tabula rasa* encountering such stories as if they were serial broadcasts from an Orwellian Ministry of Truth.[4] Acquiring an explicit understanding of folk psychology by being told stories by adults is nothing like being taught a set of explicit principles, rules or regulative propositions. Only if we have the model of folk psychology as a 'set of propositions' in mind would it be right to follow Goldman in saying that few children "have mothers who utter [folk psychological] platitudes" (Goldman 1992a: 107).

In general, engaging with narratives is not a passive affair: it presupposes a wide range of emotive and interactive abilities. To appreciate stories children must be capable, at least to some degree, of imaginative identification. Not only must they exercise their recreative imaginations in various ways, if they are gripped by the story they will also be responding emotively, just as they do in basic social engagements. So, I fully agree that, "what does seem important for understanding narrative is the kind of emotional resonance that one finds already in infancy, in primary intersubjectivity" (Gallagher, this volume). Indeed, as one might expect "if the emotional character of the other person is not in character with the narrative framework – with the story that I could tell about her and her circumstances – it is difficult to understand that person" (Gallagher, this volume). In this respect, I take it that "conversations about written and oral stories are natural extensions of children's earlier experiences with the sharing of event structures" (Guajardo and Watson 2002: 307). It is therefore no accident that the first pre-narrative encounters of young children are with picture books, the more advanced of which still only depict actions. They slowly graduate to properly discursive stories that describe and contextualise the various psychological attitudes of characters who find themselves embedded in increasingly complex social dramas.

Sophisticated demands are also placed on children in the course of hearing, discussing and learning from such stories. It is normal for children to be directed by caregivers to attend to the thoughts, desires, feelings of story characters and these are often explained to them by placing them in a larger context. Those who tell stories to young children generally go beyond the strict text – animating the activity by using voices, enacting character actions and reactions, and providing asides that emphasise and remind listeners of the background motivations and rationales of characters. Such exchanges are a mix of dramatic re-enactment, contextualisation, exposure to further examples of the sort which prompt further requests from listeners and opportunities for expansion from story-tellers. Throughout these interactions children must of course call on their previously acquired practical grasp of the mentalistic terms, i.e. belief, desire, hope, fear and so on. But it is important to note that such terms are not simply mentioned by story-tellers. In the course of telling a story, not only are children shown how the propositional and psychological attitudes operate in relation to one another; they are also prompted at crucial points to offer their own explanations using these terms. Thus they are asked to apply them and their capacity to do so is checked and corrected, as need be. For example, in reading stories it is normal for adults to press for answers to questions such as: "Why do you think X did that?" This is a vital developmental opportunity. In this way this story-telling is effectively a kind of boot camp: It is folk psychology 101.

Although I have been emphasising the imaginative, emotional capacities that characterise early engagements with folk psychological narratives, I also want to highlight how simple it would be for children to pick up the *structural template* of means-end reasoning from such encounters. This is important because the propositional attitudes must be inserted into this framework in the way mathematical arguments are inserted into variables. It is the folk psychological constant that lies at the heart of all coherent narrations concerning intentional attitudes. Similarity-based connectionist accounts of cognitive processing – those that trade in stereotypes, prototypes and exemplars –would suffice to explain how it is possible to derive such a simple schema from the relevant narrative encounters. Indeed, picking this up from well constructed exemplars would be easy work for our pattern-completing, form-finding brains.[5] There underlying mechanisms governing this process are therefore completely unmysterious.

Understanding reasons for action involves more than extricating the relevant template, it also requires a capacity to make sensitive adjustments for relevant factors occasion by occasion, and each will have its own novel features: encounters with folk psychological narratives helps with this too. For, although the structure of intentional psychology is a constant in all FP narratives, they vary in other aspects. Through them children also learn that many non-mentalistic factors are pertinent to why someone has acted or might act. For example, they learn that what a person believes or desires matters to the actions they take but also how their character, unique history and circumstances might affect their motivational set. These are the sorts of features, inter alia, that differ from story to story, within a single story over time – and often from protagonist to protagonist within the same story. They are prominent in nearly all interesting stories even if only in the background. Knowing how to make relevant adjustments to accommodate just such factors is necessary for the skilled application of folk psychology. The simplest person-narratives engender this kind of practical knowledge by introducing children to distinct characters and their specific background beliefs and desires, particular agendas, unique histories, personality traits and so on. Although the stories in which they figure are at first quite simple, they become more sophisticated over time.

The main point is that these stories have precisely the right properties for familiarising children, not only with the core mentalistic framework, but also with the rudimentary norms governing its practical application. By putting examples of people acting for reasons on display, they show both how the items in the mentalistic toolkit can be used together to understand reasons in general, as it were, but also how and when these tools might be used – i.e. what to adjust for – in specific cases. They not only teach children this but they also give some hints about how to make the relevant adjustments (e.g. a character with suspicious tendencies is likely to form certain beliefs in such and such a situation, etc.). Encounters with such stories looks ideally suited to provide children with the requisite specialised know-how – i.e. to teach them how to apply folk psychology, with sensitivity, in everyday contexts.

This involves more than extracting the formal schema of the practical syllogism. By means of robust examples folk psychological story-telling gives insight into the behaviour of core propositional attitudes *in situ* – how they normally relate with respect to one another and other psychological players, i.e. emotions, perceptions, etc. And this 'mental set' is placed in a still wider context in such stories. They also introduce a range of stock characters and personality types, set scripts for behaviour in specific situations and familiar plot-lines. All of this prepares children for making sense of actions in terms of reasons, although this goes mostly unnoticed, or unmentioned, both during the activity itself and in most philosophical reflections on it (see Hutto 2007a, 2007b for full details).

Gallagher remarks that "our understanding of others [doesn't require] an occurrent or explicit narrative story telling: but it does require the ability to see/to frame the other person in a detailed pragmatic or social context, to understand that context in a narrative way" (Gallagher, this volume). More needs to be said about this, but I would suggest that our everyday ability to make sense of intentional actions is the exercise of the ability for explicit narration, even when the stories are short and focused; i.e. where only the explanatory relevant details are mentioned. For knowing how and what to mention is itself an important narrative skill. If I am right, it is based on a unique kind of training.

3. Pre-narrative and narrative interactions

But isn't the line I am pursuing 'too mentalistic'? For surely, "it is not the inner life or the mental life that we attempt to access, but simply the other's life in its worldly/situational contexts" (Gallagher: this volume). As long as we purge ourselves of certain misleading pictures there is a way of understanding the metaphor of the 'inner' that is quite respectable, though I agree that in the current philosophical climate its unqualified use is very likely to be misunderstood. I will say more about this in the next section, but for the moment I want to stress that there is a legitimate place for mentalistic explications and explanations, properly construed, and that these are needed for making sense of actions in ways that cannot be achieved by means of purely embodied responding.

Kerstin Dautenhahn has recently propounded what she calls the Narrative Intelligence Hypothesis (or NIH): It is a particular version of Dunbar's speculation that language may have become an efficient medium for social grooming in hominid groups when their size reached a critical ceiling (*circa* 150 members) as would have occurred during the time of *H. erectus*. The proposal is that narratives – which provided the medium for conversational gossip – may have been called upon to play this special role. Thus, "the evolutionary origin of communicating in stories co-evolved with the increasing social dynamics among our human ancestors, in particular the necessity to communicate about third-party relationships" (Dautenhahn 2002: 103–104, 2001: 252).[6]

Yet – if read in a robust way – the NIH cannot be true. For if the hominids in question lacked facility with complex languages – as is generally supposed – then they also lacked the capacity to conduct discursive conversations. At best, they would have had the capacity to form complex proto-conversational vocalisations and interactions or – thanks to their blossoming mimetic abilities – they could have communed by means of dramatic re-enactments, which is the natural precursor to narration proper. Either of these methods might have served equally well as a direct substitute for the physical grooming of individuals, ensuring social cohesion for larger groups. Moreover games, rites, and so on, as made possible by a developing mimetic culture, may even have allowed for the establishment of clearly defined, if somewhat inflexible, roles and rules. All of this could have helped to solidify within-group identities obviating the need for exhausting forms of personal social maintenance through individual physical grooming alone.[7]

In assessing the NIH, it is vital to keep in mind two importantly different ways of thinking about 'narratives'. We must distinguish those of the purely dramatic re-enactive sort and those which rely on language. Indeed, we can do better than this. To avoid confusion it is best that we distinguish the pre-narrative and the narrative more cleanly, adhering to the following stipulation: "Narrative is the vehicle of communicating representations of events between people by verbal means" (Nelson 2003: 32). A mimetic culture may have been enough to sponsor pre-narratives in the form of ritualistic dramatic re-enactments, involving established canonical forms, roles and figures. These are the obvious forerunners to myth and story, but they must not be identified with narrative practices *per se*. To my eye, this proposal allows for a more modest rendering of the NIH as the *Pre*-Narrative Intelligence Hypothesis, according to which dramatic (yet non-discursive) re-enactments of social happenings may have acted as the first kind of mimetic social glue. These activities would have had a pre-narrative format and structure (Dautenhahn 2001: 253).

This is utterly consistent with the idea that basic social engagements are the very stuff of many discursive narratives – this is because more basic social engagements are ripe for potential narration; indeed they provide much necessary fodder for spoken or written stories. Certainly the interactions of social creatures, even those only capable of harbouring intentional attitudes, engender complex, and sometimes hard to predict, dramas. Charting these, at least in part, lies at the heart of many explicit narratives. Often they focus on the dramas, tensions and unique courses of specific interpersonal relationships. To clarify, it is not as if some kinds of stories could not have been told about the actions of our ancient ancestors – their lives were surely structured enough for this – it is rather that *they*, lacking the appropriate medium and established social practices, were in no position to tell such stories to or about themselves. We must be clear about the order of appearance: narratives could not have been related orally or conversationally in the early stages of our pre-history since "there can be no narrative without narration, a point sometimes overlooked by those who see human life in terms of narratives untold or waiting to be told" (Lamarque 2004: 394).[8] On the assumption that our immediate pre-linguistic ancestors lacked complex language abilities it follows that they also lacked the resources for conducting discursive conversations and telling stories (Dunn 1991). This is why I say in the target paper that "emotions and their consequences have a kind of structure that is ripe for narration" (quoted by Gallagher: this volume).

Kerby reaches much the same conclusion in his work *Narrative and the Self*. He tries to make sense of a pre-narrative level of experience by appeal to Ricoeur's work, defending his idea that "this primordial experience has a 'pre-narrative quality' or prefiguredness that 'constitutes a demand for narrative'" (Kerby 1993: 42). As Kerby describes it, the key idea is that there is a level of human experience which *lends* itself to explicit narration – but it is not in and of itself explicitly narrated. The distinction between the implicit/explicit narration allows him to drive a wedge between two otherwise opposed stances of which, as he sees it, Mink and MacIntyre exemplify.

At one pole we find Louis Mink telling us that "Stories are not lived but told. Life has no beginnings middles or ends" (Kerby 1993: 41). Hence on this view, like Dennett's, the world is essentially devoid of meaning, thus any meaning we 'find' in it or in ourselves is transferred to it from art to life. At the opposite pole, we find MacIntyre saying, in characteristically Aristotelian style, that the very idea of an intelligible action is more basic than the notion of action itself (cf. MacIntyre 1984: 209). Talk of a pre-narrative level makes room for action and an understanding of action as purposeful in a way that does not already rest on acting for reasons or understanding actions in terms of reasons. I have tried to explicate what 'actions' of this kind would be in terms of biologically-based intentional attitudes and by appeal to the increasingly complex forms of social interaction enjoyed by certain species, those capable of recreative imagination, mimesis, etc. For, even if the actions and interactions of such beings are not driven by 'reasons of their own', they are nevertheless rich in drama.

MacIntyre's idea is that there can be no action without a narrative. Human actions, and hence meaning, are a part of the world but they don't exist without (or prior to) the linguistic activity of narration. This is true in one sense and false in another. There is equivocation here over the notion of a 'human action' – for some of our actions involve 'acting for reasons of our own' (and as such the claim is true) and sometimes we 'act' more viscerally, instinctively – in accord with our first natures (see my reply to Rudd). We sometimes act and interact as animals – human animals, to be sure. And although we can act without reasons, such actions are not unintelligible.[9]

The requirements for a person to act for a reason of their own and for being in a position to understand actions of this kind are quite peculiar. It demands a very specific and sophisticated kind of linguistic competence; this is need for telling folk psychological narratives in more ways than one.[10] It is only those linguistically competent actors that are capable of harbouring propositional attitudes and combining them logically so as to act for reasons and it is practical reasoners of this kind that are the proper subjects of *folk psychological* narratives. Commitment to some kind of sententialism is non-negotiable if we want to explain what it is for someone to act for a *reason* of their own. Sententialists claim that the having of propositional attitudes should be understood as instantiating a three-place relation in which thinkers stand in relation to sentences – adopting certain psychological attitudes towards them – and in turn, the sentences themselves stand in relation to specific states of affairs. On the traditional analysis, the meaningful parts of such sentences refer to worldly objects and the sentence as a whole is made true by the obtaining of the relevant state of affairs that it picks out (and rendered false otherwise). Sentences have just the right kind of semantic properties of reference and truth required to be the appropriate *relata* of the attitudes. But they also have internal logical forms and syntax, and thus are tailor-made to explain the computational, inferential features exhibited by propositional attitudes, assuming – as we must – that it is the *propositions* and not the attitudes that do all the interesting logical work.[11] So it was only after language and certain practices of reasoning bedded down that there were any folk who acted for reasons of their own. This is one way in which being able to act for a reason depends on language.

Moreover, only language users would have been capable of relating narratives about such reason-based actions, presenting stories about these as third personal objects of public attention. Complex language would have been necessary, not just as a basis for the *subject matter* of these stories – bouts of practical reasoning activity involving propositional attitudes – but also for the *relating* of the relevant narratives about these. I presume therefore that the former practice not only logically presupposes but also temporally pre-dates the former. It is therefore no accident that exposure to relevant conversational stimuli in early discourse is a critical determinant for folk psychological development.[12] Conversations in which people and their reasons for action are discussed *just are* a kind of *discursive* narrative. They minimally fall into the category of those that use mentalistic lexical terms and verbs – i.e. labels for mental predicates. And presumably when propositional attitudes are discussed, this is done by using the appropriate object complements – descriptions of the contents to which these attitudes relate. Importantly, the activity of relating folk psychological narratives in the form of personal conversations is always discursive (whatever particular form the discourse happens to take – i.e. spoken or sign language). So, once again, complex linguistic abilities are a must for developing a *bona fide* mentalistic understanding of actions that are performed for reasons.[13] To reiterate, command of complex linguistic forms and the related practices this enables would have added significant dimensions to social dramas, transforming them in important ways by providing (i) new and more refined ways of reflecting upon and meeting old ends and (ii) a new way of communicating about such activity, using discursive and not merely embodied dramatic forms.

Putting all of this together, it is possible to explain the kind of case Gallagher cites. He describes a situation in which two different groups of listeners hear two different types of what is essentially the same story; yet one group hears a version that mentions the mental states of characters and another group hears a version that lacks precisely this feature. Yet both groups agree when it comes to recounting the story's facts, the order of its events and its gist (apparently autistic individuals can do this sort of thing with non-mentalistic narratives too). My proposed explanation of this, in line with the above discussion, is that we can assume that the pre-narrative format and structure of the story in question remained constant across both renderings, even though the *reasons* for which the protagonists acted are only made visible in those versions that make mention of their propositional attitudes.

4. The 'narrative competence' objection

But what of the argument that Gallagher attributes to Astington: how should we respond to the claim that "to understand narrative we need access to the characters' minds, and to have the latter requires us to have TOM" (Gallagher: this volume)? Certainly, in some speculative cases, we may need to fill in the relevant details of a narrative by calling on our general knowledge, making inferences and generalisations, and perhaps – *in extremis* – by theorising or simulating. These are useful supplementary heuristics, for sure – especially when we cannot get the other's story from them directly. I deny, however, that such activities *lie at the heart* of our capacity to understand folk psychological narratives. For me this is learnt by encounters with the relevant kinds of narrative; folk psychological ones.

This raises the spectre of perhaps the most compelling worry about the NPH; i.e. that it may be circular.[14] For if children could only acquire folk psychological skills by engaging in a particular kind of narrative practice – those in which they engage with stories about reasons for action – this might suggest that they would only be in a position to understand these *if and only if* they already had a very specialized kind of narrative competence. And the trouble is that the narrative competence in question might look as if it equates to having prior 'theory of mind' abilities. Thus even if the NPH were in some weak sense the right thing to say about how folk psychological skills are acquired, our primary capacity for belief/desire psychology – so the argument goes – *must be* explained as a kind of phylogenetic inheritance: an ancient cognitive endowment. If so, the postulation of some kind of theory of mind mechanism (or ToMM) of the theory theory or simulative variety is unavoidable.

Autistic individuals seem to provide a kind of existence proof in support of this line of argument. Compared with the normal population, they have troubles dealing with *certain types* of narrative – i.e. mentalistic ones – even though they exhibit a basic narrative competence when it comes to dealing with other subject matters. Although their abilities in this regard are quite limited, let us accept that they have a general capacity for dealing with narratives *per se*. That is, they can coherently order the events in narratives that have a 'mechanical' or 'behavioural/functional' subject matter, as was revealed in a number of experiments requiring them to correctly sequence cartoon frames relating to such topics (see Baron-Cohen 1995: 72, Frith 1989: 163–5).

This is all true, but it gives us exactly no reason to suppose that autistic individuals fail to understand folk psychological narratives because they lack or have a faulty ToMM. Our basic narrative competence – our true ancient endowment – involves having a good command of language and its pragmatics and certain imaginative and interactive abilities that enable young children to get a practical grasp of the core propositional attitudes (see my replies to Goldie and Hobson for details). This is what children normally bring to the table that enables them to engage appropriately with their *first* folk psychology narratives in their preschool years. Some of these core abilities are also those that children with infantile autism lack. The decisive point is that this raft of abilities does not equate to having 'theory of mind' abilities. For this reason the 'narrative competence' objection lacks teeth.

5. Narrative competency as a basis of self-development and self-understanding

Gallagher observes that to "occupy a position within a self-narrative requires more than a minimal, non-conceptual self-awareness – it requires a conceptual, objective, narrative self that is aware of itself as having a point of view that is different from others" (Gallagher, this volume). He talks of autobiographical memory as being one critical factor amongst others that "*shapes* narrative competency – an ability to see things in a narrative framework… [It] helps to *kick-start* narrative abilities during the second year of life" (Gallagher, this volume). While I have sympathy with the general spirit of the proposal, and especially the use that is made of Nelson's work on this topic, I suspect that this way of putting things is misleading.

Like the imagined dramatic re-enactments of our hominid ancestors "children's first narrative [or better, pre-narrative] productions occur in action, in episodes of symbolic play by groups of peers, accompanied by – rather than solely through – language. Play is an important developmental source of narrative" (Nelson 2003: 28).[15] As a result, although a kind of narrative training begins in the second year of life, it is really the honing of this skill (with the active support of caregivers) that makes autobiographical memory so much as possible. There is a causal connection between the fact that only after their fluency with narration has developed beyond that of pretend play and picture books (again depicting actions) that the child can "view the self as having a specific experiential history that is different from others and thus a specific personal past and a possible specific future" (Nelson 2003: 30).[16]

It is because younger children have yet to develop a 'personal frame of reference' or capacity to give a narrative account of themselves as persons existing across time. If so this would explain why "we are typically unable to recall events that occurred before the age of around 3 years, a phenomenon known as infantile amnesia" (Harley & Reese 1999: 1338). It merits observation that not only are children budding conversationalists by age 3, it is also around this point at which "they can verbalise a number of familiar scripts in reliable sequence" (Nelson 2003: 25). So, this is also the age at which they begin to get to grip with discursive narratives.[17]

Indeed, this account of the developmental pattern is more consistent with the empirical evidence Gallagher cites. For initially "children of 2 to 4 years often 'appropriate' someone else's story as their own. Miller provides observations of appropriation by a child from a parent's account. For example, one small boy who was told by his mother in a cautionary way about having fallen off a stool when she was young retold this story later as his 'when he fell off the stool'. Miller also reports children in preschool freely appropriating" (Nelson 2003: 31).[18] Children and adults use narratives as complex linguistic objects of joint attention and also for the purposes of joint reminiscing, although they are not equal partners in this activity. In both cases narratives provide a much more sophisticated vehicle for social interaction, one with far richer resources than those of declarative sentences that are used for communicating about putative facts. Folk psychological narratives allow for discussion of what is personal and particular, thus they not only foster an understanding of what it is to act for a reason but also what is to have a history, to cut a particular trajectory through the world.

In all, quite a lot happens in the crucial pre-school and early school period. Around the 2 year mark, children are gaining a firm command of complex language and engaging in pre-narrative pretend play, learning to cope with picture books, and getting a handle on propositional desires. From the age of 3 onwards they are engaging in conversations and forging an understanding of belief. And between the ages of 3 and 5, through their encounters with folk psychological narratives, they are acquiring an understanding of reasons and beginning to foster some sense of being a person, of having a temporally extended existence and a certain kind of social face.

And the story does not end here. The capacity to understand someone's actions in terms of reasons, one's own or others, can be more or less limited. The sad fact is that early research in this territory has been overshadowed by the dominant theory or mind experimentation which has occupied the limelight of late. Nevertheless, there is "a finding from person perception research that has remained stubbornly persistent. Although preschool children display significant understanding of temporary mental states, research continues to show that they have difficulty grasping more enduring traits and they are rarely able or inclined to use such traits to explain behaviour .... The significance of this discrepancy remains unclear but it may be that young children still have trouble in achieving *stability* in their conception of the person" (Richner & Nicolopoulou 2001: 398, emphasis original).

I take it that narrative ability and self-understanding develop in tandem and that the process is nuanced, multi-faceted and probably developmentally uneven. What is clear however is that "the period from 3 to 5 years appears to be one especially crucial phase of transition in the development of children's conceptions of persons" (Richner & Nicolopoulou 2001: 398).[19]

There is much more to say about how this way of looking at things can free up our thinking about self consciousness in its different varieties – and also how it might open up new avenues for tackling the so-called paradox of self-deception and related puzzles about self-knowledge and personal identity. As it happens, these are my next set of philosophical projects. But I hope I have said enough here in reply to Gallagher to give at least a basic sketch of how I think one might begin to approach these topics (hence also meeting Hobson's fourth challenge – see my reply to Hobson).

Notes

1. The relevant forthcoming papers are Hutto 2007a, 2007b, 2007c. In fact, as a direct consequence of our interaction for this special issue Gallagher and I have agreed to co-author a paper on this topic (Gallagher & Hutto 2007).

2. Here it is important to note that there are a spectrum of narrative ways of making sense of ourselves and others. And that this claim is not at all in tension with the fact that there are *other* more primary, non-narrative ways of intersubjective engagement.

3. Culturally established texts of this sort are the most secure medium of introducing children to the folk psychological schema and training children in its application. Yet any story about reasons for action, even those related through causal conversations has the potential to re-enforce this understanding. And, of course, folk psychological narratives are most regularly relayed through conversation, despite the latter being less regimented and structured than the canonical texts used in much pre-school story-telling. Like the well-constructed and well-known fairy tale cited above, conversations about reasons will incorporate and therefore serve to introduce the already familiar lexical terms and verbs – the labels of the attitudes – and the appropriate object complements of these – examples of the propositional contents to which these attitudes relate. Still, everyday conversations describing reasons for action, unless they are well focused and extended, do not always reveal the full structure of the way the attitudes inter-relate in the way text-based folk psychological narratives do. This is because our workaday folk psychological explanations are often truncated, in line with the rules of conversational implicature.

4. It has been claimed that a poverty of the stimulus argument could be developed in this domain which would parallel Chomsky's, developed to support his claims about the existence of innate linguistic knowledge (Carruthers 2003: 71, cf. Botterill & Carruthers 1999: 52–3). Accordingly, normal developmental environments would lack ambient information, instruction and training of the right sort (or enough thereof) for acquiring folk psychology. As applied to folk psychology this argument has not been spelt out in any detail, but presumably its credibility depends on the idea that children could not possibly fashion the rich product that is folk psychology by applying their general reasoning abilities in response to impoverished stimuli.

5. A major virtue of the NPH is that it does not need to characterise this aspect of the learning process as one of 'scaling up' or 'bootstrapping'; to do so is rightly to be accused of hand waving (Gopnik 2003: 243). For in this case the training 'input' is identical to learned 'output': the structures to be acquired are clearly detectable in the exemplars – the folk psychological

narratives – themselves (this can be seen by replacing the italicised mentalistic verbs in the 'Red Riding Hood' excerpt with a series of neutral symbols). And it is well known that connectionist networks can 'learn' both lexical categories (e.g. nouns, verbs) and grammatical structures (e.g. agreement and dependence of embeddedness clauses) using their humble resources. In summarising the evidence on this score, Prinz remarks that "Elman shows that a dumb pattern detector can pick up on structural relations" (Prinz 2002: 206). Note too that the folk psychological template is a much simpler kind of structure than even the most basic of syntactic patterns. All the NPH requires to make this account credible is the assumption that the child's world is adequately populated with folk psychological narratives and that they have enough opportunities to engage with them. This seems to be the case, in most cultures.

6. The basic idea is that: "Story-telling also gives more flexibility than social grooming as to the actors and content of the stories: stories can include people that are part of the current audience, as well as absent persons, historical characters, fictional characters, etc. Stories that are told by a skilled story-teller (e.g. using appropriate body language, exploiting prosody, and possessing a rich repertoire of verbal expressions) can give very good examples of the power of words" (Dautenhahn 2001: 253).

7. This may explain why, recapitulating the dramatic re-enactments of our ancient ancestors "Children's first narrative productions occur in action, in episodes of symbolic play by groups of peers, accompanied by – rather than solely through – language. Play is an important developmental source of narrative" (Nelson 2003: 28).

8. Or more succinctly: "a story must be told, it is not found" (Lamarque 2004: 394).

9. Like Wittgenstein, "I really want to say that scruples in thinking begin with (have their roots in) instinct" (Wittgenstein 1967: § 391).

10. Plausibly, it is only after acquiring language that our ancestors were able to combine "gestures to form new meanings and [this perhaps marked] the beginnings of narrative" (Corballis 2003: 216).

11. Fodor is, for once, on the side of the angels in his long campaign to ensure that we recognise the "independence of content from functional role" (Fodor 1987: 71).

12. Empirical evidence shows that children deprived of the opportunity for conversation and narrative with siblings or caregivers, as is the case with certain classes of blind and deaf children, are stunted in their ability to understand others (cf. Garfield et al. 2001). It has been discovered that "Profoundly deaf children who grow up in hearing families often lag several years behind hearing children in their development of an understanding of false belief, even when care is taken to include only children of normal intelligence and social responsiveness in the deaf sample… it was not until aged 13 to 16 that deaf children's success rates were seen to approximate those of normally developing 4-year-old's" (Peterson & Siegal 2000: 127, see especially the summary on 138). Hence "The results of the studies… combine to suggest that the ease with which deaf children develop a theory of mind may be related to the nature and extent of their exposure to conversation in the home while growing up as preschoolers" (Peterson & Siegal 2000: 131).

13. And the fact is that "much social discourse involves personal stories… people are constantly telling stories about their own or other's thoughts and beliefs as well as actions" (Guajardo & Watson 2002: 307). Thus "Parents talk to their children about feelings, thoughts, and desires from a very young age (Brown & Dunn 1991; Dunn 1988) and the extent to which they do this is related to the extent to which children talk about such states at a later point in time (Dunn, Brown & Beardsall 1991; Moore et al. 1994). Children are exposed to mentalistic talk in stories

that are read to them and in their conversations about stories (Astington 1990, Paley 1984). And they are often audience to narratives in adult conversations" (Astington 1996: 194).

14. A good proportion of my forthcoming book is devoted to defeating this argument by demonstrating that the postulation of ToMMs of any sort is beset with insuperable logical and empirical difficulties.

15. Thus there are "two aspects of children's narrative activity which are too often treated in mutual isolation: the discursive exposition of narratives in storytelling and their enactments in pretend play" (Richner & Nicolopoulou, 2001: 408). Again I would want to talk in terms of pre-narrative and narrative activities, for the sake of clarity, but I agree with these authors that we should better understand the relation between the two.

16. The trouble is that prior to this point "at 2 years of age the child has only a few of the rudiments that enter into narrative" (Nelson 2003: 27). In line with my account of embodied expectation and mimetic abilities, at this stage if they have a sense of self it is of self-as-actor. And this is because "During this early developmental period language is being learned and used but it is not yet a vehicle for conveying the representation of narrative" (Nelson 2003: 27).

17. Until the point that children have mastered the art of using this particular kind of linguistic form "There are no insights into another's life because there is no vehicle except shared actions through which experience can be shared. The claim here is that shared experiential narratives are the symbolic vehicles available only to humans, through which such insights are gained" (Nelson 2003: 29, emphasis mine).

18. Thus a sense of self as a person with a particular past is "dependent upon language used to exchange views about self and other, primarily through narratives but also through commentary on the self by others, as well as on their own feelings, thoughts and expectations of what might happen" (Nelson 2003: 33). All of this takes, "place during the critical years when the child can enter fully into the linguistic world but is not yet a participant in formal schooling" (Nelson 2003: 22). Indeed it has been shown that "the way in which adults talk… does appear to facilitate the richness and narrative organisation of children's memory talk" (Harley & Reese 1999: 1338). Specifically, there were effects traced to individual differences in maternal expositional style, using rich versus low levels of elaboration. The authors of the study get closer to the heart of things, however, when they propose that "future research with older children could explore the role of narrative abilities instead of language skill measured just in terms of total vocabulary, in children's verbal memory development… Notably, the only measure of non-verbal memory that positively predicted children's later memory reports in this study measured event sequencing, not total number of actions recalled. Event sequencing can be viewed as a nonverbal analogue of narrative structure" (Harley & Reese 1999: 1346).

19. Even so Nelson identifies "three essential components of narrative [that]… remain weakly or non-existent in most of the narrative productions of the 3- to 5-year-old preschooler: temporal perspective, the mental as well as physical perspective of self and of different others, and essential cultural knowledge of the unexperienced world" (Nelson 2003: 28).

References

Astington, J. 1990. "Narrative and the Child's Theory of Mind." In *Narrative Thought and Narrative Language*, B.K. Britton and D. Pellegrini (eds), 151–72. Hillsdale, New Jersey: Erlbaum.

Astington, J. 1996. "What Is Theoretical About a Child's Theory of Mind?: A Vygotskian View of Its Development." In *Theories of Theories of Mind*, P. Carruthers and P. Smith (eds). Cambridge: Cambridge University Press.

Baron-Cohen, S. 1995. *Mindblindness: An Essay on Autism and Theory of Mind*. Cambridge, MA: MIT Press.

Botterill, G. and Carruthers, P. 1999. *The Philosophy of Psychology*. Cambridge: Cambridge University Press.

Brown, J.R. and Dunn, J. 1991. "'You can cry, mum': The Social and Developmental Implications of talk about Internal States." *British Journal of Developmental Psychology* 9: 237–56.

Carruthers, P. 2003. "Moderately Massive Modularity." In *Minds and Persons*, A. O'Hear (ed.), 67–89. Cambridge: Cambridge University Press.

Corballis, M.C. 2003. "Gestural Origins of Language." In *Language Evolution*, M. Christiansen and S. Kirby (eds), 201–218. Oxford: Oxford University Press.

Dautenhahn, K. 2001. "The Narrative Intelligence Hypothesis: In Search of the Transactional Format of Narratives in Humans and Other Social Animals." In *Proceedings of the Fourth International Cognitive Technology Conference: CT 2001: Instruments of Mind*, M. Beynon, C.L. Nehaniv and K. Dautenhahn (eds), 248–66. Berlin, Heidelberg: Springer-Verlag.

Dautenhahn, K. 2002. "The Origins of Narrative." *International Journal of Cognition and Technology* 1: 97–123.

Dunn, J. 1988. *The Beginnings of Social Understanding*. Cambridge: Cambridge University Press.

Dunn, J. 1991. "Understanding Others: Evidence From Naturalistic Studies of Children." In *Natural Theories of Mind*, A. Whiten (ed.), 51–61. Oxford: Blackwell.

Dunn, J., Brown, J.R. and Beardsall, L. 1991. "Family Talk About Emotions and Children's Latter Understanding of Other's Emotions." *Developmental Psychology* 27: 448–55.

Gallagher, S. and Hutto, D.D. 2007. "Primary Interaction and Narrative Practice: From Empathic Resonance to Folk Psychology." In *The Shared Mind: Perspectives on Intersubjectivity*, J. Zlatev, T. Racine, C. Sinha and E. Itkonen (eds). Amsterdam/Philadelphia: John Benjamins.

Garfield, J.L., Peterson, C.C. and Perry, T. 2001. "Social Cognition, Language Acquisition and the Development of the Theory of Mind." *Mind and Language* 16: 494–541.

Goldman, A. 1992a. "In Defense of the Simulation Theory." *Mind and Language* 7: 104–19.

Gopnik, A. 2003. "The Theory Theory as an Alternative to the Innateness Hypothesis." In *Chomsky and His Critics*, L.M. Antony and N. Hornstein (eds), 238–54.

Guajardo, N.R. and Watson, A. 2002. "Narrative Discourse and Theory of Mind Development." *The Journal of Genetic Psychology* 163: 305–25.

Fodor, J.A. 1987. *Psychosemantics*. Cambridge, MA: MIT Press.

Frith, U. 1989. *Autism: Explaining the Enigma*. Oxford: Blackwell.

Harley, K. and Reese, E. 1999. "Origins of Autobiographical Memory." *Developmental Psychology* 35: 1338–48.

Hutto, D.D. 1997. "The Story of the Self: The Narrative Basis of Self-Development." In *Critical Studies: Ethics and the Subject*, K. Simms (ed.), 61–75. Amsterdam: Rodopi.

Hutto, D.D. 2003b. "Folk Psychological Explanations: Narratives and the Case of Autism." *Philosophical Papers* 32: 345–61.

Hutto, D.D. 2004. "The Limits of Spectatorial Folk Psychology." *Mind and Language* 19: 548–73.
Hutto, D.D. 2007a. *Folk Psychological Narratives: The Socio-Cultural Basis of Understanding Reasons*. Cambridge, MA: MIT Press.
Hutto, D.D. 2007b. "Folk Psychology without Theory or Simulation." In *Folk Psychology Reassessed*, D.D. Hutto and M. Ratcliffe (eds). Dordrecht: Springer.
Hutto, D.D. 2007c. "The Narrative Practice Hypothesis." In *Narrative and Understanding Persons*, D.D. Hutto (ed.). Cambridge: Cambridge University Press.
Kerby, P. 1993. *Narrative and the Self*. Indiana: Indiana University Press.
Lamarque, P. 2004. "On Not Expecting Too Much From Narrative." *Mind and Language* 19: 393–408.
Lillard, A. 1997. "Other Folk's Theories of Mind and Behaviour." *Psychological Science* 8: 268–74.
MacIntyre, A. 1984. *After Virtue*. London: Duckworth.
Moore, C., Furrow, D. and Chiasson, L. 1994. "Developmental Relationships between the Production and Comprehension of Mental Terms." *First Language* 14: 1–17.
Nelson, K. 2003. "Narrative and the Emergence of a Consciousness of Self." In *Narrative and Consciousness*, G.D. Fireman, T.E.J. McVay and O. Flanagan (eds), 17–36. Oxford: Oxford University Press.
Paley, V.G. 1984. *Boys and Girls: Superheroes in the Doll Corner*. Chicago, IL: Chicago University Press.
Peterson, C. and Siegal, M. 2000. "Insights into Theory of Mind from Deafness and Autism." *Mind and Language* 15: 123–45.
Prinz, J. 2002. *Furnishing the Mind: Concepts and Their Perceptual Basis*. Cambridge, MA: MIT Press.
Richner, E.S. and Nicolopoulou, A. 2001. "The Narrative Construction of Differing Conceptions of the Person in the Development of Young Children's Social Understanding." *Early Education and Development* 12: 393–432.
Wittgenstein, L. 1967. *Zettel*. Oxford: Basil Blackwell.

Index

In the *Consciousness & Emotion Book Series (C&EB)* the following titles have been published thus far or are scheduled for publication:

3 **CHAFE, Wallace:** The Importance of Not Being Earnest. The feeling behind laughter and humor. *Expected February 2007*

2 **MENARY, Richard (ed.):** Radical Enactivism. Intentionality, Phenomenology and Narrative. Focus on the philosophy of Daniel D. Hutto. 2006. ix, 255 pp.

1 **ELLIS, Ralph D. and Natika NEWTON (eds.):** Consciousness & Emotion. Agency, conscious choice, and selective perception. 2005. xii, 330 pp.